Ecology
in the
Antarctic

Ecology in the Antarctic

Papers presented at a meeting held on
11 October 1979 organised by the
Linnean Society of London

Edited by W. N. Bonner and R. J. Berry

Reprinted from the Biological Journal of the Linnean
Society, Volume 14, Number 1, 1980

Published for the Linnean Society of London

ACADEMIC PRESS

London   New York   Toronto   Sydney   San Francisco

ACADEMIC PRESS INC. (LONDON) LIMITED
24/28 Oval Road
London NW1
(Registered Office)

US edition published by
ACADEMIC PRESS INC.
111 Fifth Avenue
New York
New York 10003

Printed in Great Britain by
The Whitefriars Press Ltd., London and Tonbridge

Foreword

The motives which drive ecologists to work in the Antarctic may not always be of a sort to weigh with committees allocating research funds. Many scientists delight in the combination of physical and intellectual challenge which the far south offers and the attraction of its austere and almost unviolated beauty may be stronger than that of a purely scientific objective. Politics might play a part, since at the present a nation's influence in the Antarctic club depends to a large extent on its research effort, but does not seem to do so to any untoward extent. Fortunately there are reasons for carrying out research in Antarctic ecology which can stand up better than these to the cynical scrutiny of the science administrator. Antarctic ecosystems are distinctly different from any others. The isolation of the continent and its associated islands has meant that few plants and animals have been able to colonise them and their ecosystems are correspondingly less complex. The Antarctic seas are not similarly insulated from invasion but the Antarctic Convergence clearly demarcates an enormous area of sea with remarkably uniform and distinctive characteristics. The terrestrial, freshwater and marine environments of the Antarctic present more extreme conditions than anywhere else on Earth and it is often under such conditions that ecological principles are revealed most clearly. The Arctic, with its land connexions to temperate regions allowing in a rich variety of plants and animals and its confusion of currents in its seas, is different and although it has the advantage of being nearer home does not necessarily provide an alternative area for the investigation of many of the ecological problems of the polar environment.

To these academic reasons for studying Antarctic ecology must be added the economic one. The Southern Ocean is productive—although probably not so highly productive as has sometimes been suggested—and short food chains concentrate biomass into large populations of a few species. In the past some of these species, fur seals, elephant seals and whales, have been over-exploited and, indeed, provide some of the most publicised examples of the stupidity of allowing short-term economics to have priority in the utilisation of a biological resource. With the world food problem becoming ever more serious, other Antarctic marine animals such as krill and fish are now being harvested, but there is an awareness that harvesting must be regulated if over-fishing is not again to destroy the resource and drastically alter the ecological balance of the Antarctic seas. Whether practical control measures can be formulated and agreed upon before it is too late is open to question, but it is a hopeful sign that species of economic value are being recognised as components in an ecosystem which must be understood as a whole if really effective measures to regulate exploitation are to be devised. The looming possibility that Antarctic mineral resources, such as oil, may be exploited gives an added reason for having a thorough understanding of Antarctic ecosystems so that probable effects of pollution may be assessed.

Research on ecosystems requires sustained and detailed work over many years on a wide variety of aspects and it is in this type of research that an organisation such as the British Antarctic Survey can excel. The papers in this symposium volume, all by members of the Survey, are evidence that it has, indeed, excelled. The introductory paper, after an admirable sketch of the history of the Survey, sets its biological work in context. The succeeding papers, which deal with organisms as diverse as bacteria and elephant seals and with the main environments— terrestrial, freshwater and marine, relate their particular subject matters to the operation of the ecosystems as a whole. It is particularly welcome that studies of microbial activity are included; although micro-organisms have long been recognised as the principal agents in recycling, field studies on their activities have been sparse until recently and it is of especial interest to learn how they operate under the adverse conditions of the Antarctic. Several papers deal with the always intriguing question of how animals adapt in metabolism and life-cycle to survive so well in the Antarctic. The paper on Scotia Sea zooplankton is doubtless the forerunner of many others on this subject since the British Antarctic Survey is participating in a major way in the international BIOMASS programme, one of the objects of which is to provide an understanding of the ecology of krill as a basis for framing proper regulations for the krill fishery. Bird studies sometimes tend to be a thing apart and little related to the rest of biology, but it is a particular merit of the paper on the seabirds of South Georgia to put them in perspective as an important component of the marine ecosystem.

The first problem in any Antarctic research is to get the scientist and his equipment to the right place at the right time. Logistics receive scarcely any mention in these strictly scientific papers but the work could not have been accomplished without the help of ships and boats, often operated under exceptionally difficult conditions, and well-found bases. Co-operation between those responsible for these facilities and scientists is not always smooth—even the usually imperturbable Captain Cook, first of the Antarctic explorers, is reputed to have exclaimed "Curse the scientists, and all science into the bargain!"*. No doubt such things are still said but the science of the British Antarctic Survey would be nowhere without the efficient and adaptable support of its logistics division.

The Symposium on Antarctic Ecology held under the auspices of the Linnean Society provided an excellent survey of the subject as well as presenting exciting new material and I am sure that this record of its proceedings will be valued by a wider audience. Our gratitude must be expressed to the Linnean Society for organising the Symposium and to Professor R. J. Berry and Mr W. N. Bonner for so ably editing this volume.

G. E. FOGG
Chairman, Scientific Advisory Committee
of the British Antarctic Survey

---

* *The Journals of Captain James Cook on his Voyages of Discovery, Vol. II*, edited by J. C. Beaglehole: Cambridge University Press for the Hakluyt Society, 1969: xlvi.

Contents

British biological research in the Antarctic

W. N. BONNER

Life Sciences Division, British Antarctic Survey,
Natural Environment Research Council,
Madingley Road, Cambridge CB3 0ET, England

Accepted for publication January 1980

A tradition of biological research in the Antarctic was established by Cook 200 years ago. This tradition has been built on by other British expeditions, notably the 'Discovery' Investigations. The British Antarctic Survey, which arose from Operation Tabarin and the Falkland Islands Dependencies Survey, now carries out a programme of coordinated and continuous biological research. The Atlantic sector of the Antarctic, in which the Survey operates, is of key importance biologically. The Antarctic provides a striking biological contrast between a species-poor and very barren terrestrial ecosystem and the species-rich and productive ocean which surrounds it. Severe climatic conditions and great isolation (a contrast to the Arctic) characterize the Antarctic environment. Work at the Survey's biological research stations is designed to study the distribution and interactions of organisms and communities, how they have adapted to Antarctic conditions, and which by their abundance may be deemed successful. Research is done into terrestrial, fresh-water and marine systems. Additionally, there is a major research programme into the biology, environment and principal predators of krill, *Euphausia superba*. The Antarctic is a laboratory where opportunities exist for natural experiments to test theories and elucidate basic biological problems.

KEY WORDS: – adaptation – Antarctic – climate – decomposition – ecosystem – *Euphausia superba* – isolation – krill.

It is more than two hundred years since Captain Cook on his voyage of discovery in 1773–1775 penetrated the Antarctic and set a tradition of British biological research there by taking with him the naturalist Johann Forster on 'Resolution' to record the natural curiosities encountered on the voyage (Cook, 1784). Cook's voyage, and many notable British expeditions that followed, were primarily for the purpose of geographical exploration; biological research was perforce fitted in on an opportunistic basis. Despite this, considerable advances were made in what were very often not very convenient circumstances. Everyone has heard of the efforts to obtain Emperor Penguin embryos from the Cape Crozier rookery in the winter of 1911, so dramatically described by Apsley Cherry Garrard in *The Worst Journey in the World* (Cherry-Garrard, 1922). The scientific results of that particular endeavour were not great. Much more significant, though far less well known, were the researches of men like Joseph Hooker, who accompanied Sir James Clark Ross to the Antarctic in 1839–1843 (Hooker, 1847) and members of the Scottish National Antarctic Expedition in 1902–1904 (Brown, Mossman & Pirie, 1906).

The sealers, who combed the island groups and the accessible coasts of the Antarctic Peninsula in their search for fur seal skins and elephant seal oil, did not add much to our knowledge of the biology of the region, though an exception must be made in the case of James Weddell, who in the course of several sealing voyages between 1820 and 1824 made many careful biological observations (Weddell, 1825).

The development and rapid expansion of the modern Antarctic whaling industry, which was established in South Georgia in 1904 and in the South Shetland Islands the following year, prompted the British Colonial office to set up the 'Discovery' Investigations, which commenced their field studies in 1925 (Hardy, 1967). These were financed by the money raised from the duty levied on whale oil produced in the Falkland Island Dependencies and were intended to make scientific investigations on the biology of whales and their environment with a view to providing the necessary data on which a rational control of the whaling industry could be based. Although control of the whaling industry proved to be far beyond the powers of the Falkland Island Dependencies administration, the scientific results of these investigations, published as the impressive series of 'Discovery Reports', have added much to our knowledge of the oceanography and marine biology of the Antarctic, with especial emphasis on the South Atlantic sector, while their pioneer studies on whale biology have set the standard for the rest of the scientific community.

The British Graham Land Expedition of 1934–1937 which worked on the west coast of the Antarctic Peninsula, made important biological discoveries, particularly in respect of seals and penguins (Bertram, 1940; Roberts, 1940), This expedition was the first to recognize the need for continuous biological research over a range of disciplines, in the Antarctic.

The organization responsible today for British biological research in the Antarctic had its origin in the Second World War as the naval operation 'Tabarin'. This established a base at Deception Island in the South Shetland Islands, and two in the Antarctic Peninsula area—one at Port Lockroy, Wiencke Island, and the other at Hope Bay, Trinity Peninsula. At the end of the war, 'Tabarin' was replaced by the Falkland Island Dependencies Survey which continued to operate in that sector of the Antarctic bounded by latitudes 20° West and 80° West. A further sixteen bases were established, five of which are at present occupied throughout the year.

In 1959 the United Kingdom became a signatory to the Antarctic Treaty, which amongst other things ensured that the area south of 60° South latitude was to be used for peaceful purposes only and, by leaving territorial claims in abeyance, that scientific research and cooperation should continue without political interference. In 1962 that part of the Falkland Islands Dependencies that was covered by the Antarctic Treaty was redesignated the British Antarctic Territory, and the Falkland Islands Dependencies Survey was renamed the British Antarctic Survey (BAS). Although 'Tabarin' and the Falkland Islands Dependencies Survey had served political as well as scientific ends, participation in the International Geophysical Year, 1957–1958, and subsequent programmes, showed that the British work in the Antarctic could be justified by its science alone. In 1967 BAS eventually became a component body of the Natural Environment Research Council and thus achieved a more permanent status (Laws, 1976).

Although the area of operations of the Survey and its predecessors (Fig. 1) was not chosen on biological grounds, it has turned out to be a key area for Antarctic biological research. The dominant features of the Antarctic as an environment for living organisms are its severe climate and its great isolation. In the British

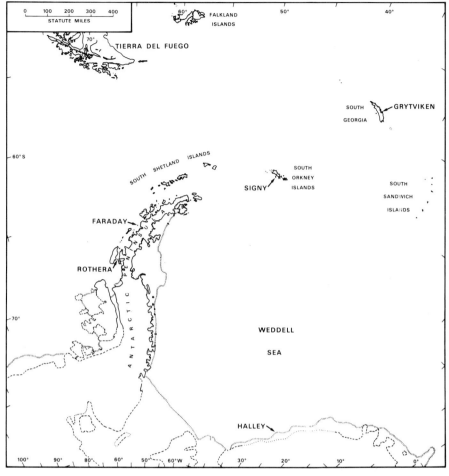

Figure 1. Location of British Antarctic Survey bases.

Antarctic Territory, Antarctica makes its closest approach to other continental land masses where the Antarctic Peninsula reaches out towards the tip of South America from which it is separated only by the 800 km wide Drake Passage. The Antarctic Peninsula, together with the islands and island groups of South Georgia, South Sandwich, South Orkney and South Shetland, provide a latitudinal transect of conditions of increasing polarity, where unique opportunities exist for studying the response of organisms and systems to gradients of increasing isolation and severity of climate.

Biologically the Antarctic consists of two contrasting areas. The Southern Ocean (with a surface area of about 31 million km²) is continuous with the waters of the three other Southern Hemisphere oceans and is separated from them by the Antarctic Convergence, where cold dense Antarctic Surface water dips sharply beneath the warmer less dense Sub-antarctic water (Deacon, 1937). The Southern Ocean supports a species-rich and locally highly productive marine ecosystem characterized by unique short food-chains. The terrestrial systems, on the other hand, are both limited in extent (of the 14 million km² of surface area in Antarctica only about 2% is free from snow or ice in any part of the year) and composed of species-poor communities which are relatively unproductive (Holdgate, 1977).

The Antarctic shares with the Arctic the severe climate and extreme seasonality of day-length, but in most other respects it affords a complete contrast. Terrestrial systems in the Arctic for the most part communicate freely with the plant and animal communities of temperate areas. Isolation is not an important factor, and this is reflected in the much greater species diversity shown by Arctic terrestrial communities, with a consequent increase in complexity, particularly where the higher forms are concerned.

To exploit the opportunities for fruitful research offered by these contrasts organized biological research is needed. In the early years of the Falkland Islands Dependencies Survey much valuable work was done on limited projects which represented the research interests of the workers involved. Thus the work on pygoscelid penguins (Sladen, 1958) and on the Southern Elephant Seal (Laws, 1953, 1956a, b) has added much to our knowledge of these species but has not contributed in a major way to our understanding of Antarctic biology as a whole. However, in 1961 a coordinated programme of biological work covering terrestrial, freshwater and marine ecosystems, was begun at Signy Island (lat. 60°43'S; long. 45°36'W) in the South Orkney Islands, where the first wholly biological research station in Antarctica was established in 1964 (Holdgate, 1965). Signy Island was particularly suitable as the location of such a station. Lying at the mouth of the Weddell Sea, and invested with pack-ice for several months each year, it has a fully polar marine environment. On land there is a uniquely wide range of terrestrial habitats on both base-rich and base-poor substrates, and examples of nearly all the types of Antarctic freshwater body (Smith, 1972; Collins, Baker & Tilbrook, 1975; Heywood, 1967). Analogues of most of the maritime Antarctic terrestrial and freshwater habitats can be found within convenient travelling distance of the research laboratory, built in 1964.

In 1969 a research station was re-opened at South Georgia (lat. 54°17'S; long. 36°30'W) and its programmes expanded to include biology in its disciplines. South Georgia provides an interesting contrast with Signy Island. Conditions on land are less severe than at the South Orkneys, although about 60% of the island is covered by permanent ice, and in many respects the terrestrial ecosystems can be regarded as sub-Antarctic, with well-developed communities of vascular plants although arborescent forms are absent (Smith & Walton, 1975). The island is totally surrounded with Antarctic surface water, however, so that the marine ecosystem is similar to that at the South Orkneys. South Georgia and its off-lying islands support large seasonal colonies of seals and sea-birds which subsist on the high production of the sea in the neighbourhood of the island.

Besides these two main research stations, other British Antarctic Survey bases, though not used regularly for biological research, provide a polar transect extending over 70° of latitude from South Georgia and other islands on the Scotia Ridge to the far south of the Antarctic Peninsula, the dispersal route from South America.

Initially much of the research had to concentrate on the description and classification of the organisms present. In the Antarctic it has been necessary in most cases to start from scratch without the advantage of the published taxonomic keys, the existence of which scientists in the U.K. and other developed areas can often take for granted. For most groups this preliminary taxonomic phase is now complete, or nearly so, and more sophisticated ecological and physiological research has developed. Because of the importance of the severe conditions in the winter, and the great fluctuations experienced on land in spring and autumn, it is important that the research is based on year-round observations and experiments (except for migratory species) and the majority of scientists overwinter for two consecutive seasons in the Antarctic. Contact with supervisors or advisors in the United Kingdom is maintained by teleprinter and adequate laboratory facilities are available at the two biological research stations.

In the terrestrial field, systematic botanical collections throughout the maritime Antarctic and South Georgia date from 1960 and from these have been developed descriptive floras and phytosociological accounts (e.g. Greene, 1964; Smith, 1972). This work is still being added to on an opportunistic basis and has made possible the ecological studies that have followed, notably a significant contibution to the I.B.P. Tundra Biome studies (Callaghan, Smith & Walton, 1976) and subsequent research. At Signy Island a pair of contrasting moss sites, one a dry moss-turf, the other a wet moss-carpet, were instrumented and have been studied in detail for ten years. These sites were chosen because they are typical and widespread communities of the island and the northern maritime Antarctic as a whole, and afforded sufficiently large uniform stands to permit adequate long-term sampling (Tillbrook, 1973). Energy flow and seasonal abundance of most of the important groups are now reasonably well-known and a synthesis of some of the results in the form of models of processes is now possible (Davis, 1980, this volume). Decomposition and nutrient cycling at low temperatures and the response of the microbial flora to the sudden changes associated with freeze-thaw cycles are of particular interest. The ease with which these changes can be simulated in the laboratory has provided a powerful tool for the study of micro-organism dynamics and decomposition (Wynn-Williams, 1980, this volume). Studies of decomposition of plant materials *in situ* have contrasted the slow but unique degradation patterns in Signy Island tundra with much faster rates at sub-Antarctic South Georgia. Such generally slow rates of decay, and the absence of herbivores (with the exception of a few invertebrates) in the Antarctic allow many Antarctic plants to be used for the study of the demography of current populations back through several generations (Callaghan, 1977; Collins, 1976). Relative growth rates and standing crop levels in some of the South Georgia communities are very high, comparable to some temperate communities (Smith & Walton, 1975). Micro-climatological measurements reveal the surprisingly wide range of temperatures experienced in the microhabitats occupied by the plants and animals. During much of the summer, conditions for plant growth are much more favourable than temperatures measured in a meteorological screen would suggest. Amongst vegetation, temperatures exceeding 30°C at Signy Island and 40°C at South Georgia have been recorded (Walton, 1977; Smith & Walton, 1975). Conversely, severe conditions and rapid fluctuations are regularly experienced by the biota and adaptations to tolerate or exploit these are important. Experiments under controlled conditions have shown that many Antarctic plants can photosynthesize well below 0°C and can recover their activity rapidly even after being frozen. For many invertebrates freezing means death, and survival strategies, which include the production of anti-freezes in their body fluids, have been studied using the Antarctic mite *Alaskozetes antarcticus* as an example (Block, 1980, this volume). The unique occurrence of a single species of predatory mite, *Gamasellus racovitzia,* facilitates studies on predator-prey relationships, and the feeding of micro-arthropods on microbes is clarified by low species-diversity in both groups. The introduction of brown rats, house mice and reindeer into South Georgia by sealers and whalers in the 19th and present centuries has provided an opportunity to study the effects of perturbation by natural agents on native ecosystems. Whilst reindeer at South Georgia have increased greatly they have not shown the sudden devastating crash characteristic of other island populations of reindeer (Leader-Williams, in press). This is perhaps associated with the fact that their staple diet at South Georgia is tussock grass (*Poa flabellata*) and not lichens.

The lakes and ponds of Antarctica are the most limited ecosystems found there. Conditions within them are severe and even the warmest are frozen to depths of 1–2 m for 8–12 months of the year. Consequently they are virtually isolated from external influences for most of each year and form ideal natural laboratories. BAS has played the major role in Antarctic freshwater research since the programme of coordinated studies was started at Signy Island in 1962. Certain physical, chemical and biological properties of all seventeen lakes on the island are monitored regularly and detailed studies are made on selected lakes. Light rather than temperature is the main controlling factor for plant growth. Although ice transmits light well, even a thin covering of snow can reflect and absorb up to 95% of incident radiation. The extent of snow cover is more dependent on strong winds, which can sweep snow away, than it is on precipitation itself. On Signy Island the spring phytoplankton community is adapted to low light conditions resulting in a maximum chlorophyll *a* level while the lakes are still ice-covered. The higher light levels after the thaw appear to inhibit these species and activity falls. However, more light-tolerant algal species produce a further peak of activity during the open-water period (Light, Ellis-Evans & Priddle, in press). An interim study of chemical factors influencing phytoplankton production is now being carried out. The clear lakes support dense stands of moss and benthic algae even at depths in excess of 15 m. These are capable of utilizing extremely low light levels, remaining active for all but two months of each year, but appear unable to increase productivity appreciably under the higher light conditions of summer (Priddle, 1980). In contrast, benthic algae in shallow water are frozen for a large part of each year and become very active in summer (Fogg & Horne, 1970). Similar rich aquatic vegetation occurs in the lakes of continental Antarctica where arid conditions permit little terrestrial vegetation, leading Light & Heywood (1975) to suggest that Antarctic vegetation is predominantly aquatic. The majority of lake animals are nektobenthic, feeding unselectively on epiphytic benthic plants and detritus, and are therefore independent of the brief seasonability of the phytoplankton. Predators are few and mainly appear in summer when the other species are most abundant (Heywood, Dartnall & Priddle, 1979).

Retreat of the ice on Signy Island has left a series of lakes in all stages of development from proglacial lakes on ice to highly enriched lakes near the sea shore. This evolutionary succession is described by Priddle & Heywood (1980, this volume). The enclosed system of an Antarctic lake affords an opportunity for interesting comparisons in geochemical cycling with lakes in other latitudes where wind disturbance caused water movement throughout the year. BAS are currently collaborating with the Freshwater Biological Association to study nutrient cycling in Signy Island and English Lake District lakes. The role of bacteria in nutrient cycling at the water sediment interface is also being studied. Future studies will include the interactive role of bacteria and benthic algae in the carbon cycle. Study of interactions between terrestrial and freshwater microflora is simplified by low species diversity and the sudden influx of melt-water during the spring.

The Antarctic marine ecosystem offers the widest field for research and the one with the greatest application to modern needs for maximizing food harvests for the world's increasing population. Early marine research in British Antarctic Survey was largely confined to the near-shore ecosystem. Because of seasonal ice-cover, collecting methods in the Antarctic must differ from those used in more temperate latitudes. Sampling by SCUBA divers through holes cut in the sea-ice with a chain saw has proved an effective method, as well as providing an improved and more precise form of sampling for quantitative studies. Year-round observations have shown that near-shore primary production from phytoplankton is concentrated in a limited period of the summer; seaweeds and benthic micro-algae make a concurrent but smaller contribution. Ice-associated micro-algae make a significant and characteristically polar contribution to production (Whitaker, 1977; Richardson & Whitaker, 1979). The continental shelf supports a high biomass of invertebrates which continues into the sub-littoral zone as a rich in-fauna of burrowing molluscs, annelids and crustaceans. The benthos is affected by ice-scour from grounded icebergs and pack-ice, so that the epifauna (and seaweeds) are restricted to sheltered habitats, such as vertical rock faces or crevices. Temperatures in this marine environment are low, but very stable, a striking contrast to conditions in the terrestrial habitats. Because of this, adaptations of marine organisms have followed a different course from those of terrestrial invertebrates. Clarke (1980, this volume) shows that low basal metabolic rates, slow growth and slow protein synthesis rates enable marine invertebrates to exploit more effectively the food resources which seasonally may be very small. Life cycles and reproductive strategies must also adapt to the short period of high production in the Antarctic summer (White, 1977). Planktonic larvae of benthic invertebrates are rare in the Antarctic, probably because they are less able to exploit the brief abundance of phytoplankton during the summer bloom. Most invertebrates produce a few large yolky eggs from which advanced juveniles emerge after a long development. This is illustrated by work on prosobranch molluscs (Picken, 1980, this volume), one of the many groups of the inshore fauna studied at Signy Island.

Inshore fish in the Antarctic show particularly interesting adaptations, both physiological and biochemical, to low temperature. A unique adaptation of the channichthyid fish, found in no other vertebrate, is the absence of all haemoglobin and erythrocytes. These fish have large hearts which pump large volumes of low viscosity blood through wide vessels at low pressure and are able to compete favourably with sympatric conventional fish in the cold, oxygen-rich waters of the Antarctic (Twelves, 1972). Biochemical adaptations occur in the muscle and enzyme systems of Antarctic fish, involving changes in the myosin, actin and calcium regulatory proteins which modulate the ATP-ase activity, enabling them to function efficiently at very low temperatures (Johnston & Walesby, 1977).

With the collapse of some major fisheries in the north, and the establishment of exclusive economic zones for fishing there has been a great surge of interest in marine resources in the Antarctic, particularly krill, *Euphausia superba*. Because of the key role of krill in the Antarctic marine ecosystem, and the unknown effects that krill exploitation might have on other components of the ecosystem, BAS has embarked on a programme on the biology of krill, its principal predators and its environment (Bonner, Clarke, Everson, Heywood, Whitaker & White, 1978). This programme will build on the base of knowledge already established by the 'Discovery' investigations. The RRS 'John Biscoe', one of the Survey's two ships, has been equipped as a marine sampling platform and is participating in the international cooperative programme BIOMASS (Biological Investigations of Marine Antarctic Systems and Stocks), sponsored by SCAR, SCOR, IABO and ACMRR*. Krill is the dominant Antarctic zooplankton and its characteristic habit of forming dense swarms is closely associated with its role as the principal prey species for many species of fish, squid, birds and seals. An understanding of the swarming behaviour of krill is essential to interpret observations on the abundance of krill in net hauls or on echograms, a subject discussed by Everson & Ward (1980, this volume).

The abundant and diverse colonies of breeding seabirds found at Bird Island provide a useful means for investigating the utilization of marine resources by the different species. Antarctic birds show little fear of man and food samples can be collected without causing undue disturbance. Examination of these samples, coupled with study of breeding strategies in several pairs of closely similar species (for example, Black-browed and Grey-headed Albatrosses; South Georgia and Common Diving Petrels) shows how the food resources are divided between them. In some cases chick-feeding periods are complementary between species-pairs, so that direct competition for food is reduced, while in others there may be species differences in the frequency with which chicks are fed, allowing one species to exploit more distant feeding grounds than another. More frequently, however, differences are found in the detailed composition of diets (Croxall & Prince, 1980, this volume). A further extension of these trophodynamic studies has been the use of seabirds as sampling devices for oceanic squid, which have proved difficult to catch by conventional methods.

Most Antarctic seabirds are long-lived and at Bird Island banding records extend back over 20 years. Such populations of known age and recorded breeding history provide powerful tools for demographic studies. Antarctic seabirds, particularly penguins, are major predators of krill, ranking with whales and seals. Distribution studies of birds and monitoring fluctuations in their numbers can provide useful information on krill abundance, which may prove difficult to record in other ways (Croxall & Prince, 1979).

The intensive exploitation of fur and elephant seals in the past has created natural perturbation experiments from which results can now be harvested. Antarctic fur seals, nearly exterminated in the 19th century, are now recovering at a faster rate than any other seal population (Laws, 1973; Payne, 1977). This may be related to the great reduction in baleen whales which has allowed the

---

* Scientific Committee on Antarctic Research; Scientific Committee on Oceanic Research; International Association for Biological Oceanography; and Advisory Committee on Marine Resources Research, respectively.

increase of krill stocks, on which the fur seals also feed. Rapidly expanding populations such as this provide opportunities for studies of colonization and the effects of crowding on breeding success and social behaviour.

The study of mammalian populations in general was greatly advanced when Laws (1953) showed that age and time of first breeding could be determined from the examination of incremental layers in teeth. This discovery, first made on the elephant seal, has since been applied to other mammalian groups, but research on elephant seals still continues. Comparative studies of elephant seals at South Georgia, where heavy exploitation was practised till 1964 and at Macquarie Island where the seals had not been disturbed for many years, showed differences in sex ratios and growth rates that were thought to be the result of sealing. Sex ratios at South Georgia have now reverted to the presumed natural values, but differences in growth rates remain, which appear to be intrinsic and may be related to food availability (McCann, 1980, this volume).

No nation has made a greater contribution to the study of Antarctic biology than the United Kingdom. Improved facilities and the accumulation of expertise mean that we can continue to exploit the scientific challenge offered by this great natural laboratory. The immediate relevance of studies on a vast and exploitable resource such as krill is apparent. Some of the other research is less easily related to practical problems as they affect us at home, though this need not detract from their value to science, and as history repeatedly shows us, it is never possible to say of a piece of research that it has no applied value. Despite the financial stringency of present times, BAS remains among the leaders in the scientific exploration of Antarctica, maintaining a tradition going back more than 200 years.

REFERENCES

BERTRAM, G. C. L., 1940. The biology of the Weddell and Crabeater seals. *British Graham Land Expedition 1934–37 Scientific Reports, 1* (1): 1–139.

BLOCK, W., 1980. Survival strategies in polar terrestrial arthropods. *Biological Journal of the Linnean Society, 14:* 29–38.

BONNER, W. N., CLARKE, A., EVERSON, I., HEYWOOD, R. B., WHITAKER, T. M. & WHITE, M. G., 1978. *Research on Krill in Relation to the Southern Ocean Ecosystem by British Antarctic Survey.* International Council for the Exploration of the Sea, C.M. 1978/L: 23. 6 pp. mimeo.

BROWN, R. N. R., MOSSMAN, R. C. & PIRIE, J. H. H., 1906. *The Voyage of the 'Scotia'.* Edinburgh & London: William Blackwood.

CALLAGHAN, T. V., 1977. Adaptive strategies in the life cycle of South Georgian graminoid species. In G. A. Llano (Ed.), *Adaptations within Antarctic Ecosystems:* 981–1002. Washington: Smithsonian Institution.

CALLAGHAN, T. V., SMITH, R. I. L. & WALTON, D. W. H., 1976. The I.B.P. Bipolar Botanical Project. *Philosophical Transactions of the Royal Society of London (B), 274:* 315–319.

CHERRY-GARRARD, A., 1922. *The Worst Journey in the World.* London, Bombay & Sidney: Constable.

CLARKE, A., 1980. A reappraisal of the concept of metabolic cold adaptation in polar marine invertebrates. *Biological Journal of the Linnean Society, 14:* 77–92.

COLLINS, N. J., 1976. Growth and population dynamics of the moss *Polytrichum alpestre* in the maritime Antarctic. Strategies of growth and population dynamics of tundra plants 2. *Oikos, 27:* 389–401.

COLLINS, N. J., BAKER, J. H. & TILBROOK, P. J., 1975. Signy Island, Maritime Antarctic. In T. Rosswall & O. W. Heal, *Structure and Function of Tundra Ecosystems. Ecological Bulletins (Stockholm),* No. *20:* 345–374.

COOK, J., 1784. *A Voyage Towards the South Pole and Around the World,* 2 vols. London: W. Strahan & T. Cadell.

CROXALL, J. P. & PRINCE, P. A., 1979. Antarctic seabird and seal monitoring studies. *Polar Record, 19* (123): 573–595.

CROXALL, J. P. & PRINCE, P. A., 1980. Food, feeding ecology and ecological segregation of seabirds at South Georgia. *Biological Journal of the Linnean Society, 14:* 103–131.

DAVIS, R. C., 1980. Peat respiration and decomposition in Antarctic terrestrial moss communities. *Biological Journal of the Linnean Society, 14:* 39–49.

DEACON, G. E. R., 1937. The hydrology of the Southern Ocean. *'Discovery' Reports, 15:* 1–124.

DREW, E. A., 1977. The physiology of photosynthesis and respiration in some Antarctic marine algae. *British Antarctic Survey Bulletin,* No. *46:* 59–76.

EVERSON, I. & WARD, P., 1980. Aspects of Scotia sea zooplankton. *Biological Journal of the Linnean Society, 14:* 93–101.

FOGG, G. E. & HORNE, A. J., 1970. The physiology of Antarctic freshwater algae. In M. W. Holdgate (Ed.), *Antarctic Ecology:* 632–638. London & New York: Academic Press.

GREENE, S. W., 1964. The vascular flora of South Georgia. *British Antarctic Survey Scientific Reports,* No. *45:* 58 pp.

HARDY, A., 1967. *Great Waters.* London: Collins.

HEYWOOD, R. B., 1967. Antarctic ecosystems. The freshwater lakes of Signy Island and their fauna. *Philosophical Transactions of the Royal Society of London (B), 261:* 347–362.

HEYWOOD, R. B., DARTNALL, H. J. G. & PRIDDLE, J., 1979. The freshwater lakes of Signy Island, South Orkney Islands, Antarctica. Data sheets. *British Antarctic Survey Data, 3:* 46 pp.

HOLDGATE, M. W., 1965. Biological research by the British Antarctic Survey. *Polar Record, 12 (80):* 553–573.

HOLDGATE, M. W., 1977. Terrestrial ecosystems in the Antarctic. *Philosophical Transactions of the Royal Society of London (B), 279:* 5–25.

HOOKER, J. D., 1847. *The Botany of the Antarctic Voyage of H.M. Discovery Ships 'Erebus' and 'Terror' in the Years 1839–1843. Flora Antarctica Parts 1, 2.* London: Reeve Bros.

JOHNSTON, I. A. & WALESBY, N. J., 1977. Molecular mechanisms of temperature adaptation in fish myofibrillar adenosine triphosphatases. *Journal of Comparative Physiology, 119:* 195–206.

LAWS, R. M., 1953. The Elephant seal (*Mirounga leonina* Linn.) I. Growth and Age. *Scientific Reports of the Falkland Islands Dependencies Survey,* No. *8:* 62 pp.

LAWS, R. M., 1956a. The Elephant seal (*Mirounga leonina* (Linn.)) II General, social and reproductive behaviour. *Scientific Reports of the Falkland Islands Dependencies Survey,* No. *13:* 88 pp.

LAWS, R. M., 1956b. The Elephant seal (*Mirounga leonina* (Linn.) III. The physiology of reproduction. *Scientific Reports of the Falkland Islands Dependencies Survey,* No. *15:* 66 pp.

LAWS, R. M., 1973. Population increase of fur seals at South Georgia. *Polar Record, 16 (105):* 856–858.

LAWS, R. M., 1976. British research in the Antarctic. *Journal of the Royal Society of Arts* (October 1976): 630–645.

LEADER-WILLIAMS, N., in press. Populations ecology of reindeer on South Georgia. *Proceedings of the Second International Reindeer/Caribou Symposium* Røros, 1979.

LIGHT, J. J., ELLIS-EVANS, C. & PRIDDLE, J., in press. Phytoplankton ecology in an Antarctic lake. *Freshwater Biology.*

LIGHT, J. J. & HEYWOOD, R. B., 1975. Is the vegetation of continental Antarctica predominantly aquatic? *Nature, 256:* 199–200.

McCANN, T. S., 1980. Population structure and social organization of the Southern Elephant Seals, *Mirounga leonina* (L.). *Biological Journal of the Linnean Society, 14:* 133–150.

NORDENSKJÖLD, Ö., 1905. *Antarctica, or Two Years amongst the Ice of the South Pole.* London: Hurst & Blackett.

PAYNE, M. R., 1977. Growth of a fur seal population. *Philosophical Transactions of the Royal Society of London (B), 279:* 67–79.

PICKEN, G. B., 1980. Reproductive adaptations of Antarctic benthic invertebrates. *Biological Journal of the Linnean Society, 14:* 67–75.

PRIDDLE, J., 1980. The production ecology of benthic plants in some Antarctic lakes I. *In situ* production studies. *Journal of Ecology, 68:* 141–153.

PRIDDLE, J. & HEYWOOD, R. B., 1980. Evolution of Antarctic lake ecosystems. *Biological Journal of the Linnean Society, 14:* 51–66.

RICHARDSON, M. G. & WHITAKER, T. M., 1979. An Antarctic food chain: observations on the interaction of the amphipod *Pontogenia antarctica* Chevreux with ice-associated micro-algae. *British Antarctic Survey Bulletin,* No. *47:* 107–115.

ROBERTS, B. B., 1940. The breeding behaviour of penguins with special reference to *Pygoscelis papua* (Forster), *British Graham Land Expedition, 1934–37 Scientific Reports, 1:* 195–254.

SLADEN, W. J. L., 1958. The Pygoscelid penguins: I. Methods of study. II. The Adelie penguin, *Pygoscelis adeliae* (Hombron and Jacquinot). *Scientific Reports of the Falkland Islands Dependencies Survey,* No. *17:* 97 pp.

SMITH, R. I. L., 1972. Vegetation of the South Orkney Islands with particular reference to Signy Island. *British Antarctic Survey Scientific Reports,* No. *68:* 124 pp.

SMITH, R. I. L. & WATSON, D. W. H., 1975. South Georgia, Sub-antarctic. In T. Rosswall & O. W. Heal (Eds), *Structure and Function of Tundra Ecosystems. Ecological Bulletins,* No. *20:* 399–423.

TILBROOK, P. J., 1973. The Signy Island Terrestrial reference sites. I. An Introduction. *British Antarctic Survey Bulletin,* Nos. *33 & 34:* 65–76.

TWELVES, E. L., 1972. Blood volume of two Antarctic fishes. *British Antarctic Survey Bulletin,* No. *31:* 85–92.

WALTON, D. W. H., 1977. Radiation and soil temperatures 1972–74: Signy Island Terrestrial Reference Sites. *British Antarctic Survey Data,* No. *1:* 49 pp.

WEDDELL, J., 1825. *A Voyage Towards the South Pole, Performed in the Year 1822–24.* London: Longman. Hurst, Rees, Orme, Brown & Green.

WHITAKER, T. M., 1977. Sea-ice habitats of Signy Island (South Orkneys) and their primary productivity. In G. A. Llano (Ed.), *Adaptations within Antarctic Ecosystems:* 75–82. Washington: Smithsonian Institution.

WHITE, M. G., 1977. Ecological adaptations by Antarctic poikilotherms to the polar marine environment. In G. A. Llano (Ed.), *Adaptations within Antarctic Ecosystems:* 197–208. Washington: Smithsonian Institution.

WYNN-WILLIAMS, D. D., 1980. Seasonal fluctuations in microbial activity in Antarctic moss peat. *Biological Journal of the Linnean Society, 14:* 11–28.

Seasonal fluctuations in microbial activity in Antarctic moss peat

D. D. WYNN-WILLIAMS

Life Sciences Division, British Antarctic Survey,
Natural Environment Research Council,
Madingley Road, Cambridge CB3 OET, England

Accepted for publication January 1980

The Signy Island terrestrial reference sites epitomize unpolluted maritime Antarctic tundra. The extreme transition from the harsh Antarctic winter to the milder summer facilitates studies of the effects of freeze–thaw cycles on microbial activity in moss peat. Seasonal monitoring of peat oxygen uptake showed a transient spring peak at *c.* 0°C, attributed to microbial utilization of dissolved organic carbon (DOC). After a more gradual temperature-linked summer increase, autumnal freeze–thaw cycles stimulated a final pre-winter peak. The transient climaxes were associated with blooms of saccharolytic yeasts and microfungi. The bacterial population stabilized after a spring increase but then diversified as DOC became rate-limiting. Effects of pre-monitored spring freeze–thaw cycles on late-winter peat cores were simulated in a Gilson respirometer. *In vitro* perturbations demonstrated the regulatory effects of DOC availability, water content and temperature on peat respiration and microfloral composition. Comparative respirometry and loss in tensile strength of interred cotton strips showed a difference in decomposer activity beneath a relatively dry *Polytrichum–Chorisodontium* turf and a wet *Calliergon–Cephaloziella* carpet. This was associated with water content and anaerobiosis. Cellulolysis accelerated during the growing season and increased with depth, despite anaerobic conditions. Estimates of annual bryophyte decomposition are presented for use in an Antarctic ecosystem model.

KEY WORDS:– terrestrial – tundra – Antarctic – peat – microbiology – decomposition – respiration – simulation – freeze–thaw – cellulolysis.

CONTENTS

INTRODUCTION

Antarctica is isolated from any major conurbations and industry which emit both chemical and microbial contaminants (Allen, Grimshaw & Holdgate, 1967) although scientific stations may cause local contamination. Terrestrial microbio-

11

logical studies in the Antarctic therefore offer an ideal opportunity to determine baseline soil microbial population composition and decomposer activity in virtually undisturbed tundra. There are no terrestrial vertebrates, besides land-nesting birds, and the vegetation comprises simple floristically-poor bryophyte and lichen dominated communities (Smith & Gimingham, 1976) which with their associated immature soils have a limited microflora and microfauna. Such ecosystems are best developed in the less severe environment of the maritime Antarctic (Holdgate, 1977) where the vegetation and soil are subjected to well defined spring and autumn freeze–thaw transitions. The activity and composition of the peat-soil microflora in relation to seasonal temperature changes was investigated at Signy Island, South Orkney Islands (lat. 60° 43′S, long. 45° 38′W), where winter air temperatures are commonly between −20° and −30°C but midsummer temperatures reach 5°C with maxima of c. 10°C.

The Signy Island terrestrial reference sites (SIRS) were selected near Gourlay Peninsula (Tilbrook, 1973) with convenient access to the British Antarctic Survey research station, equipped for microbiological work. Two contrasting sites were established—a relatively dry moss turf community site (SIRS 1) on a bluff dominated by *Polytrichum alpestre* Hoppe and *Chorisodontium aciphyllum* (Hook. f. et Wils.) Broth., and a wet moss carpet community in a shallow basin (SIRS 2) dominated by *Calliergon sarmentosum* (Wahlenb.) Kindb., *Calliergidium austro-stramineum* (C. Muell.) Bartr., *Drepanocladus uncinatus* (Hedw.) Warnst. and the liverwort *Cephaloziella varians* (Gottsche) Steph. (Smith, 1972).

The SIRS were established to provide a wide range of floristic and faunistic data for synthesis into a model of ecosystem energy dynamics for maritime Antarctic tundra peat, comparable with other International Biological Programme (IBP) sites (Flanagan & Veum, 1974). Microbial decomposer activity is a major component in the model. The microbial population of a range of Signy Island soil types has been surveyed by Heal, Bailey & Latter (1967) and Bailey & Wynn-Williams (in press). Baker (1970a, b, 1974) and Baker & Smith (1972) examined the population of *Chorisodontium* peat on the west coast of the island comparable with SIRS 1. Overall decomposition in this peat was assessed by Dixon respirometry of whole core sections (Baker, 1970a), litter bags containing air-dried peat cores re-interred, loss in dry weight of *Chorisodontium* stem sections with depth (time) assuming no vertical compression, and by bulk density measurements at various depths (Baker, 1972). Rates of peat decomposition varied with the degree of compression which itself varied with vegetation cover (Fenton, in press) and with seasonal fluctuations in temperature, peat water content and nutrient availability.

The aims of the present research were five-fold: (1) an assessment of microbial decomposition of biological materials ranging from dissolved organic carbon (DOC), such as sugars, to macromolecules such as cellulose; (2) determination of the effects on decomposer activity of seasonal microclimatic changes such as temperature, moisture content and nutrient availability; (3) demonstration of the biological importance of spring and autumn freeze–thaw transitions; (4) simulation *in vitro* of freeze–thaw cycles and perturbations such as amendments with nutrients; (5) investigations of different peat decomposition rates by respirometry *in vitro* and cotton strip decomposition *in situ* at different depths beneath the dominant moss species at SIRS to provide data for the SIRS ecosystem model (Davis, 1980, this volume).

METHODS

The SIRS have been fully described by Tilbrook (1973) and Collins, Baker & Tilbrook (1975). Peat cores of 27 mm diameter were sampled to 12 cm depth beneath *Polytrichum* and *Chorisodontium* on SIRS 1 and *Calliergon* and *Cephaloziella* on SIRS 2. In winter the sites were frozen for *c.* seven months and a power drill with corer attachment was used; in summer a sterilized steel hand-corer and syringe system was employed. Routinely eight replicate cores were cut aseptically into 1–3, 3–6, 6–9 and 9–12 cm sections for direct injection into sterile base cones (Quickfit, CNB34) of special Gilson respirometry flasks (Parkinson & Coups, 1963). Four more cores were similarly sectioned and subsampled for microbiological counting. Viable bacterial counts were obtained on modified casein peptone starch agar (CPSA, IBP code 0200. xxxx. 01.08.3; Rosswall, 1971) amended with peat expressate and 50 mg l^{-1} each of Nystatin (E. R. Squibb & Sons, Moreton, Merseyside) and Actidione (The Upjohn Company, Michigan, USA). Yeasts and micro-fungi were counted on Sabouraud dextrose agar (SDA, IBP code 015. xxxx. 01.04.1) amended with 250 mg l^{-1} sodium propionate and 30 mg l^{-1} Aureomycin (Lederle Laboratories Division, Cyanamid of Great Britain Ltd., Gosport). Spread plates were incubated at 10°C for 14 days before counting. Full details of all procedures are given in Wynn-Williams (1979).

In summer the screening of peat cores for oxygen uptake and the treatment of subsamples were completed within 12 h of field sampling. Winter cores were used as soon as possible or stored at −10°C. Laboratory procedures were conducted on a cooled bench at 0–5°C.

The basic procedure for Gilson respirometry is given in Wynn-Williams (1979). Measurements were made at ambient field temperature and at a standard 5°C relative to synthetic control cores of wet cotton wool. In simulation experiments, peat temperature was monitored in an accessory core using an Edale thermistor thermometer (Grant Instruments Ltd.).

The collection and storage of peat cores at −10°C for subsequent *in vitro* simulation of the four critical seasonal periods shown in Fig. 1 is summarized in Table 1. In each case, 1–3 cm depth whole core sections were subjected to freeze–thaw cycles in a Gilson respirometer comparable with those monitored in the field. Certain cores were desiccated at 0–5°C in a chamber containing silica gel for 20–40 h to investigate microbial moisture requirements for respiration. Amendments with dissolved organic carbon (DOC) entailed aseptic pipetting of 0.5 ml aliquots of 0.1% w/v (rather than 0.5% as in Wynn-Williams, 1979) glucose or mannitol solution evenly on to the surface of cores in base cones before replacing them in Gilson flasks. *Polytrichum* peat cores from the autumn 1976 Gilson respirometry simulation were also subjected to analysis of carbon dioxide evolution using an Analytical Development Company Series 225 infra-red gas analyser (IRGA).

The technique of cotton strip insertion is described in Latter & Howson (1977) and the characteristics of different fabrics are reviewed in Walton & Allsopp (1977). The strips of unbleached calico (170 gm^{-2}) 35 cm long by 10 cm wide were autoclaved and inserted into pre-cut slits in peat *in situ* to a depth of 15–20 cm using a strip of aluminium as a guide. Twenty replicate strips were placed in each of *Polytrichum*, *Chorisodontium*, *Calliergon* and *Cephaloziella* in late autumn (March 1977). Ten replicates were removed after the spring thaw had reached *c.* 15 cm depth (January 1978). However, skuas removed so many strips that another series was

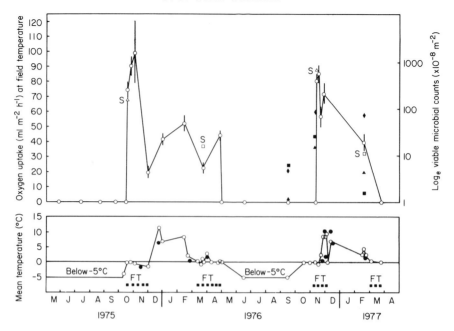

Figure 1. Seasonal variation for 1975–1977 in microbial population and oxygen uptake (mean ± s.e.) at ambient ground temperature, 1–3 cm beneath *Polytrichum alpestre* at SIRS 1. ○, *Polytrichum* data; △ S, integrated maximum oxygen uptake in simulation; □ S, basal uptake in simulation; ◆, bacteria ▲, yeasts; ■, fungi; ●, comparative SIRS 2 ground temperature; _ FT _ , period of freeze–thaw cycling.

inserted to monitor autumn decomposition between the period of basal activity in late summer and the pre-winter freeze–thaw cycles. After recovery and examination for discoloration, the strips were washed but not scrubbed, and then dried for storage and treatment as described in Latter & Howson (1977). Threads were picked off the strips with fine forceps to the required width. After equilibration at 80% r.h. at room temperature for a week, the tensile strength (TS) of the strips was measured at 80% r.h. and 24° C by Biodeterioration Information Centre, University of Aston, Birmingham.

Fluctuations in peat temperature were monitored in the field using an Edale thermistor thermometer and a Grant microclimate recorder. The measurement of other environmental factors including peat water content, pH and loss on ignition is described by Wynn-Williams (1979).

RESULTS

Seasonal fluctuations in peat respiratory activity

In Fig. 1, oxygen uptake by peat at 1–3 cm depth beneath *Polytrichum* illustrates the seasonal fluctuation of total decomposer activity, most of which is probably due to the microflora (Fenton, 1978) which was further substantiated by the present simulation experiments. Respiration during winter was undetectable although it was measured at −1°C in drained, re-frozen cores. The spring thaw stimulated maximal activity despite the temperature remaining around or even slightly below 0°C. This period was one of frequent freeze-thaw cycles but field

Table 1. Collection and storage of peat cores used in simulations indicated in Fig.
1 and Table 2

Vegetation cover	Simulation	Equivalent field sample date	Simulation core collection date	Condition when sampled	Duration of frozen storage (months)
Polytrichum	Spring 1975	17 Oct. 1975	13 Oct. 1975	Frozen	11
Polytrichum	Autumn 1975	22 Mar. 1975	13 Oct. 1975	Frozen	11
Polytrichum	Spring 1976	12 Nov. 1975	20 Oct. 1976	Frozen	2
Polytrichum	Autumn 1976	17 Feb. 1975	4 Feb. 1976	Thawed	5
Chorisodontium	Spring 1976	28 Oct. 1975	25 Oct. 1976	Thawed	None

measurements could only yield integrated values of respirometry activity for practical reasons. The results for 1975 showed a sharp post-spring decline in activity followed by a midsummer increase and late summer decline associated with temperature changes. Autumnal freeze–thaw cycles also stimulated a sharp increase in oxygen uptake but at half the maximal level. The demonstration of reproducibility of these maximal and basal levels of activity by simulations *in vitro* (Fig. 1, 1975–76) using cores collected before the spring thaw (Table 1) indicated a 'microcosm' system suitable for perturbation studies. The predictive potential of such a system was supported by the similarity in peat activity changes between the 1975 and 1976 seasons.

The system also facilitated estimating the size and composition of viable microbial populations associated with respiratory changes. Counts in the 1976–77 season (Fig. 1) showed an increase in all three microbial groups—bacteria, yeasts and micro-fungi—in spring. However, they responded differently during the remainder of the growing season. The bacteria remained relatively constant in number but increased in species diversity; after a large spring increase relative to the low winter population size, yeast numbers declined during the summer; the glucose utilizing micro-fungi decreased greatly in numbers after the spring bloom, but this effect may be exaggerated by the spread plate method of enumerating fungal colony-generating units.

Simulation in vitro *of seasonal changes*

The peat temperature cycling of the 1976–77 growing season was reproduced *in vitro* using cores collected shortly before the spring thaw (Table 1) to give the oxygen uptake data in Fig. 2. Each freeze–thaw cycle gave a peak of respiratory activity (S.E. always $< 8\%$ of the peak) which increased in two stages, possibly reflecting the decrease in saccharolytic fungal biomass with increasing yeast biomass. Regression analysis of log yeast count g^{-1} wet weight on incubation time (h) confirmed an exponential population increase ($r = 0.970$, $P < 0.05$, $N = 4$, $y = 0.18x + 9.591$). The bacterial biomass remained relatively constant and therefore probably non-influential. Regression analyses showed no demonstrable correlation between bacterial, yeast or fungal biomass and oxygen uptake in the simulation. However, oxygen uptake (μl oxygen h^{-1} ml^{-1} suspension) was shown to correlate ($r = 0.924$, $P < 0.001$, $N = 12$) with viable yeast counts ($\times 10^{-2}$ ml^{-1}) in a homogenate of 50 g of *c.* 3 cm depth *Polytrichum* peat in 300 ml of diluent. The regression oxygen uptake (y) on yeast counts (x) was given by $y = 0.0011x + 0.077$.

Table 2. *Effect of freeze–thaw cycles on viable microbial counts and oxygen uptake in 1–3 cm depth* Polytrichum *peat cores relative to continuously thawed controls*

Simulation	Sample	Initial freeze-thawed/thawed core data ratio and subsequent percentage change				
		Bacteria	Yeasts	Fungi	Total	Oxygen uptake
Spring 1976†	Initial	1.20	1.30	1.30	1.30	1.02
	After 7 F/T* and prolonged incubation	−85	+78	−23	c. +76	+17
Autumn 1977††	Initial	2.21	1.24	1.95	1.86	1.15
	After 4 F/T	−57	−90	+45	−80	−21
	After 7 F/T	−58	−42	ND	−81	−30
	After prolonged incubation	+45	+243	ND	+243	−14

F/T　Freeze–thaw cycle; T, continuously thawed.
*　　After 4F/T the ratio was 2.3 (+125%) and after 7 F/T it was 4.0 +74%).
†　　For microbial counts, $N = 4$ in the F/T series and 2 in the T series;
　　　for oxygen uptake, $N = 5$ in the F/T series and 6 in the T series.
††　For microbial counts, $N = 3$ in the F/T series and 2 in the T series;
　　　for oxygen uptake, $N = 8$ in the F/T series and 4 in the T series.
ND　Not determined.

A comparison of the different effects of freeze–thaw cycles on peat cores sampled before spring and later in the growing season is shown in Table 2. The yeast population particularly reflects the probable relative availability of DOC in spring and autumn. Freeze–thaw cycling was slightly deleterious to oxygen uptake in autumn cores relative to continuously thawed controls whose population increased uninterrupted.

Integration of the respiratory responses to the freeze–thaw cycles yielded a simulated spring maximum for 1976 very similar to the observed field value (Fig. 1). The mean simulated basal value (Fig. 2) after cessation of freezing was likewise similar to the equivalent autumnal value recorded *in vivo* in mid February 1977 (Fig. 1).

Microbial counts m^{-2} *in vivo* could be approximately equated to counts g^{-1} fresh weight *in vitro* by the conversion: counts $m^{-2} \equiv$ counts g^{-1} fresh weight $\times 1.733 \times 10^4$, assuming a mean ($\pm$ S.E.) wet weight of eight simulation cores of 9.925 ± 0.184 g and a core surface area of 5.726 cm^2. The initial microbial population of the spring simulation cores was similar to the equivalent late winter population of September 1976 (Fig. 1). Neither bacterial, yeast or micro-fungal simulation populations were initially more than two to three times larger than in equivalent field samples despite prolonged frozen storage. However, after the spring freeze–thaw cycles in the field the bacterial population was conversely ten times larger than the equivalent simulation population. Although the yeast population *in vivo* increased tenfold in early spring, this exponential increase was attained within 120 h *in vitro* after only four freeze–thaw cycles, only stabilizing after c. 300 h (Fig. 2). Such an increase was not apparent *in vivo* (Fig. 1), possibly owing to dilution of the developing population by leaching which could not occur in the closed simulation system. Conversely, although initially similar in size to the yeast population, the saccharolytic micro-fungal population decreased tenfold within the same 120 h period *in vitro*.

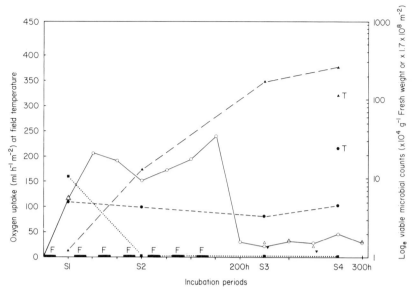

Figure 2. Simulation of Spring 1976 temperature cycling in peat 1–3 cm beneath *Polytrichum alpestre* at SIRS 1. O, oxygen uptake by thawed cores after freezing; △, oxygen uptake by continuously-thawed cores; ●, bacteria; ▲, yeasts; ■, fungi; T, continuously thawed; F, freeze.

Slight elevation in peat temperature above 0°C during spring has several concurrent effects: drainage of interstitial ice as melt-water permits gaseous exchange within the peat; inorganic nutrients from the air and fauna are mobilized (Northover & Allen, 1967); DOC is leached from frost-damaged microbial, macrofloral and microfaunal cells percolating downwards into the oligotrophic peat.

Direct evidence of the importance of DOC as a respiratory substrate is given in Table 3. Glucose was consistently stimulatory and mannitol slightly less so. Amendment with water was occasionally deleterious owing to saturation but was stimulatory in late summer peat from *Chorisodontium* owing to desiccation in the field. DOC, probably mainly intracellular, must accumulate quite rapidly during winter as indicated by near maximal levels of oxygen uptake shown in cores from all sites after thawing and screening at the standard temperature of 5°C (Fig. 3) in June and September 1976.

Total peat respiration and microbial counts decreased with depth and varied with vegetation cover according to aeration-limiting water content. Table 4 shows that decrease in oxygen uptake with increasing depth was twice as fast beneath *Calliergon* in the wet moss carpet (mean 1975–76 growing season water content of 1573% dry weight ± 155% S.E.) than beneath *Polytrichum* in the drier moss turf (moisture content of 511% dry weight ± 30% S.E.) suggesting a sharp *Eh* gradient. Oxygen uptake in 1–3 cm depth SIRS 1 peat was occasionally more than twice that at SIRS 2 (Fig. 3), consistent with increasingly anaerobic conditions due to waterlogging. This was implied, although not confirmed, by the blackening of silver-plated stakes by sulphide production in peat beneath *Cephaloziella* (Fig. 4). Table 5 suggests a linear decrease in aerobic respiration with increasing depth beneath *Chorisodontium* and *Calliergon* but a non-linear decrease beneath *Polytrichum* and *Cephaloziella*. The reasons for these differences were not

Table 3. Effect on oxygen uptake of amending peat 1 to 3 cm beneath *Polytrichum* and *Chorisodontium* with dissolved organic carbon (DOC) *in vitro*

Cover	Simulation	Amendment†	Replicates $(N)^*$	Pre-amendment mean O_2 uptake (ml h^{-1} m^{-2} ± S.E.)	Post-amendment mean O_2 uptake (ml h^{-1} m^{-2} ± S.E.)	% change due to amendment
Polytrichum	Spring 1976	Glucose	4	30.3 ± 7.0	38.2 ± 6.8	26.0
		Water	4	22.0 ± 5.5	23.7 ± 4.4	7.7
		None	2	31.4 ± 1.3	33.6 ± 0.6	7.0
Polytrichum	Autumn 1976	Glucose	6	99.2 ± 21.1	129.0 ± 25.3	30.1
		Water	5	72.9 ± 9.9	69.7 ± 10.8	−4.4
Chorisodontium	Spring 1976	Glucose	3	48.1 ± 7.2	71.2 ± 0.8	48.0
		Water	2	53.3 ± 0.1	6.5 ± 2.7	23.3
		Mannitol	2	53.4 ± 10.5	63.7 ± 8.3	19.1
		None	1	101.9	107.9	5.9

* Replicates include all cores amended as indicated, whether pre-desiccated, freeze–thawed, or continuously thawed.
† 0.5 ml of 0.1% (w/v) solution or sterile distilled water per 11.5 cm^3 core.

Table 4. Variation in annual total aerobic peat respiration with depth at the Signy Island Reference Sites in 1975–76

Depth zone (cm)	Annual oxygen uptake (cm depth^{-1} m^{-2})							
	Polytrichum		*Chorisodontium*		*Calliergon*		*Cephaloziella*	
	ml × 10^{-3}	Ratio†	ml × 10^{-3}	Ratio	ml × 10^{-3}	Ratio	ml × 10^{-3}	Ratio
0 to 1	300.0*	16.7	—	—	69**	11.5	—	—
1 to 3	107.0	6.0	125.5	9.9	69.9	11.7	64.3	3.4
3 to 6	39.9	2.2	68.9	5.4	30.7	5.1	27.8	1.5
6 to 9	21.9	1.2	41.4	3.3	12.8	2.1	27.5	1.5
9 to 12	18.0	1.0	12.7	1.0	6.0	1.0	18.8	1.0

* Data for growing shoots (Collins 1975).
** Data for comparable *Drepanocladus* from Collins (1975).
† Relative to the lowest rate in each profile.

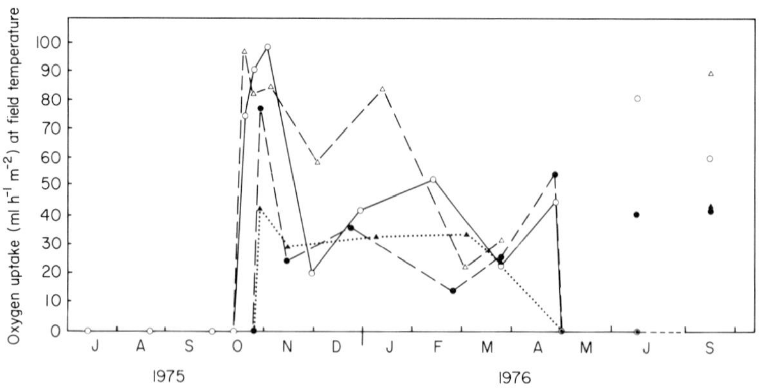

Figure 3. Comparison of 1975–1976 seasonal variation in oxygen uptake by peat from relatively dry SIRS 1 and wet SIRS 2 at ambient ground temperature. Winter values for June and September 1976 were potential rates only, at 5° C. ○, *Polytrichum;* △, *Chorisodontium;* ●, *Calliergon;* ▲, *Cephaloziella.* Open symbols, SIRS 1; closed symbols, SIRS 2.

Table 5. Regression analyses of total annual respiration (oxygen uptake ml m^{-2}) against depth of SIRS peat (1–12 cm)

Vegetation cover	x	y	N	r	P	Regression slope	Constant
Polytrichum	Depth	O_2 uptake	4	−0.931	0.1	−18462	226,402
Chorisodontium	Depth	O_2 uptake	4	−0.992	0.01	−23498	290,114
Calliergon	Depth	O_2 uptake	4	−0.980	0.02	−14593	161,553
Cephaloziella	Depth	O_2 uptake	4	−0.923	0.1	−7511	133,783
Polytrichum	Depth	$\log_e O_2$ uptake	4	−0.973	0.05	−0.165	12.499
Chorisodontium	Depth	$\log_e O_2$ uptake	4	−0.952	0.05	−0.219	13.077
Calliergon	Depth	$\log_e O_2$ uptake	4	−0.996	0.01	−0.246	12.418
Cephaloziella	Depth	$\log_e O_2$ uptake	4	−0.943	0.1	−0.086	11.868
Calliergon	LTS*	O_2 uptake	4	−0.993	0.01	−5,479	133,588

* Annual loss in tensile strength (kg cm^{-1}) relative to the depth zones between 1 and 12 cm.

associated with peat water content and were not clarified by a log transformation of the data. However, anaerobiosis was not a limiting factor for aerobic respiration at 1–3 cm beneath *Polytrichum*. This was shown by the similarity of oxygen uptake $(x: \mu g\,h^{-1})$ to concurrent carbon dioxide evolution $(y: \mu g\,h^{-1})$ measured by IRGA. The regression equation was $y = 0.065x + 0.668$ and $r = 0.815$, $P < 0.01$, $N = 12$. Conversely, estimates of decomposition rates at SIRS 2 indicated that aerobic respiration was inadequate to explain the turnover of organic matter. Anaerobic decomposition may explain the discrepancy. Although not implying causation, this was supported by the negative correlation between annual total aerobic respiration and loss of tensile strength of cotton strips with respect to increasing depth in *Calliergon* peat only (Table 5). This was consistent with a gradient becoming progressively anaerobic with increasing depth, not apparent beneath *Cephaloziella* where the peat was mainly anaerobic to within 1.5 cm of the surface (Fig. 4). SIRS 1 peat was generally aerobic down to 30 cm but may be locally microaerophilic.

Cotton strip decomposition

Table 6 summarizes losses in tensile strength of strips inserted on the day preceding the first major ground frost of winter (March 1977). Replication was reduced to an unreliable level by skua interference at the *Chorisodontium* site in summer, and to only four strips in the *Calliergon* site. The resulting data should therefore be considered with caution. The strips inserted in late summer 1978 showed little decomposition, much variation, and many increased in tensile strength relative to the insertion control mean. The series was therefore omitted from Table 6. The trend of increasing decomposition with increase in depth beneath *Polytrichum, Chorisodontium* and *Calliergon* (Table 7) continued to 18.5–21 cm depth but the latter was insufficiently replicated to include in the analyses. A close correlation was observed between yellow discoloration of the strips and loss in tensile strength (Table 7). Decomposer activity increased after spring in *Polytrichum* turf except near the surface where variation was considerable. This trend was also apparent in the *Calliergon* carpet but not in *Cephaloziella* where high water content and anaerobic conditions may obscure the summer increase which may occur at a time of DOC-limitation as suggested by respirometric data.

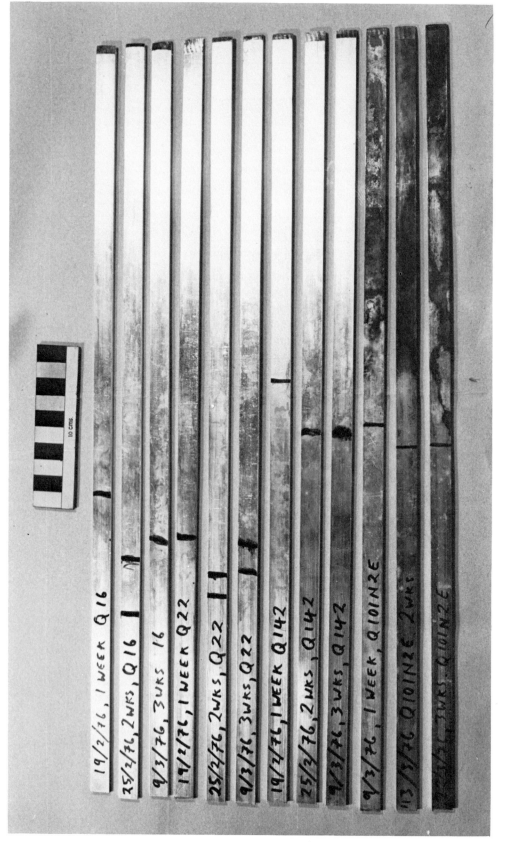

Figure 4. Crude indication of anaerobiosis by sulphide-blackening of silver-plated stakes over periods of 1, 2 and 3 weeks *in situ*. Q 16, *Chorisodontium*; Q 22, *Polytrichum*; Q 142, *Calliergon*; Q 10 IN2E, *Cephaloziella*. Marker lines indicate the position of the vegetation surface at the time of insertion and at recovery.

Table 6. Loss in tensile strength (kg cm^{-1}) of cotton strips inserted in SIRS 1 and SIRS 2 at the onset of winter 1977, relative to mean strength of insertion controls (13.5 ± s.e. 0.6 kg cm,$^{-1}$ N = 23)

Vegetation cover	Period	N	1–3	3.5–6	6.5–9	9.5–12	12.5–15	15.5–18	Depth 1–18 cm Total
					Depth (cm)				
Polytrichum	Spring (74 days)	10	1.8	0.8	0.3	0.9	3.9**	5.3**	13.1
	Season† (127 days)	10	0.7	1.4	0.9	3.2**	7.0**	10.6**	23.8
	Summer†† (53 days)	—	+1.0	0.6	0.6	2.3	3.1	5.3	10.8
Chorisodontium	Spring	10	1.3	3.0**	3.7**	4.0**	4.9**	5.3**	22.2§
Calliergon	Spring	10	+1.5**	+0.7	0.4	0.2	+0.2	0.3	+1.6
	Season	4	+0.4	1.8**	3.8**	4.0**	2.5**	2.8*	14.6
	Summer	—	1.2	2.5	3.4	3.9	2.8	2.5	16.2
Cephaloziella	Spring	10	2.0**	2.7**	2.6**	2.4**	2.8**	2.4**	15.0
	Season	8	3.8**	2.6**	4.0**	4.4**	5.4**	3.5**	23.7
	Summer††	—	1.7	+0.1	1.3	2.0	2.6	1.1	8.7

** Significance at $P < 0.01$.
† Growing season (spring plus summer) from initial thaw to first ground frost (127 days).
‡ By difference.
§ A single remaining full growing season replicate gave a 1–18 cm depth total LTS of 28.0 kg cm^{-1} (used in approximating the annual total for SIRS 1).

The losses in TS of wet strips, given in Tables 6 and 7, were internally consistent. However, when applying the combined IBP data regression equation relating loss in TS to weight loss (Latter & Howson, 1977) allowance must be made for the considerable difference in TS of the same fabric at 65% r.h. and 22°C (Heal, Howson, French & Jeffers, 1974) and at 80% r.h. at 24°C. In the absence of a TS/r.h. calibration curve, an approximate correction may be made by direct proportion. The TS values in Table 8 were therefore multiplied by the ratio of the mean insertion control TS at 'Hut Bank', Signy Island in 1970–71

Table 7. Significant regressions of loss in tensile strength (LTS) of cotton strips on increasing depth at SIRS 1 and SIRS 2

Vegetation cover	x	y	N	r	P	Regression slope	Constant
Polytrichum	Depth (1–18 cm)	Spring LTS*	6	0.748	0.10	0.270	−0.338
		Season** LTS	6	0.916	0.01	0.662	−2.185
		Summer† LTS	6	0.974	0.001	0.391	−1.847
	Yellowing (1–18 cm)†† (Scale 1 to 3)	Season LTS	23	−0.754	0.01	8.627	29.801
Chorisodontium	Depth (1–18 cm)	Spring LTS	6	0.960	0.001	0.250	1.376
Calliergon	Depth (1–18 cm)	Season LTS	6	0.894	0.02	0.106	−1.390

* LTS, loss in tensile strength (kg cm^{-1}).
** Season, growing season (spring plus summer) from initial thaw to first ground frost (127 days).
† By difference.
†† Dominance of yellow patches on decomposing strips.

Table 8. The relationship between loss in tensile strength (TS) of cotton strips and cellulose decomposition in bryophyte tissue at the Signy Island Reference Sites between March 1977 and March 1978

Series	Final TS (kg) 1–18 cm depth strips after one season**	Equivalent weight† (g m⁻² of cloth)	Equivalent weight loss (g m⁻² of cloth)	Weight loss of cloth (%)	Cellulose in vegetation cover (%)††	Weight loss of bryophyte tissue due to cellulose decomposition y⁻¹ (%)
Control	195.4	303.3	—	—	—	—
SIRS 1*	172.4	283.5	19.8	6.5	29.9	1.9
SIRS 2*	179.4	289.5	13.8	4.5	16.0	0.7

*   After correction for proportional and total vegetation cover.
** Total mean tensile strength of the six series of frayed strips totalling 14.5 cm width representing 1–18 cm depth. Growing season of 127 days.
†   Derived from the combined IBP data regression equation ($N = 1264$), weight $= 1.09$ TS $+ 135$ (Latter & Howson, 1977), after correcting for TS at 65% r.h./TS at 100% r.h. $= 0.79$.
†† Crude fibre data from *Polytrichum alpestre* (= SIRS 1 turf) and *Tortula robusta* (= SIRS 2 carpet) from South Georgia (R.I.L. Smith, pers. comm.).

(10.6 kg cm⁻¹ at 65% r.h.) (Heal *et al.,* 1974) to that at SIRS in the present study (13.5 kg cm⁻¹ at 80% r.h.) before using the regression equation. The values derived in Table 8 permit estimation of loss in weight of bryophyte tissue *in situ* due to cellulose decomposition. Such estimates complement the respirometric estimates of annual decomposition made in Table 9.

Table 9. Annual total peat respiration for the Signy Island Reference Sites during 1975–1976

Vegetation cover or site	Annual respiration (litres O₂m⁻²) and decomposition (g m⁻²)*							
	1–12 cm depth peat total		Total minus summer peak**		Total minus spring simulation basal§		Total minus peak and basal	
	R	D	R	D	R	D	R	D
Polytrichum	454.3	534	366.6	431	309.6	364	221.9	261
Chorisodontium	578.6	680	482.5	568	433.9	510	337.8	397
SIRS 1†	465.0	547	384.4	452	340.1	400	259.5	305
SIRS 1 (mean§§)	344.4	405	—	—	—	—	—	—
Calliergon	288.7	340	271.0	319	—	—	—	—
Cephaloziella	351.1	413	351.1	413	—	—	—	—
SIRS 2††	300.1	353	284.6	335	—	—	—	—
SIRS 2 (mean§§)	240.6	283	—	—	—	—	—	—

*   Assuming that 1 mg dry weight of organic matter is oxidized by 0.85 ml O₂ (Petrusewicz & Macfadyen, 1970).
** Under DOC-limited conditions for the microflora, a large proportion of this contribution in excess of the declining microbial contribution is probably due to below-ground plant biomass and microfauna.
§   The spring simulation (1976) basal respiration rate was probably mainly due to below-ground plant biomass and microfauna.
§§ Based on mean spring and autumn values for a mean growing season of 151 days for SIRS 1 and 181 days for SIRS 2 (Davis, 1980).
†   Corrected for a *Polytrichum: Chorisodontium* cover ratio of 32:68 and a total vegetation cover of 86.3%. Growing season 187 days.
†† Corrected for a *Calliergon:Cephaloziella* cover ration of 87:13. Growing season 187 days.
—   Not determined.
R, Respiration; D, decomposition.

Estimation of annual decomposer activity

The summer of 1976 was longer than average (c. 187 day for SIRS 1 compared with an average of 151 day) so that the integrated annual respiration values given in Table 9 were larger than the mean values used by Davis (1980) in deriving decomposition rates for the SIRS communities.

Two main corrections were applied to total peat respiration in assessing the microbial contribution: firstly, to compensate for the probable proportional increase in the non-saprophytic contribution during summer temperature elevation under DOC-limited conditions; and secondly, to subtract the post-spring basal respiratory level in the simulation of spring 1976, assuming this to be mainly non-microbial after DOC depletion. Both these corrections were exaggerated, but they indicated that the true microbial contributions to annual peat respiration, and *ipso facto* decomposition, were in the range of 260 to 465 l oxygen m^{-2} (mean c. 340 l m^{-2} for SIRS 1 and c. 240 l oxygen m^{-2} for SIRS 2 as used by Davis, 1980).

DISCUSSION

The seasonal fluctuation in respiratory activity shown at SIRS 1 was similar to that found beneath *Chorisodontium* on the west coast of Signy Island (Baker, 1970a). However, a different response was found in the yeast population of the two areas despite the similarity of their exceptionally large numbers (Baker, 1970b). The SIRS 1 population showed a distinct increase suring the spring thaw, unlike the erratic fluctuations of the west coast yeast numbers at the same depth. This may relate to the presence of permafrost at the west coast site, absent at SIRS 1. However, in both cases the populations decreased markedly with increasing depth, consistent with their downward translocation from their phyllosphere origin by water percolation as suggested by Baker (1970b).

The spring yeast: bacterial biomass ratio *in vivo* at SIRS 1 was 12:1, but was c. 1500:1 *in vitro*. This characteristic preponderance of yeasts in Signy Island peat was also found at the west coast site where the ratio was 500:1 (Baker, 1970b). The discrepancy between *in vivo* and *in vitro* ratios was probably due to the absence of drainage of the suspended population from cores *in vitro* which affects vertical distribution in the field.

The vertical distribution of bacteria was more variable between comparable sites. The population decreased with increasing depth at the SIRS, and although not linearly correlated with depth, it was maximal at the surface in 'Hut Bank' at Signy Island (Bailey & Wynn-Williams, in press). However, Baker (1970b) found an increase with depth in the west coast *Chorisodontium,* possibly a characteristic of an elevated pure moss bank raised above permafrost, in contrast to the mixed *Polytrichum–Chorisodontium* turf at SIRS 1.

An increase in the entire microbial population during the spring thaw has been reported at all comparable maritime and coastal continental Antarctic sites investigated. The post-spring decline was, however, variable. The bacterial population declined rapidly in the Signy Island west coast moss bank (Baker, 1970a) and in coastal continental Antarctic protoranker (*Bryum-* and lichen-bearing 'soil' No. 3) from hills above the U.S. base at McMurdo Sound (Boyd, & Boyd, 1963), but only gradually at Spring Point and Hope Bay (Antarctic Peninsula) and Deception Island (South Shetland Islands) (Margni Castrelos,

1971). However at SIRS 1 the bacterial population size remained relatively constant as its composition diversified with changing substrate quality. At the SIRS and the west coast site the yeast population declined rapidly after the spring bloom, probably because of an inability to decompose substrates other than the rapidly-utilized sugars released by frost-damaged cells (Ivarson & Gupta, 1967). The microfungal population also declined at the SIRS but recovered later in the growing season as the population adapted or diversified to utilize macromolecular substrates, consistent with the cotton strip data presented here.

Regression analyses did not show any close correlation between bacterial, yeast or fungal biomass and oxygen uptake *in vivo* or in simulation except for yeasts in culture. Similar independence was found in the *Chorisodontium* bank (Baker, 1970b). This was consistent with the relative changes of the proportions of the microbial population shown by the non-correlation of numbers between any two groups. Such trends implied adaptability of the population to changing conditions. DOC released from frost-damaged cells was exploited by saccharolytic yeasts, fungi and bacteria in spring and to a lesser extent in autumn. During the summer, DOC was probably limiting as shown by the positive respiratory response on amending with sugars (Table 3). This was paralleled by increasing cellulolytic activity with increasing depth and with advancing growing season as DOC became depleted. Bacterial multiplication was stimulated *in situ* by glucose amendment of an organic-poor soil at Paradise Harbour, Antarctic Peninsula (65°S) in midsummer (Boyd, Rothenberg & Boyd, 1970).

It was noticeable that total peat respiratory activity was independent of temperature during spring, only showing a temperature related increase later in the summer. Baker (1970a) showed a bacterial decline as the peat temperature rose. Such effects, clearly shown in the simulation of spring 1976, were indicative of DOC-dependence early in the growing season and a close correlation with nutrient release by freeze–thaw cycling in the 'zero curtain' temperature range (Chambers, 1966). Allen *et al.* (1967) showed that inorganic nutrients were unlikely to be rate-limiting at the SIRS.

The similarity between seasonal field data and the simulation of spring 1976 exemplified the suitability of Antarctic peat for detailed studies of microbial physiological responses to seasonal variation. Such 'microcosms' have been employed in studies of Arctic tundra (Coleman, 1973; Bååth *et al.,* 1978) but in each case the soil structure was disrupted before treatment, in contrast to whole peat core sections in the present study. The simulation of spring 1976 demonstrated the stimulatory effect of freeze–thaw cycles on respiratory activity which evoked an increase in yeast numbers but not in bacterial or microfungal counts. (Table 2). This was consistent with the known saccharolytic activity of yeasts during the period of readily available DOC at a favourable pH (4.4 and 5.0 at 1–3 cm depth in SIRS 1 and SIRS 2, respectively). Yeast and bacterial populations both increased during the simulation of autumn 1977, but did so faster in continuously thawed cores. These observations indicated that part of the microbial population itself was killed by freeze–thaw cycling as also shown in sub-Arctic tundra by Campbell, Biederbeck & Warder (1970). Prolonged incubation in the present simulations reduced oxygen uptake to a constant basal level, lower in spring than in autumn. It is probable that the difference between the two basal levels reflected the progressive adaptations of the peat microbial population to decomposition of more diverse substrates, in addition to residual

DOC, as the growing season advanced. This effect was impossible to reproduce in the small time scale of the simulation studies.

The simulation revealed the fine balance between desiccation and waterlogging of peat, associated with limitation of aerobic respiration. The decreasing levels of oxygen uptake with increasing depth (Table 4) were due to a combination of (1) increasing distance from the source of respiratory substrate (the growing bryophytes and algae), (2) the decreasing microbial population size, particularly with respect to yeasts, (3) the decreasing amount of below-ground viable plant biomass and microfauna, and (4) increasingly micro-aerophilic conditions. The latter factor was most pronounced at SIRS 2, beneath *Calliergon* and especially *Cephaloziella* (Fig. 4). The steepness of the aerobic to anaerobic gradient (Table 5) was inversely proportional to the peat water content, which was greatest beneath *Cephaloziella*. This saturation-related trend was also apparent between sites (Fig. 3). Aerobic respiration beneath *Polytrichum* and *Chorisodontium* was similar, consistent with fully aerobic conditions indicated by the similarity of oxygen uptake to carbon dioxide evolution by IRGA. However, *Calliergon* and *Cephaloziella* aerobic peat respiration was considerably lower without evident accumulation of organic matter at SIRS 2. This implied that anaerobic decomposition was significant.

This was illustrated by similar rates of decomposition of cotton strips between 1 and 18 cm in anaerobic *Cephaloziella* compared with the relatively aerobic *Polytrichum* and *Chorisodontium* sites (Table 6). The rate beneath *Calliergon* was apparently less, possibly due to the increase in tensile strength of some strips, previously reported for Signy Island by Latter & Howson (1977) which was partly explained by differential removal of wax or from the cementing action of soil mucilage impregnated in the cloth fibres. All measurements at Signy Island may therefore be underestimates. After correcting for the different test r.h. in the two studies, the data in Table 6, expressed as loss of tensile strength (LTS) cm^{-1}, were comparable with the data of Heal *et al.* (1974) 3 cm^{-1} because the original test strip width was 2.5 cm per test level except for the 2.0 cm between 1 and 3 cm depth. The loss in tensile strength beneath *Polytrichum* (Table 6) showed a positive correlation with increasing depth (Table 7). This trend increased in significance during the growing season as the gradient steepened, especially when measured over a full growing season. A similar correlation was found beneath *Chorisodontium*. This overall trend at SIRS 1 confirmed the increasing decomposition rate with increased depth shown at the Signy 'Hut Bank' site of the IBP in 1970–71 and a *Polytrichum* bank on Observation Bluff, Signy Island in 1975–76 (Fenton, 1978), contrasting uniquely with all other IBP tundra sites (Heal *et al.*, 1974). A strong correlation was observed between loss of tensile strength and yellow microbial discoloration in strips in the lower depths of *Polytrichum* peat (Table 7). Although not implying causation, it is therefore probable that yellow bacterial colonization was associated with cellulolysis at SIRS 1, either in active decomposition or in utilization of the DOC released from the fibres.

At SIRS 2, the equivalent decomposition gradient was not as steep beneath *Calliergon* (Table 7) and not significant beneath *Cephaloziella,* probably reflecting the more uniformly anaerobic or micro-aerophilic conditions due to saturation.

The estimates of annual loss in weight of bryophyte tissue (Table 9) by cellulose decomposition at the SIRS were based on a generalized regression curve of weight loss on tensile strength loss at all IBP tundra sites (Latter & Howson,

1977). No other sites had sufficiently similar edaphic and climatic characteristics to justify using a more specific equation. Crude fibre was taken as mainly cellulose in the bryophyte biomass. The loss of bryophyte cellulose was twice as rapid at SIRS 1 than at SIRS 2, commensurate with the greater fibre content of *Polytrichum* and *Chorisodontium* than in *Calliergon* and *Cephaloziella*. The pro-duction–decomposition balance for cellulose should therefore remain stable at both sites.

Much of the evidence presented here suggests that a high proportion of peat respiration at the SIRS was microbial. Nevertheless, there were various other contributions. *Polytrichum* has a dense tomentum of rhizoids in the upper zone of the decomposing peat. No reliable estimates of stem and rhizoid dark respiration per square metre are available but it should be considerably less than that of *Polytrichum* growing shoots (Collins, 1975) given in Table 4 because of the much smaller below-ground biomass, as yet not accurately quantified. Other sources of below-ground aerobic respiration included algae, protozoa, nematodes, rotifers, tardigrades and micro-arthropods (Collins *et al.*, 1975). As these sources of data require further qualification and standardization, they will not be discussed here. However, some compensation for the below-ground plant biomass contribution at SIRS 1 and 2 can be made as shown in Table 9. During the summer, DOC was rate-limiting as shown by glucose amendment, so that the temperature elevation was only markedly effective on autotrophic biomass, mainly bryophyte stems and rhizoids. The proportion of the non-microbial contribution was therefore probably greatly increased in summer so that subtraction of the summer peak reduced the overestimate of annual microbial respiratory activity. The lowest level of peat respiration was detected immediately after the spring decline, at which time DOC was probably minimal and the microbial population has not diversified greatly to decompose macromolecular subtrates. Again the below-ground non-microbial biomass contribution to oxygen uptake was large and subtraction of this basal level of activity may correct the microbial contribution even further. In both these corrections, the amounts subtracted will be excessive, but the resulting values for microbial activity in the SIRS provide a range within which lies the mean value used by Davis (1980) in the SIRS ecosystem model.

It has been possible to monitor seasonal physiological responses of the indigenous microbial population of maritime Antarctic tundra peat before significant human impact. Such baseline studies have predictive potential which could prove useful if the exploitation of Antarctic terrestrial resources is pursued.

ACKNOWLEDGEMENTS

I am grateful to Dr R. M. Laws, Director of the British Antarctic Survey, for permission to publish this work. I thank the personnel of Signy Island Research Station (1975–1977) for all their help, and in particular J. C. Ellis-Evans for extracting the cotton strips in 1978. I am also grateful to Dr K. Seal of the Biodeterioration Information Service, University of Aston, Birmingham, for tearing the cotton strips. Finally I thank Dr W. Block and many other colleagues for their help and invaluable discussion.

REFERENCES

ALLEN, S. E., GRIMSHAW, H. M. & HOLDGATE, M. W., 1967. Factors affecting the availability of plant nutrients on an Antarctic island. *Journal of Ecology*, 55: 381–396.

BÅÅTH, E., LOHM, U., LUNDGREN, B., ROSSWALL, T., SÖDERSTRÖM, B., SOHLENIUS, B. & WIREN, A., 1978. The effect of nitrogen and carbon supply on the development of soil organism populations and pine seedlings: a microcosm experiment. *Oikos, 31:* 153–163.

BAILEY, A. D. & WYNN-WILLIAMS, D. D., in press. Soil microbiological studies at Signy Island, South Orkney Islands. *British Antarctic Survey Bulletin.*

BAKER, J. H., 1970a. Yeasts, moulds and bacteria from an acid peat on Signy Island. In M. W. Holdgate (Ed.), *Antarctic Ecology:* 717–722. London: Academic Press.

BAKER, J. H., 1970b. Quantitative study of yeasts and bacteria in a Signy Island peat. *British Antarctic Survey Bulletin,* No. 23: 51–55.

BAKER, J. H., 1972. The rate of production and decomposition of *Chorisodontium aciphyllum* (Hook. f. & Wils.). *British Antarctic Survey Bulletin,* No. 27: 123–129.

BAKER, J. H., 1974. Comparison of the microbiology of four soils in Finnish Lapland. *Oikos, 25:* 209–215.

BAKER, J. H. & SMITH, D. G., 1972. The bacteria in an Antarctic peat. *Journal of Applied Bacteriology, 35:* 589–596.

BOYD, W. L. & BOYD, J. W., 1963. Soil microorganisms of the McMurdo Sound area, Antarctica. *Applied Microbiology, 11:* 116–121.

BOYD, W. L., ROTHENBERG, I. & BOYD, J. W., 1970. Soil microorganisms at Paradise Harbour, Antarctica. *Ecology, 51:* 1040–1045.

CAMPBELL, C. A., BIEDERBECK, V. O. & WARDER, F. G., 1970. Simulated early spring thaw conditions injurious to soil microflora. *Canadian Journal of Soil Science, 50:* 257–259.

CHAMBERS, M. J. G., 1966. Investigations of patterned ground at Signy Island, South Orkney Islands: II Temperature regimes in the active layer. *British Antarctic Survey Bulletin,* No. 10: 71–83.

COLEMAN, D. C., 1973. Compartmental analysis of "total soil respiration": An exploratory study. *Oikos, 24:* 361–366.

COLLINS, N. J., 1975. *Studies on the Productivity of Antarctic Bryophytes.* Ph.D. Thesis: University of Birmingham, 125 pp.

COLLINS, N. J., BAKER, J. H. & TILBROOK, P. J., 1975. Signy Island, Maritime Antarctic. In T. Rosswall & O. W. Heal (Eds), *Structure and Function of Tundra Ecosystems. Ecological Bulletin, 20:* 345–374. Stockholm: Swedish Natural Research Council.

DAVIS, R. C., 1980. Peat respiration and decomposition in Antarctic moss communities. *Biological Journal of the Linnean Society, 14:* 39–49.

FENTON, J. H. C., 1978. *The Growth of Antarctic Moss Peat Banks.* Ph.D. Thesis: University of London, 162 pp.

FENTON, J. H. C., in press. The rate of peat accumulation in Antarctic moss banks. *Journal of Ecology, 68.*

FLANAGAN, P. W. & VEUM, A. K., 1974. Relationships between respiration, weight loss, temperature and moisture in organic residues in tundra. In A. J. Holding *et al.* (Eds.) *Soil Organisms and Decomposition in Tundra:* 249–278. Stockholm: IBP Tundra Biome Steering Committee.

HEAL, O. W., BAILEY, A. D. & LATTER, P. M., 1967. Bacteria, fungi and protozoa in Signy Island soils compared with those from a temperate moorland. In J. E. Smith (Organizer), *A Discussion on the Terrestrial Antarctic Ecosystem. Philosophical Transactions of the Royal Society (B), 252:* 191–197.

HEAL, O. W., HOWSON, G., FRENCH, D. & JEFFERS, J. N. R., 1974. Decomposition of cotton strips in tundra. In A. J. Holding *et al.* (Eds.), *Soil Organisms and Decomposition in Tundra:* 341–362. Stockholm: IBP Tundra Biome Steering Committee.

HOLDGATE, M. W., 1977. Terrestrial ecosystems in the Antarctic. In V. Fuchs & R. M. Laws (Organizers), *A Discussion on Scientific Research in Antarctica. Philosophical Transactions of the Royal Society (B), 279:* 5–25.

IVARSON, K. C. & GUPTA, U. C., 1967. Effect of freezing on free sugars in soil. *Canadian Journal of Soil Science, 47:* 74–75.

LATTER, P. M. & HOWSON, G., 1977. The use of cotton strips to indicate cellulose decomposition in the field. *Pedobiologia, 17:* 145–155.

MARGNI, R. A. & CASTRELOS, O. D., 1971. Las bacterias del Antárctico y su relación con la época del año. *Contirbución del Instituto Antárctico Argentino, 141.* Buenos Aires: Instituto Antárctico Argentino.

NORTHOVER, M. J. & ALLEN, S. E., 1967. Seasonal availability of chemical nutrients on Signy Island. In J. E. Smith (Organizer). *A Discussion on the Terrestrial Antarctic Ecosystem. Philosophical Transactions of the Royal Society, (B), 252:* 191–197.

PARKINSON, D. & COUPS, E., 1963. Microbial Activity in a Podzol. In J. Doeksen & J. van der Drift, *Soil Organisms:* 167–175. Amsterdam: North Holland Publishing Company.

PETRUSEWICZ, K. & MACFADYEN, A., 1970. *Productivity of Terrestrial Animals. IBP Handbook 13.* Oxford & Edinburgh: Blackwell Scientific Publications.

ROSSWALL, T., 1971. List of media used in microbiological studies. *Swedish Tundra Biome Technical Report, 8.* Stockholm: Swedish Natural Research Council.

SMITH, R. I. L., 1972. Vegetation of the South Orkney Islands with particular reference to Signy Island. *British Antarctic Survey Scientific Report, 68:* 1–124.

SMITH, R. I. L. & GIMINGHAM, C. H., 1976. Classification of cryptogamic communities in the maritime
    Antarctic. *British Antarctic Survey Bulletin,* No. *43:* 25–47.
TILBROOK, P. J., 1973. The Signy Island terrestrial reference sites. I. An introduction. *British Antarctic Survey
    Bulletin,* Nos. *33 & 34:* 65–76.
WALTON, D. W. H. & ALLSOPP, D., 1977. A new test cloth for soil burial trials and other studies on cellulose
    decomposition. *International Biodeterioration Bulletin, 13:* 112–115.
WYNN-WILLIAMS, D. D., 1979. Techniques used for studying terrestrial microbial ecology in the maritime
    Antarctic. In A. D. Russell and R. Fuller (Eds.) *Cold Tolerant Organisms in Spoilage and the Environment. Society
    for Applied Bacteriology Technical Series, 13:* 67–82.

Survival strategies in polar terrestrial arthropods

WILLIAM BLOCK

Life Sciences Division. British Antarctic Survey,
Natural Environment Research Council,
Madingley Road, Cambridge CB3 OET, England

Accepted for publication January 1980

Three components of the survival strategy of a terrestrial Antarctic mite, *Alaskozetes antarcticus* (Acari: Cryptostigmata) are considered: overwintering survival, energetics and life history. Supercooling is an important feature of its cold tolerance, whilst elevation of standard metabolism allows activity at low temperatures, both of which contribute to a long development and maximum survival of individuals in the population. These are facets of the overall survival strategy evolved by such a species in response to the Antarctic terrestrial environment, but which may be widespread in polar invertebrates.

KEY WORDS:—strategies–arthropods–supercooling–energetics–cold adaptation–life cycles.

CONTENTS

INTRODUCTION

Survival is often regarded as the keynote to the existence of invertebrate poikilotherms in terrestrial habitats of polar regions. But, as Williams (1966) pointed out, "the central biological problem is not survival as such, but the design for survival". It is these designs or strategies which are the concern of this paper. The term strategy may be defined as a set of co-adapted traits, designed by natural selection, to solve particular ecological problems.

Adaptations of animals, both invertebrate and vertebrate, may be viewed as solutions to problems posed by environments. The solutions have evolved by natural selection. By the study of such solutions or adaptations in poikilotherms, it is possible to deduce certain aspects of the underlying strategy of the species or animal group in relation to its environment.

An analogy of this type extends naturally to terrestrial invertebrates living in extreme environments such as those characterized by low temperatures. As such, low environmental temperatures present two major problems to poikilotherms by (a) producing a general deceleration of metabolism resulting in reduced activity, feeding and growth, and (b) exposure to extreme low temperatures resulting in freezing of the tissues. In the former case, lower metabolic rates are more general and the seasonal time available for activity is much reduced, whilst in the latter, the proximity of snow and ice accentuates the freezing effect by seeding of ice crystals through the body surface.

Invertebrate animals living in polar and other low temperature habitats have evolved both physiological and ecological adaptations which are solutions to these two problems. The aims of this paper are to examine three components of the overall survival strategy of polar arthropods: overwintering survival, energetics and life history pattern, to highlight some of the more important solutions adopted and thereby contribute to a knowledge of their environmental biology. This paper will concentrate on terrestrial arthropods in general (see Block, in press, for a review) and on the Antarctic mite, *Alaskozetes antarcticus* (Michael) (Acari: Cryptostigmata) in particular, about which there is a considerable amount of information. The picture is far from complete, but hopefully such a treatment will aid future research in this field.

Alaskozetes is a large (200–300 µg adult live weight) cryptostigmatid mite belonging to the Family Podacaridae. When adult it is *c.* 1 mm in length and dark brown in colour. There are four post-embryonic life stages besides the adult: a six-legged larva and three eight-legged nymphal stages (proto-, deuto- and trito-nymph). All stages are slow moving. *Alaskozetes* is both a herbivore and a detritivore feeding on lichens, foliose algae and organic debris mainly of vertebrate origin. In the field, the mite is found in a variety of habitats ranging from moss and organic material to the undersides of stones and rocks. Occasionally it occurs in dense local aggregations of several thousands of individuals representing all life stages. This species has been extensively studied at Signy Island, South Orkney Islands in the maritime Antarctic zone.

OVERWINTERING SURVIVAL

The major environmental stresses for land arthropods in polar habitats are temperature, both minimum and maximum levels, and at times, desiccation due to freezing of free water and exposure to high winds. A recent study (Young & Block, 1980a) allows the definition of the cold tolerance strategy adopted by *Alaskozetes* (Table 1). The main feature is that this species, in common with the majority of polar arthropods examined, is freezing susceptible, i.e. freezing is lethal for all individuals in all life stages. Individuals avoid freezing by super-cooling, which is enhanced by glycerol in the body fluids. In addition, juveniles of this species are slightly more cold tolerant than adults, which has implications for the life cycle (see below). Furthermore, the utilization of a low temperature cue (overall decline from 0° to −10°C) to bring the mechanism into operation, and the direct effect of desiccation to promote glycerol production, are both of considerable adaptive significance in this animal.

Table 1. Summary of the cold tolerance strategy of *Alaskozetes antarcticus* (after Young & Block, 1980a)

a.	Freezing susceptible
b.	Survive sub-zero temperatures by supercooling
c.	Gut contents detract from supercooling ability
d.	Individuals supercool to $-26°C$
e.	Supercooling enhanced to $-31°C$ with glycerol
f.	Supercooling point and glycerol concentration directly correlated
g.	Significant increases in glycerol concentration caused by low temperature and desiccation
h.	Photoperiod has no effect on glycerol levels
i.	Juveniles are more cold tolerant than adults

This mechanism of low temperature survival by extensive supercooling has been widely reported in micro-arthropods (Acari and Collembola), spiders, scorpions, beetles and several other insects (Sømme, 1964) together with terrestrial pulmonates, marine invertebrates, Antarctic fish and reptiles. The alternative strategy of freezing tolerance, in which individuals survive tissue freezing, appears to be less widespread in poikilotherms (see Miller, 1978 for a review).

Consideration of the thermal regime in the habitats of *Alaskozetes* at Signy Island, shows that the species is uniquely adapted to its maritime Antarctic environment. Figure 1 shows 10-day mean temperatures together with extreme minimum and maximum temperatures recorded on the surface of a moss turf in a typical year (Walton, 1977). Mean temperatures ranged from $+9.6°$ to $-18.1°C$, whilst the extreme minimum recorded was $-26.5°C$ and the maximum exceeded $30°C$ in that year. In an average year it appears that *Alaskozetes* is well able to survive winter temperatures by supercooling alone without the additional protection afforded by polyols such as glycerol. Conversely, during the five months of the short austral summer, the mites are subjected to much higher temperatures above freezing, albeit for short periods of time, possibly only a few hours.

Prior to the onset of winter at Signy Island, mean daily temperatures at the ground surface (Walton, 1977) are close to $0°C$ for c. 4–6 weeks with minimal fluctuations. This is also the period when an increasing proportion of the hourly temperature records occur in the $0°$ to $-5°C$ range (Fig. 2). In March–April 1972, 60–80% of the hourly data were in this zone, as compared to 40–60% in the $0°$ to $+5°C$ range. An abrupt transition was observed in May, which coincided with winter freeze-up. Chambers (1966) monitored eight to nine separate freeze-thaw cycles at 1 cm depth in a fine rock debris site during an autumn period, and totals of 19 to 23 such cycles per year in a study at Signy Island. The results of experimental work on *Alaskozetes* (Young & Block, 1980a) suggest that much of its additional cold hardiness is built up during the pre-winter period, when successive waves of freeze-thaw temperature oscillations occur.

Melt-off with its concomitant temperature rise occurs rapidly at Signy Island, normally in October or early November. Ten-day mean temperatures rise above $0°C$ (Fig. 1), and there is a rapid reversal of temperatures from just below $0°C$ to just above zero (Fig. 2). For between 5–6 months each year the land fauna at Signy Island is subject to continuous freezing temperatures, but it should be

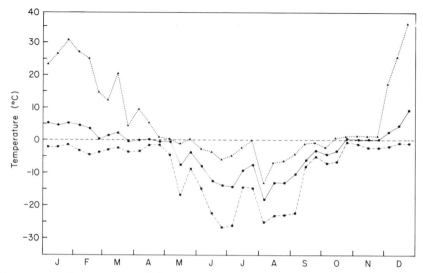

Figure 1. Annual temperature cycle for the surface of a moss turf community at Signy Island in a typical year (1972), which is representative of the thermal regime experienced by *Alaskozetes antarcticus*. ●—● 10 day mean temperature; ■ - - ■, minimum temperature; ▲ . . . ▲, maximum temperature.

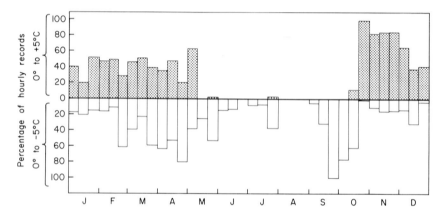

Figure 2. Proportions of hourly temperatures in the 0° to −5°C and 0° to +5°C zones per 10-days which were recorded at the surface of a moss turf at Signy Island in 1972.

pointed out that freezing tolerant arthropods have not been found there. The effects of such an annual temperature cycle on the life history of *Alaskozetes* are discussed below.

ENERGETICS

The partitioning of the energy ingested and assimilated to the pathways of respiration and production by poikilotherms living in polar habitats is a critical feature of their survival strategies. Although oribatid (cryptostigmatid) mites have generally lower metabolic rates than other comparable sized invertebrates, it has been demonstrated that *Alaskozetes* has an elevated rate of standard metabolism compared to temperate orbatids (Block & Young, 1978). It is able therefore to partly avoid the depressant effect of low temperatures on activity, feeding, growth and reproduction. It is adapted to maintaining its biological functions in the temperature range $-4°$ to $+15°C$ (Block, 1977; Young, 1979a; Young & Block, 1980b), which are generally prevalent during daytime in summer at Signy Island. Young (1979a) has postulated that lowering of the activation energy for certain reactions may constitute part of the mechanism behind the metabolic cold adaptation of this mite.

In terms of diurnal and seasonal temperature fluctuations, *Alaskozetes* does not compensate metabolically for such changes (Young, 1979b). Such a mechanism enables it to exploit the relatively warm conditions of the austral summer, and to conserve its energy resources in low temperature conditions. In other words, metabolic conformity may be of greater strategic value than metabolic regulation to these animals in polar enviroments. However, Prosser (1975) has suggested that highly variable thermal environments are associated with the ability to undergo metabolic compensation, and clearly, *Alaskozetes* is an exception to this. It may be that limitations of the Antarctic terrestrial environment are responsible rather than the control of metabolism by important biochemical substances (Precht, Christopherson, Hensel & Larcher, 1973).

The relationship of the metabolic response to temperature has been used to assess an invertebrate's overall performance. The model proposed by MacLean (1975) illustrated some of the limitations imposed by temperature on poikilotherm energy budgets. In type I of the MacLean model, A (assimilation rate) is greater than R (respiration rate) at all temperatures normally encountered by the animal, thus allowing a favourable energy balance (with positive P–production). In type II, A increases more rapidly with rising temperature than R, and thus the amount of energy available for growth increases with temperature. Such an animal may be unable to complete its life cycle at low temperatures because of an unfavourable energy balance. Type III (R increases more rapidly with temperature than A) is the pattern of an obligate polar species, which is able to maintain a positive energy balance only at low temperatures. Polar terrestrial invertebrates may be grouped under type I or III, and evidence is accumulating which shows that Antarctic oribatids such as *Alaskozetes,* have several features of the obligate polar form. Feeding and energy studies of this and other related Antarctic species are currently in progress.

LIFE HISTORY

Within the life cycle of oribatid mites there are several critical periods when survival of the individual is at greater risk than at other times. These include the time of egg hatch for the larva, and successively the four moults to complete the development: larva→ proto-→ deuto-→ trito-nymph→ adult. During moulting the mites are especially vulnerable to desiccation and extremes of temperature. These two environmental stresses are accentuated in the maritime Antarctic environment, where sub-zero temperatures occur frequently in summer, and free water may be at a premium due to rapid freeze-thaw cycles (Chambers, 1966).

It is pertinent to review briefly our knowledge of the biology of a typical polar acarine in order to develop a hypothesis concerning its overall life history strategy (Table 2). Oviposition by *Alaskozetes* occurs in spring and throughout the Antarctic summer (Strong, 1967; Tilbrook, 1973), with females carrying up to 12 eggs (usually 4–6 eggs per female). Prelarvae are found within the eggs inside the female, but do not hatch immediately after deposition. Development times for the larva and the three nymphal stages at field temperatures are probably long

2

Table 2. Life history strategies of oribatid mites in temperate and polar environments

Parameter	Temperate	Polar
Population density	High in summer and autumn	High in summer
Oviposition	Spring to mid-summer	Spring and through-out summer
Development (egg-adult)	Variable: 23–275 days	At least 1 year
Longevity	1–3 years	2 + years
Mortality	Temperature extremes, desiccation	Freezing
Metabolic rate	Low	Low with elevation
Cold tolerance (freezing susceptible)	Supercooling	Supercooling

(Block, unpublished data). Individual longevity estimated from field experiments shows considerable variation, but adults may live for longer than one year, whilst nymphal longevity estimates range between 4–9 months dependent on instar and environmental conditions. Examination of field populations and dense aggregations of *Alaskozetes* in spring, shows considerable overwintering mortality probably from freezing. Life cycle length (egg to adult) is long compared to temperate species (see Mitchell, 1977 for review), being at least one year. As all postembryonic stages overwinter, a mixed population of all the nymphal instars and mature individuals is found in all seasons, which is comparable to some prostigmatid mites (Goddard, 1979). Growth and development is limited to the period mid-October to April, and Fig. 3 shows a postulated life cycle for *Alaskozetes.* As both juveniles and adults overwinter, it is advantageous that the juveniles are at least as cold hardy as the adults to ensure survival of the species. This is particularly important in a severe Antarctic winter.

Evidence from culture studies shows that females of *Alaskozetes* oviposit on several occasions after reaching maturity, and that an individual may breed in at least two successive summers. The advantages of iteroparity (repeated breeding) for a polar terrestrial invertebrate are many (Fig. 4). Once the female has reached breeding condition after a long, slow and energetically costly development, egg production occurs when environmental conditions allow, and iteroparity combined with extended individual longevity of both sexes will enhance the survival potential of the species. Semelparity or 'big bang reproduction' would appear to have no place in such a life history strategy.

Life cycles lasting longer than one year occur in many (but not all) Arctic invertebrates (MacLean, 1975, & in press). Species with annual life cycles may have been eliminated from such tundra faunas by a succession of severe summers. Temperature and length of the Antarctic growing season (Fig. 1) determine the long life cycle of *Alaskozetes,* which in turn exposes the animal to increased

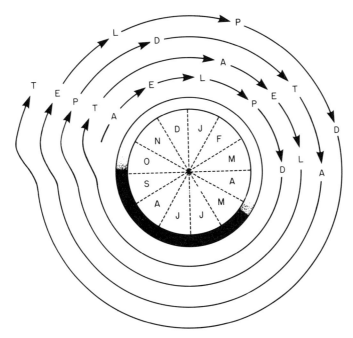

Figure 3. Postulated life cycle of *Alaskozetes antarcticus* under maritime Antarctic conditions. E: egg, L: larva, P: proto-nymph, D: deuto-nymph, T: trito-nymph, A: adult. Inner sections indicate possible snow cover and months: J, January; F, February; etc.

mortality. Thus the population must be able to sustain the additional mortality incurred during prolonged development in order for it to survive there. *Alaskozetes* appears to have evolved the strategy of increasing the probablity of survival by cold tolerance mechanisms and maximizing reproduction by oviposition over a long time period and repeated breeding. Adult body size, growth rate and environmental severity have interacted to produce such a pattern.

It is a fashionable proposition to place an Antarctic species such as *Alaskozetes* into the r- and K- selection continuum (Dobzhansky, 1950; Pianka, 1970). In this species selection has favoured slow development with delayed reproduction, decreased mortality, longevity > 1 year, and with only a small proportion of the total energy intake devoted to breeding. But *Alaskozetes* also has a small body size, few breeding periods per year and lives in a lax competitive situation, all features of an r-strategist. It is difficult, on present evidence, to suggest that *Alaskozetes* is more of an r- or K-strategist, and due to the highly seasonal nature of its environment a polymorph between opportunism and stability may result. This contrasts with the oribatid mites of some hot desert systems, which are r-strategists (Wallwork, in press). The effects of stable and fluctuating environments on the development of r- and K-strategies in relation to juvenile and adult mortalities have been discussed by Stearns (1976), Southwood (1977) and others. Terrestrial mites occupy relatively stable environments in the maritime Antarctic with well defined, predictable changes in season and resource availability. Also, on the available evidence for field survival and longevity combined with increased juvenile cold tolerance, it is thought that adult mortality may be more variable than that of the immatures. Thus the criticism of

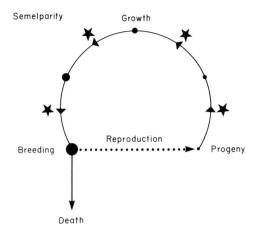

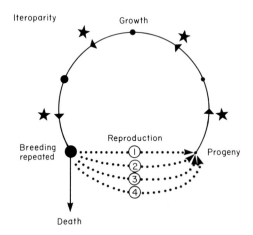

Figure 4. Generalized breeding patterns applied to oribatid life cycles. The five post-embryonic life stages are depicted commencing with progency (=larva). ★, timing of moults at which mortality is greatest.

the usefulness of the 'r–K approach' (Stearns, 1977) is upheld by the present data for *Alaskozetes*. It is interesting to note the suggestion of Clarke (1979) that the Antarctic marine benthic environment appears in some cases to favour the evolution of K-strategies in the fauna. It may be that the effects of low temperature, acting in different ways in the terrestrial and marine environments of polar regions, are fundamental to the widespread evolution of such life cycles.

CONCLUSIONS

Several adaptations are exhibited by polar arthropods such as the mite *Alaskozetes,* which overcome the ecological and physiological problems posed by the severe Antarctic environment. Low temperature effects of metabolism are overcome by elevation of standard metabolic rate, or cold adaptation, which enable individuals to function at temperatures which immobilize their temperate counterparts. Freezing of the tissues at extreme low temperatures is avoided by a complex supercooling mechanism initiated primarily by low temperature cues heightened by the desiccating atmosphere at freeze-up. These physiological adaptations have enabled the evolution of a life history pattern which incorporates several features which are similar to those described for a K-strategist. Thus, *Alaskozetes* appears to be closely adapted to its polar environment, which supports Wallwork's (1973) contention that representatives of the Family Podacaridae have undergone a long period of evolution in the southern polar region.

The preliminary analysis presented here illustrates some of the more prominent features of the underlying adaptational strategy of the Antarctic mite, *Alaskozetes antarcticus*. It is well able to endure the winter severities of its environment, as well as being able to capitalize on the shorter, favourable summer periods to grow, develop and reproduce. Such features are part of an overall strategy which is probably typical of polar arthropods and may well be representative of many other terrestrial invertebrates living in low temperature habitats.

SUMMARY

The Antarctic terrestrial mite *Alaskozetes antarcticus* (Cryptostigmata) displays many adaptational features in respect of its low temperature environment which are demonstrated in its overwintering survival, energetics and life history. Such adaptations may be typical of the strategies adopted by a wide range of terrestrial invertebrates living in similar environments.

ACKNOWLEDGEMENTS

I thank many of my colleagues in the British Antarctic Survey for helpful discussions, and Roger Worland for assistance with two of the Figures.

REFERENCES

BLOCK, W., 1977. Oxygen consumption of the terrestrial mite *Alaskozetes antarcticus* (Acari: Cryptostigmata). *Journal of Experimental Biology, 68:* 69–87.

BLOCK, W., In press. Aspects of the ecology and physiology of Antarctic soil fauna. In D. L. Dindal (Ed.), *Soil Biology as Related to Land Use Practices.* New York: State University of New York. (Soil Zoology Colloquium VII, Syracuse, New York, 1979).

BLOCK, W. & YOUNG, S. R., 1978. Metabolic adaptations of Antarctic terrestrial arthropods. *Comparative Biochemistry and Physiology, 61A:* 363–368.

CHAMBERS, M. J. G., 1966. Investigations of patterned ground at Signy Island, South Orkney Islands: II. Temperature regimes in the active layer. *British Antarctic Survey Bulletin.* No. *10:* 71–83.

CLARKE, A., 1979. On living in cold-water: K-strategies in Antarctic benthos. *Marine Biology, 55:* 111–119.

DOBZHANSKY, T., 1950. Evolution in the tropics. *American Scientist, 38:* 209–221.

GODDARD, D. G., 1979. The Signy Island terrestrial reference sites: XI. Population studies on the Acari. *British Antarctic Survey Bulletin,* No. *48:* 71–92.

MACLEAN, S. F., 1975. Ecological adaptions of tundra invertebrates. In F. J. Vernberg (Ed.), *Physiological Adaptation to the Environment:* 269–300. New York: Intext Educational Publishers.

MACLEAN, S. F., In press. The detritus-based trophic system. In J. Brown *et al.* (Eds), *An Arctic Ecosystem: the Coastal Tundra at Barrow, Alaska:* chapter 11. Philadelphia: Dowden, Hutchinson & Ross.

MILLER, L. K., 1978. Physiological studies of Arctic animals. *Comparative Biochemistry and Physiology, 59A:* 327–334.

MITCHELL, M. J., 1977. Life history strategies of oribatid mites. In D. L. Dindal (Ed.), *Biology of Oribatid Mites:* 65–69. New York: State University of New York, Syracuse.

PIANKA, E. R., 1970. On 'r' and 'K' selection. *American Naturalist, 104:* 592–597.

PRECHT, H., CHRISTOPHERSON, J., HENSEL, H. & LARCHER, W., 1973. *Temperature and Life.* Berlin: Springer Verlag.

PROSSER, C. L., 1975. Physiological adaptations in animals. In F. J. Vernberg (Ed.), *Physiological Adaptation to the Environment:* 3–18. New York: Intext Educational Publishers.

SØMME, L., 1964. Effects of glycerol on cold-hardiness in insects. *Canadian Journal of Zoology, 42:* 87–101.

SOUTHWOOD, T. R. E., 1977. Habitat, the templet for ecological strategies. *Journal of Animal Ecology, 46:* 337–365.

STEARNS, S. C., 1976. Life history tactics: a review of ideas. *Quarterly Review of Biology, 51:* 3–47.

STEARNS, S. C., 1977. The evolution of life history traits: a critique of the theory and a review of the data. *Annual Review of Ecology and Systematics, 8:* 154–171.

STRONG, J., 1967. Ecology of terrestrial arthropods at Palmer Station, Antarctic Peninsula. *Antarctic Research Series (American Geophysical Union), 10:* 357–371.

TILBROOK, P. J., 1973. *Terrestrial Arthropod Ecology at Signy Island, South Orkney Islands.* Unpublished Ph.D. thesis, University of London.

WALLWORK, J. A., 1973. Zoogeography of some terrestrial micro-Arthropoda in Antarctica. *Biological Reviews, 48:* 233–259.

WALLWORK, J. A., In press. Desert soil microarthropods: an 'r' selected system. In D. L. Dindal (Ed.), *Soil Biology as Related to Land Use Practices.* New York: State University of New York, (Soil Zoology Colloquium VII, Syracuse, New York, 1979).

WALTON, D. W. H., 1977. Radiation and soil temperatures 1972–74: Signy Island terrestrial reference sites. *British Antarctic Survey Data Report, No. 1.*

WILLIAMS, G. C., 1966. *Adaptation and Natural Selection.* Princeton, New Jersey: Princeton University Press.

YOUNG, S. R., 1979a. Respiratory metabolism of *Alaskozetes antarcticus. Journal of Insect Physiology, 25:* 361–369.

YOUNG, S. R., 1979b. Effect of temperature change on the metabolic rate of an Antarctic mite. *Journal of Comparative Physiology, 131:* 341–346.

YOUNG, S. R. & BLOCK, W., 1980a. Experimental studies on the cold tolerance of *Alaskozetes antarcticus. Journal of Insect Physiology, 26:* 189–200.

YOUNG, S. R. & BLOCK, W., 1980b. Some factors affecting metabolic rate in an Antarctic mite. *Oikos, 34:* 178–185.

Peat respiration and decomposition in Antarctic terrestrial moss communities

R. C. DAVIS

Life Sciences Division, British Antarctic Survey,
Natural Environment Research Council, Madingley Road,
Cambridge CB3 0ET, England

Accepted for publication January 1980

Oxygen uptake by the peat of two Antarctic bryophyte communities (a moss turf and a moss carpet) is converted to organic matter loss and used to derive the rate of decomposition. The decay rates obtained in this way are evaluated in two mathematical models which simulate the accumulation of dead organic matter (DOM) in the communities from the litter production and decomposition rate. Litter production, the extent of DOM accumulations at present on the sites and mean decomposition rates (i.e. fraction of standing crop lost per year) were 409 g m^{-2} year^{-1}, 33.5 kg m^{-2} and 0.017 g g^{-1} year^{-1} in the moss turf and 392 g m^{-2} year^{-1}, 29.6 kg m^{-2} and 0.010 g g^{-1} year^{-1} in the moss carpet respectively (all weights expressed as dry weight). Aerobic decomposition rate declined with depth in both communities. From the model's predictions it is suggested that the observed decay rate was too high in the moss turf and too low in the carpet. Possible reasons for this are discussed and suggestions made for future work.

KEY WORDS:— moss – respiration – decomposition – production – model – simulation – organic matter.

CONTENTS

Table 1. Factors affecting decomposition rate estimates in litter bag and soil respiration studies

Litter bags	Soil respiration
1. Disturbance and altered micro-climate	A. Disturbance and altered micro-climate.
2. Fragmentation of friable material during handling	B. Below ground plant respiration.
3. Heat sterilization, reinvasion time and change of substrate quality.	C. Anaerobic respiration.
4. Variation in water content of air dried material in attempt to minimize errors in 3.	D. Converting gaseous exchange to weight loss.
5. Comminution.	E. Loss of CO_2 and products of anaerobic respiration in solution.
6. Exclusion of large soil fauna.	
7. Root growth into and within bags.	

INTRODUCTION

The importance of measuring and understanding decomposition in tundra has been stressed by Heal & French (1974); as there is no herbivory it is the major pathway of organic matter degradation. Organic matter loss rates due to decomposition have been measured directly by the loss in weight of dead material placed in the field, usually in litter bags, (e.g. Heal & French, 1974; Rosswall, Veum & Karenlampi, 1975; Heal, Latter & Howson, 1978) although on a few occasions losses have been equated with soil or litter respiration (Flanagan & Veum, 1974; Bunnell, Tait, Flanagan & Van Cleve, 1977). In the latter event the decomposition rate estimates have been evaluated by comparison with results obtained through litter bag studies. Whilst this is a reasonable first approach it is not ideal, as with both methods there are often severe problems in interpretation of results due to incomplete understanding of the errors involved. These have been discussed at some length by Macfadyen (1970, & in press) and Heal & French (1974) and are summarized in Table 1.

An additional approach to evaluation would be to assess the decomposition estimates through their performance in predicting some characteristic of the ecosystem which is strongly influenced by decomposition. This is the aim of the present study and is achieved by using the decomposition rate estimates as determined by peat respiration studies to predict the extent of dead organic matter (DOM) accumulation in two Antarctic moss communities. The predictions are made through the use of two simple models which describe the dynamics of organic matter accumulation in ecosystems.

The ability of these models to simulate decomposition processes realistically will be examined here too, because the accuracy of their predictions and hence their value as a tool to assess decomposition rates will depend on this ability.

STUDY SITES

Two terrestrial moss communities on Signy Island, South Orkney Islands have been studied. One is a relatively dry moss turf of *Polytrichum alpestre* Hoppe and *Chorisodontium aciphyllum* (Hook f. et Wils.) Broth. which together cover 86% of the ground surface (27% and 59% respectively) of the site used in this study. The other is a wet and boggy moss carpet of *Calliergon sarmentosum* (Wahlenb.) Kindb. (35% cover), *Calliergidium austro-stramineum* (C. Muell.) Bartr. (27% cover) and *Drepanocladus uncinatus* (Hedw.) Warnst. (25% cover). The liverwort *Cephaloziella varians* (Gottsche) Steph. occurs abundantly in both communities. In the former it is evenly distributed between the stems of the mosses and hence its cover is difficult to estimate, whereas in the latter it forms distinct patches covering 13% of the ground surface of the site used in this study.

Two study sites were established, one for each community; these are known as the Signy Island terrestrial reference sites (SIRS) 1 and 2 for the turf and carpet community respectively. Tilbrook (1973) has given a description of the sites including edaphic, micrometeorological and topographic details.

MATERIALS, METHODS AND MODELS

Peat respiration and conversion to decomposition rate

Spring and summer mean hourly peat respiration rates (r: ml O_2 m^{-2} h^{-1}) for the top 12 cm of peat on SIRS 1 and 2 (after Wynn-Williams, 1980, this volume) have been used to calculate mean annual respiration (R: ml O_2 m^{-2} $year^{-1}$) for each site as follows:

$$R = r \times 24 \times D,$$

where D = sum of number of days in each month with a mean temperature of $0°$ C or more.

D, determined from data in Walton (1977), was 151 days on SIRS 1 and 181 days on SIRS 2.

Petrusewicz & Macfadyen (1970) indicated that for organisms utilizing plant matter as food the oxidation of 1 mg dry weight of food involves an oxygen uptake of 0.85 ml, hence the annual oxygen uptake was converted to the equivalent amount of material oxidized (i.e. lost to the system by biodegradation) by dividing R by 0.85. The value thus derived includes moss stem and rhizoid respiratory weight losses in addition to the respiratory weight losses of the decomposer organisms (invertebrate fauna and microorganisms). A correction for rhizoid respiration on SIRS 1 was made using data in Fenton (1978), but no correction has been made for stems on SIRS 1 or for any below ground plant respiration on SIRS 2. In the latter case this is not likely to cause significant errors as the moss stems quickly die below the surface and rhizoids are absent. After correcting for peat depth, based on the variation in annual respiration with depth observed by Wynn-Williams (1980: table 4), the annual loss of organic matter due to aerobic decomposer activities was expressed as a fraction of the total DOM present. This yielded an annual fractional loss rate or decomposition constant (loss in grams per gram initial weight) for each site. Maximum and minimum annual fractional loss rates were derived by equating maximum weight loss with minimum standing crop for maximum decomposition constant (k) and vice versa for minimum k.

Decomposition rates varying with depth were derived from the respiration of peat cores (of *P. alpeatre* on SIRS 1 and *C. sarmentosum* on SIRS 2) cut into horizontal sections representing depths 1–3, 3–6, 6–9 and 9–12 cm (Wynn-Williams, 1980). To obtain annual fractional loss rates for each depth the oxygen uptake of each section (after conversion to the equivalent amount of material lost in decomposition) was divided by the quantity of dead organic matter in the section. Extrapolation to greater depths was achieved by plotting decomposition rate against depth, extending the resulting curve by eye and reading from the graph.

Dead organic matter standing crop

DOM standing crop on each site was determined from measurements of peat depth and bulk density.

Peat depth measurements (cm) were made in late summer (March) 1978, when the peat was completely thawed, by inserting a metal rod vertically into the peat until it made contact with the bedrock. The rod was marked at the surface of the peat, withdrawn and the depth to which it had been inserted was measured to the nearest centimetre. This was repeated at 62 points on SIRS 2 and 150 points on SIRS 1, the locations being chosen on a stratified random basis. Bulk density was determined from ten peat cores collected from each site and treated as follows. The green moss on the surface of each core was sliced off with a sharp razor and the remainder cut into three 5 cm deep sections, discarding any peat in excess of this. Each section was dried to constant weight in an oven at 80°C. From the core surface area and section depth the volume of each section was calculated and bulk density determined from dry weight (g) divided by volume (ml).

The DOM standing crop (g m^{-2}) on each site was calculated from the product of peat depth and bulk density. The DOM standing crop is expressed as dry weight as are all weight and standing crop values in this paper.

Litter production

Litter production was not measured directly, but has been equated with net primary production (NPP). This is possible as with no herbivory all the NPP enters the decomposition cycle. NPP of the mosses growing in pure stands on Signy Island has been measured on a number of occasions (Longton, 1970; Baker, 1972; Collins, 1973, 1975; Fenton, 1978). The mean of the values given by these authors for each species has been used to derive estimates of NPP on the SIRS by correcting for the area covered by each moss species and summing for each species on each site.

Variability estimates, for litter production for each site were derived from twice the standard deviation of the mean of the NPP values for each species, compounded for the entire site following Jarman (1970).

Models

Two models relating DOM accumulation with litter production and decomposition have been used. The first is the simple model of Jenny, Gessel & Bingham (1949) (referred to as model 1) which assumes a constant litter production (L) and constant decomposition rate (k). The second (referred to as model 2) is similar to that of Jones & Gore (1978) and permits decomposition rate to be varied with depth, and hence age, of decomposing material.

The model of Jenny et al. (1949) relates the rate of change of organic matter (dX/dt) in the ecosystem to the balance between income (L) and loss (kX) as follows:

$$\frac{\mathrm{d}X}{\mathrm{d}t} = L - kX,$$

equation 1

where, L = litter production (g m^{-2} year^{-1}), X = amount of organic matter (g m^{-2}), k = annual fractional loss rate or decomposition rate, t = time (years). Both L and k are assumed constant with time and k is constant with depth and age of material. Olson (1963) showed how manipulation of equation 1 yields equation 2 which relates the change in organic matter standing crop with time:

$$X = \frac{L}{k}(1 - e^{-kt}).$$

equation 2

Equation 2 describes a rising exponential curve which reaches a steady state when $L = kX_{ss}$ (where X_{ss} equals equilibrium standing crop), that is when the litter input equals organic matter loss through decomposition. At this point $dX/dt = 0$, therefore $L - kX_{ss} = 0$ and hence:

$$L = kX_{ss}.$$

equation 3

If k and L are determined independently equation 2 can be used to predict the amount of organic matter which will accumulate in the ecosystem and by solving equation 2 iteratively for increasing values of t the course of accumulation can be followed and the time taken to attain a given DOM or a given fraction of X_{ss} can be derived.

As a first approximation to assume a constant decomposition rate may not be unreasonable, but as has often been pointed out (Minderman, 1968; Heal & French, 1974; Heal et al., 1978) decomposition rate usually varies with the age of the decomposing material, probably because simple compounds disappear rapidly whereas resistant materials decompose slowly. As age of material is closely related to its depth in the soil, particularly in moss communities where there is no faunal mixing, decomposition also varies with depth.

For this reason the model of Jenny et al. (1949) has been modified to permit k to be varied with depth. This was done by compartmentalizing the DOM into 1 cm deep sections near the surface and 5 cm deep sections below 5 cm and assigning each compartment a different k value, but which is constant for that compartment. Material is first accumulated in the upper compartment. When this attains a given DOM the excess overflows into the compartment below and so on. The model is run iteratively until either the loss rate, which increases steadily as the amount of organic matter accumulates, reaches 99% of the litter production or the DOM standing crop becomes excessively large without a decline in the rate of accumulation.

RESULTS

Peat respiration and decomposition rates

The organic matter weight losses due to oxidation by decomposer organisms (Table 2) were derived from a mean oxygen uptake of 95.0 and 55.4 ml O$_2$ m^{-2} h^{-1} on SIRS 1 and 2 respectively (after Wynn-Williams, 1980:

Table 2. Total peat respiration in the moss turf and carpet communities of the Signy Island terrestrial reference sites corrected for peat depth and rhizoid respiration (the moss turf only) giving fauna plus microbial respiration which is equated with decomposition. Variability estimates in parentheses

	Respiration (g m^{-2} year^{-1})	
	Moss turf	Moss carpet
Total peat respiration (1–12 cm)	405 (186–624)	283 (113–453)
Total peat respiration corrected for entire peat depth	574 (264–885)	288 (115–461)
Rhizoid respiration	3 (3–30)	—
Fauna and microbial respiration	571 (261–855)	288 (115–461)

Table 3. Litter production, annual weight loss of material due to decomposer activity and annual fractional loss rate (decomposition constant) in the moss turf and carpet communities of the Signy Island terrestrial reference sites. Variability estimates in parentheses

	Moss turf	Moss carpet
Litter production (g m^{-2} year^{-1})	409 (351–478)	392 (306–566)
Weight loss due to decomposition (g m^{-2} year^{-1})	571 (261–855)	288 (115–461)
Decomposition constant	0.017 (0.008–0.026)	0.010 (0.004–0.017)

table 9). The respiratory weight loss in the moss turf was about twice that in the carpet, giving the moss turf the higher decomposition rate (Table 3).

The decay rates for SIRS 1 (Table 3) are comparable with those obtained by direct measures of weight loss of material in situ. Annual fractional loss rates measured in other moss turf communities on Signy Island have been reported between 0.013 and 0.024 (Baker, 1972) and between 0.001 and 0.01 (Fenton, 1978). However, the rates for SIRS 2 (Table 3) seem low. In other Signy Island moss carpet communities loss rates have been given as 0.25, 0.14 (Collins, 1975), 0.077, 0.083 and 0.015 (Fenton, 1978). The decay rate of 0.008 for SIRS 2 may be an underestimate as anaerobic respiration was not measured. It should be noted that below ground plant respiration rate has not been measured and subtracted and this may have boosted the decay rate estimates. The latter applies particularly to SIRS 1 where the moss stems may be living and capable of regeneration to a depth of 25 cm (Longton, 1972).

Changes in decomposition rate with depth are shown in Table 4. In both moss communities decay rate was greatest near the surface and declined with depth. At depths greater than those indicated the decomposition rate was assumed constant at 0.009 on SIRS 1 and 0.001 on SIRS 2.

Table 4. *Variation in annual fractional loss rate with depth in the moss turf and carpet communities of the Signy Island terrestrial reference sites*

Depth (cm)	Moss turf	Depth (cm)	Moss carpet
1–3	0.083	1–3	0.040
3–6	0.026	3–6	0.018
6–9	0.012	6–9	0.006
9–12	0.011	9–12	0.003
12–24	0.009	12–15	0.001

Dead organic matter standing crop

The peat depth, bulk density and standing crop on SIRS 1 (in each case given as mean $\pm$ 1 standard error) were 24.3 ± 0.4 cm, 0.138 ± 0.003 g ml^{-1} and 33.5 ± 0.9 Kg m^{-2} respectively. On SIRS 2 the values were 15.0 ± 0.7 cm, 0.197 ± 0.006 g ml^{-1} and 29.6 ± 1.7 Kg m^{-2}. The moss turf has a greater depth and standing crop of peat than the moss carpet.

Litter production

Estimates of litter production are given in Table 3. Despite having different species composition the two communities have similar levels of production with a mean of c. 400 g m^{-2} year^{-1}.

Simulation results

Introduction

Model 1 was run five times for SIRS 1 and five times for SIRS 2 using different combinations for the value of L and k. In the initial run the mean value of L and mean value of k were used. In the second and third runs k was held constant at its mean value while L was set first a maximum and then minimum. In the fourth and fifth runs L was constant at its mean while k was set at its maximum and then minimum.

Model 2 was run only twice, once for each site using the decomposition rates in Table 4 and the mean value of L. These simulations were performed in order to investigate the consequences of using a decay rate which varied with depth as opposed to a constant rate.

It should be noted that the models assume the moss cover to be complete from the outset, whereas in reality cover will be patchy during the colonization stages. The NPP per unit area of moss may be the same as in later stages, but NPP m^{-2} will be less until 100% cover is attained. For this reason the initial development of the moss communities, which may be greatly prolonged, is not expected to fit the models predictions. However once a complete cover has been attained the organic matter accumulation rates and the steady state DOM standing crop should be similar to those predicted by the models.

Model 1 simulations

The results of simulations using the moss turf data are shown in Fig. 1 and those for the moss carpet data in Fig. 2. The simulations were terminated in each

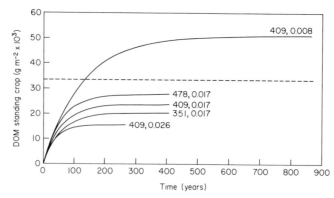

Figure 1. Predicted changes in dead organic matter standing crop with time in the moss turf community of Signy Island terrestrial reference site 1 using model 1. Numbers alongside each curve are litter production followed by decomposition constant. − − − indicates present DOM standing crop on the site.

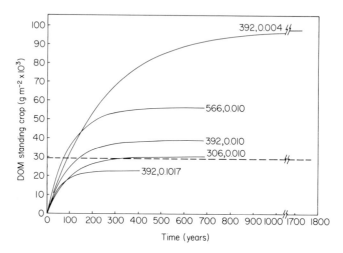

Figure 2. Predicted changes in dead organic matter standing crop with time in the moss carpet community of Signy Island terrestrial reference site 2 using model 1. Numbers alongside each curve are litter production followed by decomposition constant. − − − indicates present DOM standing crop on the site.

case when the amount of organic matter accumulated reached 99.9% of the predicted steady state value. Both sets of simulations show a wide range in the standing drop at equilibrium (X_{ss}) and the time to reach equilibrium. Furthermore the extreme values are associated with the upper and lower values for k rather than L. This suggests that the key to accurate predictions lies in a more precise measure of decomposition rate.

Four of the five simulations of the moss turf yielded an equilibrium standing crop of organic matter below that already present on the site. By analogy with other moss turf communities on Signy Island peat is likely to be accumulating (Collins, 1976), and this suggests that the estimate of decomposition rate in the moss turf is too high. On the other hand, four of the five simulations of the moss carpet predicted an equilibrium standing crop in excess of the present crop and as moss carpets do not generally attain greater depths than the SIRS 2 (Collins, 1976) this suggests that the estimate of decay rate is too low.

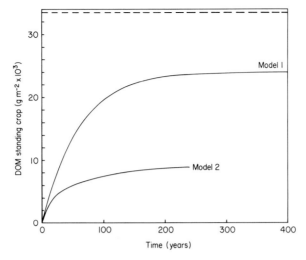

Figure 3. Comparison of predicted changes in dead organic matter standing crop with time in the moss turf community of Signy Island terrestrial reference site 1 using models 1 and 2. − − − indicates present DOM standing crop on the site.

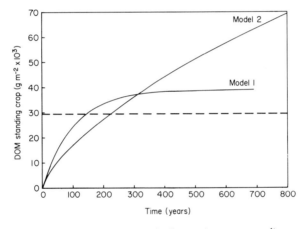

Figure 4. Comparison of predicted changes in dead organic matter standing crop with time in the moss carpet community of Signy Island terrestrial reference site 2 using models 1 and 2. − − − indicates present DOM standing crop on the site.

Assuming that these conclusions are not a consequence of using a constant decay rate then the data suggest that errors in measuring decomposition rate from peat respiration studies differ for the two sites.

Model 2 simulations

The predicted course and extent of peat accumulation on SIRS 1 and 2 using model 2 are shown in Figs 3 & 4 respectively. The simulations from model 1 using the mean values of L and k are also included in Figs 3 & 4 for comparison. In both, the predictions from model 2 differ markedly from those of model 1, but do not give an improved outcome. Thus the predicted equilibrium standing crop in the moss turf from model 2 was only half that with model 1 and the prediction for the moss carpet with model 2 was far too high (Fig. 4).

These findings support the earlier conclusions that: (1) a more detailed and precise measure of decomposition rates in moss turves and carpets are required before accurate simulations of the dynamics of such Antarctic communities can be undertaken, and (2) that the decomposition rate estimates for the moss turf are too high and for the moss carpet are too low.

DISCUSSION

Three important conclusions can be drawn from this study. Firstly aerobic peat respiration measurements when converted to an equivalent amount of organic matter oxidized provide decomposition rates which are comparable with those obtained from direct methods for moss turves, but which appear to be too low for moss carpets. Secondly, from a comparison of the two models it is clear that precision in measuring the composition rate is essential for a better understanding of the biomass dynamics of the systems. Thirdly, failure of the two models to yield equilibrium DOM standing crops equivalent to the majority of moss turves and carpets on Signy Island is thought to be due not to inadequacies in the models, as the theoretically more sound model 2 gave less accurate predictions than model 1 when run with the same basic data. Rather the failure is thought to be due to errors in the estimates of decay rate.

To obtain realistic simulations both the moss turf and carpet decay rates would need to be adjusted, down in the former case and up in the latter. Similar adjustments were needed by Sandhaug, Kjelvik & Wielgolaski (1975) and Jones & Gore (1978) who used litter bags to determine the decay rates employed in modelling tundra and bog ecosystems respectively. Thus the problems and errors are no less in direct measures of decomposition than in respiration rate measures. In addition, as the majority of the factors in Table 1 are unquantified it is not easy to decide which method is most suitable on a general basis. However, as moss tissue from these communities is friable and hence susceptible to damage and weight loss during handling it is not suitable for litter bag studies. Peat respiration studies are therefore preferred. Furthermore, respiration methods being more sensitive are better for experimental studies and in attempting to solve the problems (Table 1) greater insight into the functioning of the systems would be gained.

The main factors causing the decomposition rates presented here to differ from the actual rate of decomposition are (1) below ground plant respiration, particularly in the moss turf, (2) anaerobic respiration and the loss of anaerobic decomposition products in solution, particularly in the moss carpet, and (3) the conversion of gaseous exchange to amount (weight) of organic matter decomposed. In addition errors in extrapolating laboratory measures of respiration to the field and in integrating instantaneous rate estimates over periods of up to a year may be important. Solving these problems must be a priority in future decomposition studies on moss turf and carpet communities in the Antarctic.

ACKNOWLEDGEMENTS

I should like to thank Dr R. M. Laws for permission to publish this work. I am grateful to Dr D. D. Wynn-Williams for allowing me to use his data and to Drs W. Block and A. J. Burn for valuable discussion and comments on the manuscript. Mr S. Hutchinson assisted in field work.

REFERENCES

BAKER, J. H., 1972. The rate of production and decomposition of *Chorisodontium aciphyllum* (Hook. f. et Wils.) Broth. *British Antarctic Survey Bulletin*, No. *27:* 123–129.

BUNNELL, F. L., TAIT, D. E. N., FLANAGAN, P. W. & VAN CLEVE, K., 1977. Microbial respiration and substrate weight loss. I. A general model of the influences of abiotic variables. *Soil Biology and Biochemistry*, *9:* 33–40.

COLLINS, N. J., 1973. Productivity of selected bryophyte communities in the maritime Antarctic. In L. C. Bliss & F. E. Wielgolaski (Eds), *Primary Production and Production Processes, Tundra Biome:* 177–183. *Proceedings of the Conference, Dublin, Ireland, 1973.* Edmonton, Alberta, Canada: Tundra biome steering committee.

COLLINS, N. J., 1975. *Studies on the Productivity of Antarctic Bryophytes.* Ph.D. thesis, University of Birmingham, England.

COLLINS, N. J., 1976. The development of moss-peat banks in relation to changing climate and ice cover on Signy Island in the maritime Antarctic. *British Antarctic Survey Bulletin,* No. *43:* 85–102.

FENTON, J. H. C., 1978. *The Growth of Antarctic Moss Peat Banks.* Ph. D. thesis, University of London, England.

FLANAGAN, P. W. & VEUM, A. K., 1974. Relationships between respiration, weight loss, temperature and moisture in organic residues on tundra. In A. J. Holding *et al.* (Eds), *Soil Organisms and Decomposition in Tundra:* 249–277. Stockholm, Sweden: Tundra biome steering committee.

HEAL, O. W., & FRENCH, D. D., 1974. Decomposition of organic matter in tundra. In A. J. Holding *et al.* (Eds), *Soil Organisms and Decomposition in Tundra:* 279–309. Stockholm, Sweden: Tundra biome steering committee.

HEAL, O. W., LATTER, P. M. & HOWSON, G., 1978. A study of the rates of decomposition of organic matter. In O. W. Heal & D. F. Perkins (Eds), *Production Ecology of British Moors and Montane Grasslands:* 136–159. *Ecological studies,* Vol. 27. Berlin: Springer-Verlag.

JARMAN, M., 1970. *Examples in Quantitative Zoology.* London: Edward Arnold.

JENNY, H., GESSEL, S. P. & BINGHAM, F. T., 1949. Comparative study of decomposition rates of organic matter in temperate and tropical regions. *Soil Science, 68:* 419–432.

JONES, H. E. & GORE, A. J. P., 1978. A simulation of production and decay in blanket bog. In O. W. Heal & D. F. Perkins (Eds), *Production Ecology of British Moors and Montane Grasslands:* 160–186. *Ecological studies,* Vol. 27. Berlin: Springer-Verlag.

LONGTON, R. E., 1970. Growth and productivity of the moss *Polytrichum alpestre* Hoppe in Antarctic regions. In M. W. Holdgate (Ed.), *Antarctic Ecology,* Vol. *2:* 818–837. London: Academic Press.

LONGTON, R. E., 1972. Growth and reproduction in northern and southern hemisphere populations of the peat-forming moss *Polytrichum alpestre* with reference to the estimation of productivity. *Proceedings of the 4th International Congress I–IV, Helsinki, 1:* 259–274.

MACFADYEN, A., 1970. Soil metabolism in relation to ecosystem energy flow and to primary and secondary production. In J. Phillipson (Ed.), *Methods of Study in Soil Ecology:* 167–172. Proceedings of the Paris Symposium of UNESCO-IBP, 1967.

MACFADYEN, A., in press. Activity of soil biota during succession from old field to woodland. In D. L. Dindal (Ed.), *Soil Biology as related to Land Use Practices.* ISSS Soil Zoology Symposium, Syracuse, New York, 1979.

MINDERMAN, G., 1968. Addition, decomposition and accumulation of organic matter in forests. *Journal of Ecology, 56:* 355–362.

OLSON, J. S., 1963. Energy storage and the balance of producers and decomposers in ecological systems. *Ecology, 44:* 322–331.

PETRUSEWICZ, K. & MACFADYEN, A. 1970. *Productivity of Terrestrial Animals: Principles and Methods. IBP Handbook No. 13.* Oxford: Blackwell Scientific Publications.

ROSSWALL, T., VEUM, A. K. & KARENLAMPI, L., 1975. Plant litter decomposition at Fennoscandian tundra sites. In F. E. Wielgolaski (Ed.), *Fennoscandian Tundra Ecosystems. Part 1: Plants and Microorganisms:* 268–278. *Ecological Studies,* Vol. 16. Berlin: Springer-Verlag.

SANDHAUG, A., KJELVIK, S. & WIELGOLASKI, F. E., 1975. A mathematical simulation model for terrestrial tundra ecosystems. In F. E. Wielgolaski (Ed.), *Fennoscandian Tundra Ecosystems. Part 2: Animals and Systems Analysis:* 251–266. *Ecological Studies,* Vol. *16.* Berlin: Springer-Verlag.

TILBROOK, P. J., 1973. The Signy Island terrestrial reference sites: I. An introduction. *British Antarctic Survey Bulletin,* Nos *33* & *34:* 65–76.

WALTON, D. W. H., 1977. Radiation and soil temperatures 1972–74: Signy Island terrestrial reference sites. *British Antarctic Survey Data,* No. *1.*

WYNN-WILLIAMS, D. D., 1980. Seasonal fluctuations in microbial activity in Antarctic moss peat. *Biological Journal of the Linnean Society, 14:* 11–28.

Evolution of Antarctic lake ecosystems

J. PRIDDLE* AND R. B. HEYWOOD†

Life Sciences Division, British Antarctic Survey,
Natural Environment Research Council,
Madingley Road, Cambridge CB3 OET, England

Accepted for publication January 1980

Antarctic lakes present a wide variety of physical, chemical and biological conditions, and are not always the simplified systems imagined by earlier workers. The volume of data on lakes of various ages now allows informed speculation on the evolution of the Antarctic lake ecosystem.

KEY WORDS: – Antarctica – biota – environment – evolution – lakes.

CONTENTS

INTRODUCTION

Most early work on Antarctic inland water bodies was primarily concerned with the identification of the species present. Data on the environment and on ecology have been collected only during the last 20 years. It is possible with this information to follow the probable evolutionary history of most Antarctic lakes, their catchment and ecosystems. Most of the ideas presented in this paper were gradually formulated during our studies on the lakes of Signy Island, South Orkney Islands, and finalized whilst preparing a classification scheme following analysis of data from a long-term monitoring programme (Heywood, Dartnall & Priddle, 1980). Additional information has been drawn from lakes on other Antarctic islands and the continent. No reference is made to the numerous smaller water bodies or to lakes on sub-Antarctic islands. A summary of the geographic position and environmental data of all the lakes mentioned in the text is given in Table 1.

* Present address: School of Plant Biology, U.C.N.W., Bangor, Gwynedd, Wales.
†To whom correspondence should be addressed.

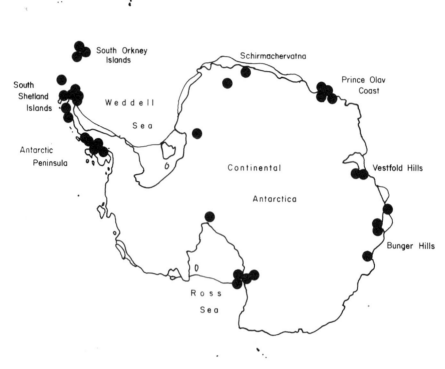

Figure 1. Map of Antarctica showing places where limnological investigations have been carried out.

The Antarctic environment

Antarctica has the severest climate and the highest mean elevation of the seven continents. Most of it is ice-covered and although it holds at least 90% of the world's fresh water, very little of this is in liquid form. Aridity is probably the major factor in the terrestrial ecology of the region (Heywood, 1977a). Antarctica is also the most isolated of the continents and this has considerably influenced the rate and nature of colonization by living organisms (Heywood, 1972, 1978; Dartnall, 1977; Dartnall & Heywood, in press). Isolation may have imposed greater selection pressure on organisms reaching the environment than the subsequent adaptation to survive there. There are few ice-free sites suitable for the development of lakes and these are restricted to offshore islands the coastal zone and a few inland nunataks and ablation areas (Fig. 1). Nearly all the lakes have arisen from glacial retreat and a few have been formed by tectonic activity. Antarctica imposes various restrictions on lake ecosystems. The severe thermal regime is the most obvious. It affects not only the temperature of the water and the period for which the lake surface is frozen, but also the availability of drainage water, the degree of weathering, the subsequent solution of minerals within the catchment, and the consequent composition of the lake waters. Ice and snow cover on the lakes further modifies a radiation regime which already changes dramatically with season.

THE MAIN EVOLUTIONARY SERIES

A small and often localized amelioration in climate or change in precipitation-ablation balance can cause glacial retreat in island, coastal and inland areas of Antarctica. The process tends to be self-accelerating in that as more rock is exposed, more radiation is absorbed creating a warmer climate which increases the rate of melting. Deglaciation stops where increased elevation of the terrain redresses the precipitation-ablation imbalance. The gradual retreat of the ice produces a succession of different lake types in each locality. Development of the physical and chemical environment parallels development of the catchments. Each generation of lakes may not always occupy the same basins because local drainage often changes with the deposition of moraine, and with scree movement. Glacial retreat is an areal as well as a temporal process and certain locations can often provide examples of lakes in various stages of evolution. The lake evolution that has and is taking place on Signy Island is shown diagramatically in Fig. 2. The first freshwater bodies to form are short-lived pools in depressions on retreating glaciers and ice fields (Type 23 of Hutchinson, 1957). These gradually enlarge until they are sufficiently deep to retain a liquid layer throughout the winter under surface ice which can be several metres thick.

Proglacial lakes on ice (Fig. 2A)

A lake of this type existed on the western shoulder of Jane Peak, Signy Island in 1955 (Matthews & Maling, 1967). The ice basin had breached and the water drained completely away by 1962 when the BAS programme of limnological research started. It is now reforming, as a shallow pool present only in summer. No observations have been made on this, or similar lakes elsewhere in Antarctica as far as we know. However ideas on the probable environment and ecosystem can be drawn from observations that have been made on slightly older forms of proglacial lake (see below). The high latent thermal capacity and high albedo of the surrounding ice will severely restrict the heat gain of the lake water. The surface will rarely thaw and any open period will be brief and intermittent throughout the summer. Water temperatures will always be below 1°C. The amount of light within the lake will be determined for most if not all the year by the depth of snow lying on the frozen surface. If, as is frequently the case, the lake is swept by geobatic winds snow cover will be negligible and at least 20% of incident light will pass down the long columnar ice crystals into the underlying water. The water will be very transparent and the light transmission will be 80–90% m^{-1}. The salt content of the water will be determined by the ionic content of the precipitation. There will be little if any exposed rock at this time. Leaching will be severely restricted by low temperatures and the brief duration and seasonality of thaw periods, and because water will not percolate through soil but run quickly over rock, permafrost and ice. Inland lakes will probably contain practically pure water at first but lakes developing near the sea will soon contain such ions as chloride, sulphate, sodium, potassium and magnesium received from wind-blown sea spray. Concentrations will remain low at first because of the relatively copious amounts of water produced during the brief melt each year. Certain algae are capable of living in ice and snow and produce a distinctive snow flora (Fogg, 1967; Kol & Flint, 1968; Kol, 1972). Clearly sufficient nutrients can be obtained from precipitation in Antarctica for their

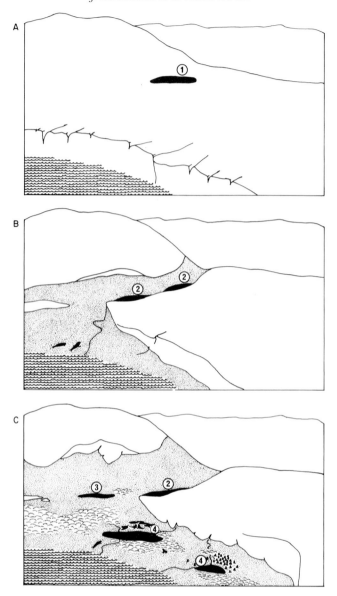

Figure 2. Lake evolution on Signy Island, South Orkney Islands: 1=proglacial lake on ice, 2=ice-dammed proglacial lake, 3=oligotrophic lake, 4=eutrophic lake.

growth. The rapidity of colonization of the lakes will therefore be determined more by the isolation of the area rather than the environmental conditions within the lakes. Algae, bacteria and fungi probably form simple communities relatively quickly.

Eventually ice melt will uncover bedrock and glacial debris within the catchment area. Lake 16, Signy Island, is a small ice basin lake which has a little ice free ground within a small catchment area. A moraine of unknown depth is being uncovered across the outflow of the lake. The mass of rocks is frozen together for most of the year and appears to dam the outflow stream allowing the lake level to rise in summer. The upper layers of moraine gradually thaw out as summer proceeds and there is some evidence of subterranean drainage in early winter before the moraine has refrozen. The lake surface rarely thaws and then only partly. There is a thin layer (approximately 80 mm) of very fine glacial sediment on the ice bottom. This is probably promoting ice melt and the further deepening of the lake by absorbing solar radiation. The lake water is a poorly buffered, chloride type reflecting the influence of precipitation and wind-blown sea spray. The silicate content is remarkably high presumably due to leaching from the sediment and limited utilization by plants. Water column chlorophyll *a* is low suggesting a poor phytoplankton. A sparse benthic vegetation covers at least part of the sediment. It consists of a thin felt composed of a *Tribonema* sp. and *Fragilaria* spp., and other diatoms including two species of the centic genus *Melosira,* which is otherwise rarely found in the Signy Island lakes. Bacteria are present in extremely low numbers. Not all nutritional groups are present so nutrient cycling is unlikely to be complete within the lake (J. C. Ellis-Evans, personal communication). Data on the fauna are incomplete. The copepod *Pseudoboeckella poppei* is present as it is in all the lakes on the island. Its reduced size suggests that it is existing on a sparse food supply (Heywood, 1970—the species was then referred to as *P. silvestri,* see Heywood, 1977b). The cladoceran *Alona rectangula* has also colonized the lake. However, the presence of the crustaceans may be misleading. They probably arrive late in the evolutionary sequence but once well established in more developed lakes they colonize less favourable environments.

With further melting the amount of exposed rock increases to form most if not all the lake basin or new lakes may develop in kettle holes in glacial debris (types 34 to 39: Hutchinson, 1957) or rock basins formed by corrasion (types 26 to 29: Hutchinson, 1957). For a period of time the lake waters will be dammed by ice or frozen moraine.

Proglacial lakes in rock basins (Fig. 2B)

These lakes may change form or even disappear as melting proceeds. Lake 17, Signy Island was included on the map published in Matthews & Maling (1967) which was based on surveys carried out in the late 1940s. It had disappeared by 1962 (Heywood, 1967). The present lake reformed in the 1972–73 summer (Heywood, Dartnall & Priddle, 1979, 1980). The water level of Lake Glubokoye, Moledezhnaya Oasis fell by 21 m when the ice dam breached near the outflow (Klokov, 1970). The maximum recorded depth is now only 13 m. The catchment of this type of lake is still mainly ice- and snow-covered. Inflowing water has a low salt content and is usually limited to a short period of the year because it is directly dependent on melt and run-off. Notable fluctuations in lake level may be caused by the rapid passage of water over the surface of ice and permafrost, especially if the catchment is large. The inflowing water will contain a heavy sediment load where glacial corrasion occurs within the catchment. The lake surfaces may remain frozen throughout the year (Upper Lake, Alexander Island); otherwise the open period is brief and intermittent because of the high thermal capacity of the ice dam or frozen moraine, the limited solar energy penetration and low temperature of the inflowing water. The transparency of the water will be determined by the sediment load and vertical transmission can be less than 10% m^{-1}. Phytoplankton development is poor because of the low nutrient content. Benthic vegetation is richer probably because of the higher nutrient content of the water just above the sediments. Filamentous algae of the genera *Zygnema, Phormidium* and *Lyngbya* have colonized the shallow areas of Lake 17 but deeper areas are bare, presumably because the considerable amounts of sediment in the water reduce irradiance and on settlement bury whatever vegetation has grown there. Bacteria numbers remain low in the water column but are higher in the sediment. All nutritional groups are present but frequently in numbers too low to make a significant contribution to nutrient cycling. The populations are similar to those occurring in the soil. However the poor nutrient status favours the development of those strains that are most able to utilize low substrate concentrations, i.e. having high substrate affinities. Consequently the proportional representation of the various strains can differ markedly between soil and lake populations (J. C. Ellis-Evans, personal communication). The fauna of these lakes is generally sparse. Six invertebrate taxa have been recorded from Lake 17 (Heywood *et al.,* 1979). The copepod *Pseudoboeckella poppei* and anostracan *Branchinecta gaini* are abundant in summer, feeding close to the bottom on detritus and epiphytic algae. There is also a carnivorous copepod *Parabroteas sarsi.* The remaining animals are a rotifer, a tardigrade and a nematode. Upper Lake remains covered with a thick layer of ice and no direct observations have been made on the flora and fauna. Many *Pseudoboeckella poppei* were seen being swept out in the outflow suggesting a large population in the lake itself (Heywood, 1977c).

Algae and lichens quickly colonize the land as the ice retreats. Mosses first appear as isolated tufts but form larger stands where the scree and glacial debris are stable. The terrestrial vegetation remains very limited in inland areas which are usually very arid but can eventually be quite extensive in coastal and island areas. In the northern areas of the Antarctic Peninsula and associated islands two flowering plants, *Deschampsia antarctica* and *Colobanthus quitensis,* may form localized but extensive swards. The development of the catchment changes the trophic status of the lakes. The change in most cases will be merely from ultra-oligotrophic to oligotrophic.

Oligotrophic lakes (Fig. 2C)

At this time the permafrost may now lie as deep as 0.5–1.0 m below the land surface. Although the inflow and outflow remain seasonal the catchment may have sufficient water-holding capacity to smooth out daily irregularities of flow. With increased residence time of ground water there may be some chemical weathering and leaching of minerals from the rock, especially under vegetation. However, the waters of the lakes are usually very poor in nutrients. Precipitation is still the major source of ions and the water is still the dilute chloride type found in the proglacial lakes. In the larger catchments inflowing water can gain an appreciable amount of heat from the underlying rocks but the main source of heat remains direct solar radiation. With the absence of ice from the basin, the lake may gain a considerable amount of heat in the brief summer. This is not normally shown by any large change in water temperature (annual range recorded on Signy Island is 0–4°C) for most of the energy is used to melt the ice cover, but in an extension of the period the lake remains ice free, two to three months. In shallow lakes a major proportion of the lake water may be involved in the formation of ice in the winter and this causes a large increase in the concentration of the major ions, an effect most clearly seen in biologically inactive ions such as chloride. This seasonal pattern of physical concentration and dilution becomes marked in lakes which thaw out completely during the summer months (Heywood, 1968; Heywood et al., 1979, 1980).

With the increased deposition of sediment at the bottom of these lakes, benthic vegetation becomes better developed and more varied. Aquatic mosses are abundant in some lakes on Signy Island (Light & Heywood, 1973; Priddle & Dartnall, 1978; Priddle, 1979). Mosses have also been reported from Lake Yukidori (Hirano, 1979), Lake Oyako (Nakanishi, 1977) and in similar lakes in the Schirmacher Oasis and Bunger Hills (Savich-Lyubitskaya & Smirnova, 1959, 1964). There is also a wide variety of algae. Parker, Samsel & Prescott (1972) recorded at least 13 taxa from Norsel Point Lake and Hirano (1979) found 39 taxa in Lake Yukidori, excluding diatoms. Algal taxonomic research on the Signy Island benthic flora is incomplete but about 150 taxa have been found by using scuba diving techniques to sample the lake troughs. Forty-eight taxa are epithytic on the mosses (Priddle & Dartnall, 1978). Cyanophytes contribute most of the biomass but diatoms present the largest number of species. Chlorophytes, both filamentous forms and desmids, are also common. The light climate is the major factor determining the distribution of the benthic vegetation and its composition. On Signy Island there is a gradation from perennial algal felts and mosses in the most transparent lakes to seasonal algal communities in lakes with a poorer light climate and in shaded areas of very clear lakes (Heywood et al., 1979, 1980; Priddle, 1979). The perennial vegetation, predominantly blue-green algae and mosses, is adapted to grow at very low irradiance (Priddle, 1980a). Growth occurs throughout most of each year but carbon fixation rates are low. The annual fixation of three benthic communities in clear Signy Island lakes ranged from 11 to 45 g C m^{-2}, with a recorded maximum daily rate of 320 mg C m^{-2} (Priddle, 1980b). The vegetation in shallow water is subject to freezing and therefore only grows in summer. It appears uniform in composition in all the Signy Island lakes and consists largely of *Phormidium* spp. with a high carotenoid concentration (Priddle & Belcher, in press). Estimates of carbon fixation by these shallow water communities suggest a high level of productivity during the short growing season. Tominaga (1977) found a daily rate of 1480 mg C m^{-2} for a similar community in Lake Kamome.

Phytoplankton communities are poorly developed in the oligotrophic lakes. Chlorophyll concentrations range from 1.6 to 3.7 mg m^{-3} in Signy Island lakes during summer (Heywood et al., 1979, 1980). Plankton primary production is also low. Parker et al. (1972) measured a particulate ^{14}C uptake rate of 0.78 mg m^{-3} h^{-1} in Norsel Point Lake, and Tominaga (1977) found particulate carbon fixation rates of 15 mg and 18 mg m^{-3} day^{-1} in the water column of Lakes Ô-Ike and Kamome, respectively. In contrast to the benthic vegetation the phytoplankton appears to be active only in the spring and summer (Light, 1977) and appears to be nutrient limited. The benthic vegetation benefits from the more nutrient rich zone of the water/sediment interface. The bacteria remain low in numbers and activity in the water column, but there is now a high diversity in the sediments. Distinct number and activity profiles due to different nutritional groups are detectable in the mud. Many of these groups are virtually absent from catchment soils and therefore there is now a distinct lake microbial flora (J. C. Ellis-Evans, personal communication).

The rich and varied benthic vegetation now supports a variety of Protozoa and invertebrates; Turbellaria, Rotifera, Gastrotricha, Nematoda, Tardigrada, Annelida and Crustacea. Most of the 43 taxa recorded from Signy Island lakes by Heywood *et al.* (1979) are only found in this type of lake. The majority of the animals are nektobenthic and feed unselectively on the epiphytic benthic plants and detritus. Few species feed in the water column because of insufficient phytoplankton in winter. Larval stages of some Crustacea are dependent on the phytoplankton however, which regulates the population levels (Heywood, 1970; Weller, 1977). Most species remain active throughout the year. Predators are few and, with the exception of the copepod, *Parabroteas sarsi,* only appear in summer when other animals are most abundant (Heywood, 1967, Dartnall, in prep.). Aquatic mosses provide a more spatially heterogeneous environment than the benthic algal felts and a specific moss-associated fauna has developed. The animals occupy niches defined by the position on leaf and stem and density of epiphyte cover (Priddle & Dartnall, 1978).

As the catchment becomes more vegetated and ice-free, the features which differentiate the oligotrophic lakes from the proglacial lakes become more strongly defined. Development of extensive bryophyte vegetation and peat banks allow longer residence times for the water in the catchment and increases the amount of organic matter entering the lakes. The terrestrial vegetation also physically traps the aerosols produced by wind blown sea spray (Allen & Northover, 1967) and the effect of the proximity of the sea is increased. Lakes in well vegetated areas close to the coast of Signy Island have chloride and sodium concentration up to 50% higher than those inland (Heywood *et al.,* 1979). The peak of development for most Antarctic lakes would currently appear to be represented by Moss Lake on Signy Island with its poor phytoplankton but relatively rich benthic community of plants and animals.

Evolution of the Antarctic lake may however continue in several ways. The Antarctic marine inshore ecosystem is highly productive and supports vast numbers of birds and seals, most of which rest and breed on land during the summer. Nutrients are transferred from the marine to the terrestrial ecosystem as these animals excrete and moult. The scale of the transfer is extreme. Signy Island is only 20 km² in area and 13.5 km² become ice- and snow-free in summer. Current breeding populations are estimated to be 216,000 penguins, 540,000 other birds (mainly petrels) (J. P. Croxall, personal communication) and 3800 fur and elephant seals (Kightley & Caldwell, in press). Opaliński (1972) estimated that birds alone may transfer as much as 100 tonnes of organic material onto the Haswell Islands each year. This can have a profound influence on lakes which have bird and/or seal colonies within the catchment.

Enriched lakes (Fig. 2C)

The nitrogen and phosphorus concentrations of these lakes are often considerably higher than in the oligotrophic lakes and both organic and inorganic carbon pools are usually high. The effects of natural enrichment are most profound in small lakes and it is in these lakes that the concentration effect associated with ice production is most pronounced in winter. Increase in ion concentrations as the water molecules freeze out is accompanied by decrease in dissolved oxygen concentration as microbial breakdown of organic matter takes place. Winter oxygen concentrations in eutrophic lakes on Signy Island range from 0.3 to 3.2 g m⁻³ whereas in oligotrophic lakes they remain between 3.1 to

8.5 g m^{-3} (Heywood *et al.*, 1979). Reducing conditions release phosphorus and dissolved organic carbon from the sediments and change the composition of the nitrogen pool.

The dominant vegetation of these lakes is a phytoplankton formed of micro- and nanno- algae (Light, 1977; Light, Ellis-Evans & Priddle, 1980). Two populations have been identified in Heywood Lake, Signy Island. A community of mainly small chlorophytes and chrysophytes produces a spring peak under the ice, characterized by high cell numbers but low production. This is succeeded by a highly productive, cryptomonad dominated community growing under the high irradiance regime of open water summer conditions. Chlorophyll *a* concentrations higher than 10 mg m^{-3} have been recorded (Heywood *et al.*, 1979). The phytoplankton can be very productive; maximum daily productivity for Heywood lake was 4 g C m^{-2} (Light *et al.*, 1980). Samsel & Parker (1972) recorded 147 mg C m^{-3} day^{-1} for Humble Island Lake and Goldman, Mason & Wood (1972) recorded 993 mg C m^{-3} day^{-1} for Skua Lake. These lakes appear to fulfil in summer the criteria for high productivity suggested by Uhlman (1978)—nutrient enrichment associated with a favourable light climate in which the critical depth is greater than that of the euphotic zone. As a result the algae are very efficient and assimilation numbers are high. The very high maximum AN value of 10.5 mg C h^{-1} mg^{-1} (chlorophyll *a*) has been calculated for the phytoplankton in Heywood Lake (Light *et al.*, 1980).

The benthic vegetation is reduced or absent from the troughs of these lakes. This appears to be due in part to insufficient underwater irradiance in spring and summer caused by the phytoplankton population and also by the high allochthonous particle concentration, especially in lakes receiving water which has drained through seal wallows. The anoxic conditions prevalent in the deepest parts of most of these lakes may also be toxic to plant life. Hydrogen sulphide is usually produced in Amos Lake and Lake 15 which are the most enriched lakes on Signy Island. Comparison of water column chlorophyll *a* measurements made regularly over several years for Heywood and Amos Lakes suggests that the nutrient loading in Heywood Lake is close to the optimum. The productivity of Amos Lake is lower in spite of its higher nutrient content (Heywood, 1978). The light climate must also be a factor because the transmission of visible light is less than 20% m^{-1} throughout the year because of the large amount of particulate seal waste present in the water. The development of the phytoplankton community is paralleled by increased numbers and activity of bacteria within the water column. A considerable amount of allochthonous organic material is usually incorporated into the sediments of these lakes. Bacterial numbers and activity remain high for a considerable depth in open structured deposits. Anaerobic bacteria become very important with increasing eutrophication. In the most affected lakes the sediments remain anaerobic for much of the year. The changes in the chemical environment and character of the vegetation have important consequences for the fauna. Fewer species colonize these lakes than the oligotrophic lakes. Rotifers are virtually absent whereas 28 species have been recorded from the oligotrophic lakes of Signy Island. The number of crustacean species are also reduced, being seven in oligotrophic Moss Lake but five and three in Heywood and Amos Lakes respectively. Two of the species in Amos Lake, the anostracan *Branchinecta gaini* and the copepod *Pseudoboeckella poppei*, probably are able to feed on the allochthonous particulate matter. The third species is the copepod *Parabroteas sarsi*. With the exception of *Branchinecta gaini*, adult Crustacea overwinter in Heywood Lake but all overwinter in the egg stage in Amos Lake, presumably because the conditions become anaerobic, and perhaps toxic with hydrogen sulphide (Heywood, 1970). Enrichment therefore results in the classical effect of increased productivity with decreased diversity (Heywood Lake) and may proceed to a stage at which the lake may be described as polluted (Amos Lake). One small lake on Signy Island is only moderately enriched and shows the intermediate condition between oligotrophy and eutrophy. Light Lake receives some water from a small bird colony. The nutrient increase is sufficient to stimulate plankton primary production. At the same time the benthic vegetation is well developed although mosses are not present (Heywood *et al.*, 1979). Similarly the fauna is almost identical to that of Moss Lake (Heywood *et al.*, 1979; Dartnall, in prep.).

In some inland ice-free areas the imbalance between precipitation and ablation is considerable and even large lakes may eventually be reduced to small highly saline pools or salt pans.

Saline lakes produced by the evaporation of fresh-water (Fig. 3A, B)

Many lakes and pools are drying up in the Schirmachervatna, Bunger Hills and South Victoria dry valleys area. There are also many dry beds. Don Juan Pond is an example of a lake in an extreme state of concentration. Beach lines indicate an original depth of 10 m but in 1961 there was only 110 mm of water (Meyer, Morrow, Wyss, Berg & Littlepage, 1962). The water is over 13 times more saline than sea water, having a total dissolved solids content (TDS) of 474 kg m^{-3} and a freezing point of $-48°C$. The lake does not freeze under normal conditions. Little fresh-water flows into the lake in summer. Harris, Cartwright & Korii (1979) have discussed annual fluctuations in chemical composition in relation to temperature. Meyer *et al.* (1962) isolated three strains of bacteria and a yeast from the lake. The organisms had a high degree of halotolerance but their ability to function under natural temperatures was questioned. More recently Siegel, McMurty, Siegel, Chen & Larock (1979) discovered an algal mat, 2–5 mm thick, covering 500–600 m^2 of a dried-out area of the lake floor. Unidentified blue-green and green algae, flagellates and bacteria were recorded. Some experimental evidence was presented which indicated that there was a trophically balanced ecosystem present, which probably became active whenever the lake level rose and covered the area.

There has been a further step along this evolutionary line. In the South Victoria Land dry valleys a climatic change in late Trilogy time (7000 years BP) caused further glacial retreat. The melt water produced entered lake basins which already contained highly saline water. Little mixing with the saline layer occurred for several reasons. The amount of inflowing water was initially small and therefore its velocity was negligible. Only wind generated turbulence could provide the considerable amount of energy necessary to overcome the extreme density differences and this was prevented because the freshwater froze immediately because of the high latent thermal capacity of the underlying brine. The permanent ice cover gradually increased in thickness until it was sufficient to insulate the liquid layer from the ambient temperatures. Solar radiation now gradually warmed up the brine and eventually melted the lower layers of ice.

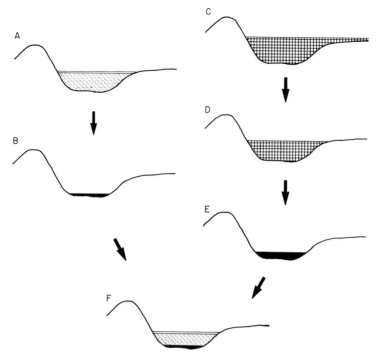

Figure 3. Saline, hypersaline and meromictic lake evolution: A, B, F from fresh-water; C, D, E, F from seawater.

Thereafter the ice cover continued to be formed at the surface and melted at the water/ice interface (Nichols, 1962; Wilson, 1964). In some cases large lakes have developed through this process.

Ectogenic meromictic lakes (Fig. 3F)

The brine layer in some lakes of this type may have arisen in a different way from that described above; from relict seawater, volcanic activity and leaching directly as brine (Heywood, 1977; Wilson, 1979). In view of the present uncertainty and controversy no attempt will be made to distinguish the origin of the lakes described in this section. The lakes contain two separate ecosystems. The lower saline layer resembles the highly saline lakes in that it is colonized by only a few microorganisms. However, solar and/or geothermal heating (Bienati, 1967; Goldman, Mason & Hobbie, 1967; Kriss & Tomson, 1973; Wilson, Holdsworth & Hendy, 1974) may raise the temperature considerably; 25, 13 and 7°C have been recorded in the monimolimnion of Lakes Vanda, Irízar and Bonney respectively. These high temperatures may modify the biological effect of the high salinities and permit some activity by the biota. The freshwater layer of the South Victoria Land dry valleys lakes is ice-covered throughout the year except for a moat round the edge in summer. Lake Irízar on Deception Island is completely ice free during the summer. It has a freely circulating mixolimnion and the stability of the two layers is entirely due to density differences. The catchments of these lakes are typically barren and the fresh-water is low in nutrients and oligotrophic. Parker et al. (1977) recorded a 50 mm thick algal felt, covering part of the floor of Lake Bonney between the bottom of a 4 m thick ice

layer and the chemocline at 14 m depth. The felt was formed of a matrix of os-
cillatoriaceous blue-green algae and 10–20 epiphytic species, mainly diatoms.
The phytoplankton was sparse and dominated by *Chlorella* and *Chlamydomonas*.
No estimate of annual production is available for the phytoplankton or
phytobenthos. The benthic felt supports a limited fauna of ciliate protozoa,
rotifers, nematodes and tardigrades. Biological data for Lake Irízar are very
limited. Several algae have been recorded from water samples and from sediment
cores but it is not clear whether the specimens were from the fresh or saline layers
(Bienati, 1967).

OTHER LAKES

Antarctica also contains lakes which have been formed by other agencies,
including the trapping of seawater by land movement, the damming of coastal
valleys by shelf ice (epishelf lakes) and volcanic activity.

Saline lakes produced by the trapping of seawater (Fig. 3C, D, E)

In several areas of coastal continental Antarctica, lakes have been formed from
the sea when fjords and bays were isolated by isostatic rebound of the land
following ice retreat. In arid areas the lakes have become very saline through
evaporation/ablation. Kerry, Grace, Williams & Burton (1977) have studied such
a lake in the Vestfold Hills. Deep Lake has a TDS content of 280 kg m^{-3} and a
freezing point of $-28°C$. The lake surface never freezes although the waters
become isothermal at $c. -14°C$ during the winter. The small inflow of fresh-water
forms a slush on the lake surface in summer which quickly ablates or mixes
through wind-generated turbulence. The present composition of the water is the
result of the concentration of seawater under low temperatures and the addition
of salts from surface run-off. The initial ionic compositions has been changed by
the selective crystallizing out of certain salts such as mirabilite ($Na_2SO_4 . 1OH_2O$)
and hydrohalite ($NaCl.2H_2O$). Mirabilite forms bands in the sediments of Deep
Lake and it encrusts the rocks bordering the shore.

Several algal taxa have been recorded from both the plankton and benthos
(Kerry *et al.*, 1977). Radiocarbon uptake experiments suggest that the planktonic
algae are making little contribution to the ecosystem (Campbell, 1978) but
significant carbon fixation by the phytobenthos has been measured (S. Wright,
personal communication). No animals have been discovered in this or similar
lakes in the area although a considerable variety of plants and animals have
colonized the brackish and freshwater lakes of the Vestfold Hills (Korotkevich,
1958; Bayly, 1978). The impoverished ecosystem of Deep Lake must therefore be
the result of the combined effects of hypersalinity and low temperature.

Epishelf lakes (Fig. 4)

Kruchinin & Simonov (1967) were the first to describe lakes of this type, lying
between the land mass of the Schirmachervatna and shelf ice. The lower layers
of the lakes were sea water in direct contact with the sea under the shelf ice.
Consequently the surface of the lakes rose and fell with the local tides. Heywood
(1977c) has described two similar lakes, Ablation Lake and Moutonée Lake, on

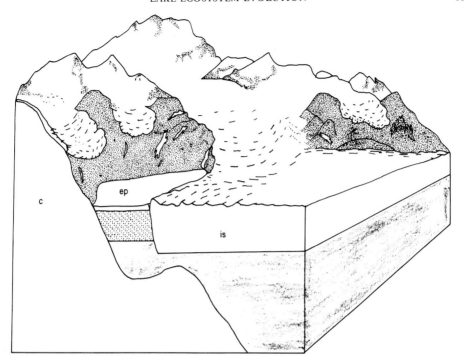

Figure 4. Epishelf lake (ep) between land (c) and floating ice shelf (is).

the coast of Alexander Island bordering George VI Sound. The lakes exist because the ice shelf is a barrier preventing melt water draining from the land into the sea. A permanent ice cover on the lakes prevents wind-generated turbulence mixing the layers within the lake basin. No chemical or biological data are available for the Schirmachervatna lakes but Heywood (1977c) describes an impoverished oligotrophic biota for the freshwater layers of the Alexander Island lakes. As far as could be determined from a preliminary scuba diving survey the benthic flora was restricted to a thin blue-green algal film on a few rocks protruding from a firm silt floor. The phytoplankton was equally sparse but a primary production rate of 60 mg C m^{-2} day^{-1} was calculated from radiocarbon uptake experiments carried out in the upper 20 m of the lake. Protozoa, rotifers, tardigrades and nematodes formed a benthic fauna in nearby pools and probably occurred in the lakes but none were caught. The copepod *Pseudoboeckella poppei* was present. The saline layer of Ablation Lake was found to contain an unidentified marine copepod (only larval forms were caught) and *Trematomus bernacchii,* a common Antarctic marine benthic fish.

Volanic lakes

Volcanoes are still active in some areas of Antarctica such as the South Sandwich Islands, South Shetland Islands and Ross Island. Some lakes may have been formed by volcanic activity. Kroner Lake on Deception Island, South Shetland Islands, occupied a shallow, circular depression in a laval plain. Fumarole activity supplied heat to the lake. Maximum recorded temperature was 10°C and the lake surface never froze over completely in winter (Stanley & Rose,

1967). The lake disappeared in 1969 following a volcanic eruption (Baker, McReath, Harvey, Roobol & Davis, 1975). New lakes were created during volcanic activity over the period 1967 to 1970.

Bacteria, fungi and algae are known to have colonized Kroner Lake (Stanley & Rose, 1967). No further data are available on this or any other lake of volcanic origin as far as we know.

DISCUSSION

The ecosystem in individual Antarctic lakes is influenced, as in other latitudes, by the character of the catchment and its effect on the lake environment. The rate and form of development of the Antarctic catchment are restricted by the low temperature regime which prevails even during the brief summer, and by the aridity of the climate in inland areas. It is in these respects and its isolation that Antarctica differs from the alpine and Arctic regions. In freshwater lakes in Antarctica an increase in biological diversity is associated with the early stages of catchment development and the deposition of sediment in the basin. Maximum diversity is reached under comparatively oligotrophic conditions. As lakes become enriched the productivity is enhanced in spite of becoming strongly seasonal. Biological diversity is however severely reduced.

The reaction of organisms to the rigorous conditions encountered in Antarctic lakes provides interesting phenomena for study at all levels from biochemistry and physiology to community ecology. The ecosystem structure of the freshwater lakes is strikingly different from that found in hot springs—the other extreme of thermal environments. In the springs the ecosystem is an easily defined trophic structure based on the few species capable of growing at temperatures in excess of 60–70°C (Brock, 1970). In most cases it must be presumed that selection pressure is located within the environment itself. In contrast the Antarctic freshwater environment is relatively favourable although temperature and light-limited growing season slow down the rate of ecosystem function. Most of the selection pressure is encountered during the process of reaching the freshwater environments across the surrounding ocean or the vast inhospitable ice-clad wastes of Antarctica itself. Consequently even the most diverse of the freshwater environments show few specialist organisms and the overall effect is a hotch-potch of opportunistic organisms conforming to an ill-defined trophic structure.

ACKNOWLEDGEMENTS

We thank Drs J. P. Croxall, H. J. G. Dartnall and J. C. Ellis-Evans (BAS) and Dr S. Wright (ANARE) for allowing us to include their unpublished material in this paper. W. N. Bonner kindly commented on a draft manuscript.

REFERENCES

ALLEN, S. E. & NORTHOVER, M. J., 1967. Seasonal availability of chemical nutrients on Signy Island. *Philosophical Transactions of the Royal Society of London (B), 252:* 187–189.

ARMITAGE, K. B. & HOUSE, H. B., 1962. A limnological reconnaisance in the area of McMurdo Sound, Antarctica. *Limnology and Oceanography, 7:* 36–41.

BAKER, P. E., McREATH, I., HARVEY, M. R., ROOBOL, M. J. & DAVIS, T. G., 1975. The geology of the South Shetland Islands. 5, Volcanic evolution of Deception Island. *Scientific Reports of the British Antarctic Survey, 78:* 81 pp.

BAYLY, I. A. E., 1978. The occurrence of *Paralabidocera antarctica* (I. C. Thompson) (Copepoda: Calanoida: Acartiidae) in an Antarctic saline lake. *Australian Journal of Marine and Freshwater Research, 29:* 817–24.

BIENATI, N. L., 1967. Estudio limnológico del Lago Irízar, Isla Decepción, Shetland del Sur. *Contribuciones del Instituto Antarctico Argentino, 111:* 36 pp.

BROCK, T. D., 1970. High temperature systems. *Annual Review of Ecology and Systematics, 1:* 191–220.

CAMPBELL, P. J., 1978. Primary productivity of a hypersaline Antarctic lake. *Australian Journal of Marine and Freshwater Research, 29:* 717–724.

DARTNALL, H. J. G., 1977. Antarctic freshwater rotifers. *Archiv für Hydrobiologie. Beihefte. Ergebnisse der Limnologie, 8:* 240–242.

DARTNALL, H. J. G. & HEYWOOD, R. B., in press. The freshwater fauna of South Georgia. *British Antarctic Survey Bulletin.*

FOGG, G. E., 1967. Observations on the snow algae of the South Orkney Islands. *Philosophical Transactions of the Royal Society of London (B), 252:* 279–287.

GOLDMAN, C. R., MASON, D. T. & HOBBIE, J. E., 1967. Two Antarctic desert lakes. *Limnology and Oceanography, 12:* 295–310.

GOLDMAN, C. R., MASON, D. T. & WOOD, B. J. B., 1972. Comparative study of two small lakes on Ross Island, Antarctica. *Antarctic Research Series, 20:* 1–50.

HARRIS, H. J. H., CARTWRIGHT, K. & KORII, T., 1979. Dynamic chemical equilibrium in a polar desert pond: a sensitive index of meteorological cycles. *Science, 204:* 301–303.

HEYWOOD, R. B., 1967. The freshwater lakes of Signy Island and their fauna. *Philosophical Transactions of the Royal Society of London (B), 252:* 347–362.

HEYWOOD, R. B., 1968. Ecology of the freshwater lakes of Signy Island, South Orkney Islands. 2, Physical and chemical properties of the lakes. *British Antarctic Survey, Bulletin* No. *18:* 11–44.

HEYWOOD, R. B., 1970. Ecology of the freshwater lakes of Signy Island, South Orkney Islands. 3, Biology of the copepod *Pseudoboeckella silvestri* Daday (Calanoida, Centropagidae). *British Antarctic Survey Bulletin,* No. *23:* 1–17.

HEYWOOD, R. B., 1972. Antarctic limnology: a review. *British Antarctic Survey* No. *29:* 35–65.

HEYWOOD, R. B., 1977a. Antarctic freshwater ecosystems: review and synthesis. In G. A. Llano (Ed.), *Adaptations within Antarctic Ecosystems:* 801–828. Washington: Smithsonian Institution.

HEYWOOD, R. B., 1977b. The correct identity of a *Pseudoboeckella* sp. (Copepoda, Calanoida) from Signy Island, South Orkney Islands. *British Antarctic Survey Bulletin* No. *45:* 147.

HEYWOOD, R. B., 1977c. A limnological survey of the Ablation Point area, Alexander Island, Antarctica. *Philosophical Transactions of the Royal Society of London (B), 279:* 27–38.

HEYWOOD, R. B., 1978. Maritime Antarctic lakes. *Verhandlungen der internationalen Vereinigung für Theoretische und Angewandte Limnologie, 20:* 1210–1215.

HEYWOOD, R. B., DARTNALL, H. J. G. & PRIDDLE, J., 1979. The freshwater lakes of Signy Island, South Orkney Islands, Antarctica: data sheets. *British Antarctic Survey Data, 3:* 46 pp.

HEYWOOD, R. B., DARTNALL, H. J. G. & PRIDDLE, J., 1980. Characteristics and classification of the lakes of Signy Island, South Orkney Islands, Antarctica. *Freshwater Biology, 10:* 47–59.

HIRANO, M., 1979. Freshwater algae from Yukidori Zawa, near Syowa Station, Antarctica. *Proceedings of the National Institute of Polar Research, Tokyo, 11:* 1–26.

HUTCHINSON, G. E., 1957. *A Treatise on Limnology. I. Geography, Physics and Chemistry.* New York: Wiley.

KERRY, K. R., GRACE, D. R., WILLIAMS, R. & BURTON, H. R., 1977. Studies on some saline lakes of the Vestfold Hills, Antarctica. In G. A. Llano (Ed.), *Adaptations within Antarctic Ecosystems:* 839–58. Washington: Smithsonian Institution.

KIGHTLEY, S. P. J. & CALDWELL, J. R., in press. The first record of a fur seal birth at Signy Island, South Orkneys. *British Antarctic Survey Bulletin.*

KLOKOV, V. D., 1970. Proryv vod iz ozera Glubokogo na stantsii Molodezhnoĭ (Water discharge from Lake Glubokoye at Molodezhnaya Station). *Informatsionnyĭ Byulleten' Sovetskoĭ antarkticheskoĭ Ekspeditsii, 77:* 96–99. (English translation: 1972, *7:* 533–535).

KOL, E., 1972. Snow algae from Signy Island (South Orkney Islands, Antarctic). *Annales Historico—Naturales Musei Nationalis Hungarici, 64:* 63–70.

KOL, E. & FLINT, E. A., 1968. Algae in green ice from the Balleny Islands, Antarctica. *New Zealand Journal of Botany, 6:* 249–261.

KOROTKEVICH, V. S., 1958. Naselenie vodoemov oagisou v Vostochnoy Antarktide. (Animal population of oasis lakes in east Antarctica). *Informatsionnyĭ Byulleten' Sovetskoĭ antarkticheskoĭ Ekspeditsii, 3:* 91–98. (English translation: 1964, *1:* 154–161).

KRISS, A. Ye., ALEKSANDROV, A. M., KOZLOVSKI, A. M., LEDENYEVA, K. V. & LEFLAT, O. N., 1968. Mikrobiologicheskie issledovaniya ozera Glubokogo vblizi stantsii Molodezhnoĭ (Microbiological research in Lake Glubokoye near Molodezhnaya Station). *Informatsionnyĭ Byulleten' Sovetskoĭ antarkticheskoĭ Ekspeditsii, 70:* 44–48. (English translation: 1969, *7:* 159–162).

KRISS, A. Ye & TOMSON, R., 1973. Origin of warm water (25.5°–27°) near the bottom of Vanda Lake in Antarctica (in Russian). *Mikrobiologiya 42:* 942–943.

KRUCHININ, Yu. A & SIMONOV, I. M., 1967. Novyĭ tip ozer v Antarktide (New type of Antarctic lake). *Informatsionnyĭ Byulleten' Sovetskoĭ antarkticheskoĭ Ekspeditsii, 66:* 12–17. (English translation: 1968, *6:* 552–555).

3

LIGHT, J. J., 1977. Production and periodicity of Antarctic freshwater phytoplankton. In G. A. Llano (Ed.), *Adaptations within Antarctic Ecosystems:* 829–837. Washington: Smithsonian Institution.

LIGHT, J. J. & HEYWOOD, R. B., 1973. Deep-water mosses in Antarctic lakes. *Nature, 242:* 535–536.

LIGHT, J. J., ELLIS-EVANS, J. C. & PRIDDLE, J., 1980. Phytoplankton ecology in an Antarctic lake. *Freshwater Biology, 10:*

McLEOD, I. R., 1964. The saline lakes of the Vestfold Hills, Princess Elizabeth Land. In R. J. Adie (Ed.), *Antarctic Geology:* 65–72. Amsterdam: New-Holland.

MATTHEWS, D. H. & MALING, D. H., 1967. The geology of the South Orkney Islands. 1, Signy Island. *Scientific Reports of the Falkland Islands Dependencies Survey, 25:* 32 pp.

MEYER, G. H., MORROW, M. B., WYSS, O., BERG, T. E. & LITTLEPAGE, J. L., 1962. Antarctica: the microbiology of an unfrozen saline pond. *Science, 138:* 1103–1104.

MURAYAMA, H., 1977. General characteristics of the Antarctic lakes near Syowa Station. (In Japanese). *Antarctic Record, 58:* 43–62.

NAKANISHI, S., 1977. Ecological studies of the moss and lichen communities in the ice-free areas near Syowa Station, Antarctica. *Antarctic Record, 59:* 68–97.

NICHOLS, R. L., 1962. Geology of Lake Vanda, Wright Valley, South Victoria Land, Antarctica. In H. Wexler, M. J. Rubin and J. E. Caskey (Eds), *Antarctic Research: the Matthew Foutaine Maurey Memorial Symposium:* 47–52. Washington, D. C.: American Geophysical Union.

OPALIŃSKI, K. W., 1972. Freshwater fauna and flora in Haswell Island (Queen Mary Land, eastern Antarctica). *Polskie Archiwum für Hydrobiologie, 19:* 377–381.

PARKER, B. C., HOEHN, R. C., PATERSON, R. A., CRAFT, J. A., LANE, L. S., STAVROS, R. W., SUGG, H. G., WHITEHURST, J. T., FORTNER, R. D. & WEAND, B. L., 1977. Changes in dissolved organic matter, photosynthetic production and microbial community composition in Lake Bonney, Southern Victoria Land, Antarctica. In G. A. Llano (Ed.), *Adaptations within Antarctic Ecosystems:* 873–890. Washington: Smithsonian Institution.

PARKER, B. C., SAMSEL, G. L. & PRESCOTT, G. W., 1972. Freshwater algae of the Antarctic Peninsula. 1, Systematics and ecology in the U.S. Palmer Station area. *Antarctic Research Series, 20:* 69–81.

PRIDDLE, J., 1979. Morphology and adaptation of aquatic mosses in an Antarctic lake. *Journal of Bryology, 10:* 517–529.

PRIDDLE, J., 1980a. The production ecology of benthic plants in some Antarctic lakes. 2, Laboratory physiology studies. *Journal of Ecology, 68:* 155–166.

PRIDDLE, J., 1980b. The production ecology of benthic plants in some Antarctic lakes. 1, *In situ* production studies. *Journal of Ecology, 68:* 141–153.

PRIDDLE, J. & BELCHER, J. H., in press. Freshwater biology at Rothera Point, Adelaide Island. 2, Algae. *British Antarctic Survey Bulletin.*

PRIDDLE, J. & DARTNALL, H. J. G., 1978. The biology of an Antarctic aquatic moss community. *Freshwater Biology, 8:* 469–480.

SAMSEL, G. L. & PARKER, B. C., 1972. Limnological investigations in the area of Anvers Island, Antarctica. *Hydrobiologia, 40:* 505–511.

SAVICH-LYUBITSKAYA, L. I. & SMIRNOVA, Z. N., 1959. Novyi vid roda *Bryum* Hedw. iz oazisa Baugera (New species of *Bryum* Hedw. from the Bunger Hills). *Informatsionyĭ Byulleten' Sovetskoĭ antarkticheskoĭ Ekspeditsii, 7:* 34–39. (English translation: 1964, *1:* 308–313).

SAVICH-LYUBITSKAYA, L. I. & SMIRNOVA, Z. N., 1964. Glubokovodnyy predstavitel' roda *Plagiothecium* Br. et Sch. v Antarktide. (A deep-water member of the genus *Plagiothecium* Br. et Sch. in Antarctica). *Informatsionyĭ Sovetskoĭ antarkticheskoĭ Ekspeditsii, 49:* 33–39. (English translation: 1964, *5:* 240–243).

SIEGEL, B. Z., McMURTY, G., SIEGEL, S. M., CHEN, J. & LAROCK, P., 1979. Life in the calcium chloride environment of Don Juan Pond, Antarctica. *Nature, 280:* 828–829.

STANLEY, S. O. & ROSE, A. H., 1967. Bacteria and yeasts from lakes on Deception Island. *Philosophical Transactions of the Royal Society of London (B), 252:* 199–207.

TOMINAGA, H., 1977. Photosynthetic nature and primary productivity of Antarctic freshwater phytoplankton. *Japanese Journal of Limnology, 38:* 122–130.

UHLMAN, D., 1978. The upper limit of phytoplankton production as a function of nutrient load, temperature, retention time of the water and euphotic zone depth. *Internationale Revue der gesamten Hydrobiologie, 63:* 353–363.

WELLER, D. L. M., 1977. Observations on the diet and development of *Pseudoboeckella poppei* (Calanoida, Centropagidae) from an Antarctic lake. *British Antarctic Survey Bulletin,* No. *45:* 77–92.

WILSON, A. T., 1964. Evidence from chemical diffusion of a climatic change in the McMurdo dry valleys 1,200 years ago. *Nature, 201:* 176–77.

WILSON, A. T., 1979. Geochemical problems of the Antarctic dry areas. *Nature, 280:* 205–208.

WILSON, A. T., HOLDSWORTH, R. & HENDY, C. H., 1974. Lake Vanda: source of heating. *Antarctic Journal of the United States, 9:* 137–138.

Reproductive adaptations of Antarctic benthic invertebrates

G. B. PICKEN*

*Life Sciences Division, British Antarctic Survey,
Natural Environmental Research Council,
Madingley Road, Cambridge CB3 0ET, England*

Accepted for publication January 1980

The majority of Antarctic benthic invertebrates so far studied do not produce pelagic larvae, but develop non-pelagically by means of egg capsules, brooding or viviparity. The predominance of protected development in the Antarctic benthos is primarily due to the short period of summer phytoplankton abundance and the low sea temperature. Such conditions make it difficult for a larva to complete pelagic development before food becomes scarce in the surface waters. Prosobranch gastropods illustrate some important aspects of Antarctic benthic invertebrate reproduction. Species which develop non-pelagically have an aseasonal or prolonged spawning period. They produce a small number of large yolky eggs which remain in the benthos and develop slowly, giving rise to large, fully competent juveniles. Conversely, one species with free development has a short, synchronous spawning period during early summer, producing larvae which can benefit from the phytoplankton bloom. Protected development by means of brooding will limit dispersion, but transport on floating algae and by anchor ice may partially compensate for this in the Antarctic.

KEY WORDS:— reproduction – Antarctic – benthic – invertebrates.

CONTENTS

INTRODUCTION

The establishment of permanent biological stations in the Antarctic has opened many hitherto neglected or impractical fields of research. Long-term observation and quantitative sampling of the shallow water benthos are now feasible and comparatively routine undertakings. In the past, the nearshore sub-

* Present address: Department of Zoology, University of Aberdeen, Tillydrone Avenue, Aberdeen AB9 2TN, Scotland.

littoral was a region poorly sampled by remote techniques from expeditionary and research vessels. Detailed investigations by SCUBA divers over the last fifteen years have now provided valuable data on the ecology of several common Antarctic benthic invertebrates. Life histories and reproduction have been studied by many workers, including Arnaud (1972), Bone (1972), Bregazzi (1972), Clarke & Lakhani (1979), Hardy (1977), Pearse (1969), Pearse & Giese (1966), Richardson (1980), Seager (1979), Shabica (1975, 1976), Simpson (1972, 1977), Thurston (1972), Walker (1972) and White (1970); the reviews by Arnaud (1974) and Dell (1972) are important reference works. The present paper is not intended to be an exhaustive review of Antarctic benthic invertebrate reproduction. I would like to outline some of the patterns, ideas and theories concerning the reproductive adaptations prevalent in the Antarctic. For the purpose of this paper, the northern limit of the Antarctic Ocean is taken to be the Antarctic Convergence.

REPRODUCTIVE ADAPTATIONS OF BENTHIC INVERTEBRATES

Marine invertebrates present a bewildering variety of life histories and reproductive adaptations. The path from zygote to adult is sometimes complex and often devious, but from the array of specific life histories some broad adaptations have been discerned. Four reproductive patterns are now recognized (Mileikovsky, 1971), two of which may be called 'free' development and two 'protected' development. This terminology was recommended by Simpson (1977) since it avoids possible confusion through the misuse of the embryological terms 'direct' and 'indirect' development. The four reproductive patterns are outlined below. This is a simplified summary of the main types of development for benthic invertebrates as a whole, and as Mileikovsky (1971) has pointed out, other schemes have been presented which are more applicable to individual taxa.

Species with free development characteristically discharge a large number of small eggs into the sea, where they develop through intermediate pelagic or non-pelagic stages. Pelagic larvae are either planktotrophic, actively swimming and feeding in the plankton of the surface waters, or lecithotrophic, essentially passive non-feeding stages, living on stored food. Non-pelagic larvae spend the majority of their life demersally, living and feeding in the fine surface sediment of the sea bed, or in the layer of water immediately above it (Thorson, 1936; Pearse, 1969).

There is no free larval stage in species with protected development. Adults produce a relatively small number of ova, and ensure a high level of survival by protecting them during development. Oviparity is the simplest form of protection, with the embryos developing within egg masses or capsules which are either attached to the substrate or freely floating in the water. Such eggs are large and yolky in comparison with those of planktotrophic species and contain sufficient food for the embryos to complete development to the juvenile state before being liberated. More protection is obtained when the developing eggs are brooded by the adult; eggs may be brooded inside or outside the parent's body, and by either sex (Arnaud, 1974). Ovoviviparous is the appropriate term for embryos which develop within the female and receive some nourishment from the maternal tissues, and yet are separated from them by egg membranes. The greatest degree of protection is afforded by viviparity, where ova with no distinct egg membrane are retained within the female genital system and receive nourishment from the adult. Both Arnaud (1974) and Simpson (1977) have pointed out difficulties and mis-understandings resulting from the imprecise use of the terms brood protection, incubation, ovoviviparity and viviparity.

Eggs shed into the water body to develop freely generally give rise to planktotrophic larvae which will eventually metamorphose and adopt the adult existence. Viviparous, protected development usually produces an advanced juvenile which will undergo no further metamorphoses. However, Thorson (1950) has emphasized that there are exceptions to both these generalities and that there is no strict correlation between the other types of oviposition and the resultant larval or juvenile form. Among species with free development there are many instances of more complicated life histories, involving more than one intermediate larval stage. The type of development exhibited is usually invariable throughout the species' geographic range, but exceptions are known. Some species may also vary in their development at different times of year or under changed environmental conditions (see Mileikovsky, 1971).

DISTRIBUTION OF REPRODUCTIVE ADAPTATIONS

Each broad type of both free and protected development is found in all the world's oceans. As data concerning marine invertebrate reproduction have accumulated, comparison has inevitably been made between the principal reproductive modes of animals in different geographic or bathymetric regions. Pelagic planktotrophic development is the most common mode, and is the principal adaptation of invertebrates from the shallow waters of tropical and temperate seas, occurring in about 70% of all benthic species (Thorson, 1950). A further 6–8% of benthic species from tropical and temperate seas produce lecithotrophic larvae. In polar oceans the majority of invertebrates studied do not produce pelagic larvae. There is a strong tendency towards non-pelagic and protected development, although planktotrophic and lecithotrophic larvae are not entirely absent (Thorson, 1936, 1950; Mileikovsky, 1971).

REPRODUCTIVE ADAPTATIONS OF POLAR BENTHIC INVERTEBRATES

The predominance of non-pelagic development in the polar ocean was first noted by Thorson (1936) who found a high frequency of protected development among Arctic benthic invertebrates. He drew comparison with data from other latitudes in the Northern Hemisphere, and showed that with increasing latitude the frequency of adaptations involving free development decreased, whereas the frequency of protected development increased. Prosobranch gastropods were cited as a particularly good example of such a latitudinal gradient in reproductive adaptation (Thorson, 1935, 1936) and similar trends have also been described for Arctic lamellibranchs (Ockelmann, 1958, 1965) and echinoderms (Einarsson, 1948). Thorson (1936) did not demonstrate latitudinal gradients in reproductive adaptations in the Southern Hemisphere, but presented evidence from the literature to show that non-pelagic development was the principal reproductive mode of benthic invertebrates from the Atlantic sector of the Antarctic Ocean.

Our knowledge of the reproduction of Antarctic invertebrates has increased substantially since Thorson made his now classic generalization. We know the reproduction of only a small number of species compared with the total fauna, but the pattern that is emerging bears out Thorson's postulate. The majority of Antarctic species whose reproduction is known have no pelagic larval stage, and there is a strong tendency towards protected development. Some of the major taxa studied in the Arctic have also been investigated in the Antarctic, and these will illustrate the predominance of protected development.

In the sponges more than 80% of the species studied are either viviparous or exhibit brood protection (Arnaud, 1974). Brood protection is the principal adaptation of the lamellibranchs (Soot-Ryen, 1951; Dell, 1964, 1972), and brood protection and viviparity are common among the echinoderms (Arnaud, 1974). More than 50% of the Antarctic ophiuroids whose reproduction is known exhibit brood protection, and this is a much higher percentage than is found in other parts of the world, including the Arctic (Mortensen, 1936). In the echinoids, two of the three Antarctic families are dominated by species which brood (Arnaud, 1974); the third family is represented by a single species which produces demersal larvae (Pearse & Giese, 1966). Seventeen Antarctic species of holothurians exhibit brood protection (Arnaud, 1974). Eleven species of crinoids are known to brood in the Antarctic (John, 1938, 1939), whereas only three other species with such an adaptation are known from the rest of the world. This high incidence of non-pelagic development contrasts with the scarcity of pelagic stages. Only the larvae of two ophiuroid species, two asteroids, one echinoid and a holothurian are known from the Antarctic plankton (Mackintosh, 1934; Thorson, 1950).

THEORIES ABOUT POLAR ADAPTATIONS

Several theories have been advanced to explain the tendency for non-pelagic and protected development among high latitude marine invertebrates. For example, non-pelagic development eliminates the hazards of pelagic existence, and also greatly increases the likelihood that juveniles will settle in a favourable environment (Ostergreen, 1912). Non-pelagic development removes the embryos from the surface waters, where osmotic difficulties may be encountered during summer at high latitudes due to dilution by freshwater run-off (Ostergreen, 1912). Such observations are undoubtedly valid, but do not provide entirely satisfactory explanations. In particular, Thorson sought an answer that would be equally true for both the Arctic Ocean, which is essentially a shallow sea surrounded by land, and the Antarctic Ocean, which is a circle of water extending into three oceans surrounding a large ice-capped continent.

Thorson (1950) proposed that in the polar oceans a combination of a short period of phytoplankton production (in terms of weeks rather than months), and low water temperature, increase the difficulty of completing a pelagic development before food becomes scarce in the surface waters. Low temperature will slow development, extending it beyond the period of phytoplankton abundance. Under conditions of limited food availability and low temperature, non-pelagic development either by large yolky eggs, brood protection or viviparity, are adaptations which will ensure the survival of offspring to the juvenile state. Non-pelagic development by demersal larvae is a similar adaptation, since sources of food will be present on the sea floor long after the phytoplankton bloom is over.

Table 1. The reproductive modes of Antarctic and sub-Antarctic prosobranch gastropods (from Picken, 1979)

Species	Source	Distribution	Development
Nacella (Patinigera) concinna	Shabica (1976)	Antarctic & Sub-Antarctic	Pelagic
Nacella (Patinigera) macquariensis	Simpson (1972)	Sub-Antarctic	Pelagic
Cantharidus coruscans	Simpson (1977)	Sub-Antarctic	Pelagic
Margarella antarctica	Picken (1979)	Antarctic	Non-pelagic
Margarites refulgens	Arnaud (1972)	Antarctic & sub-Antarctic	Non-pelagic
Pellilitorina setosa	Picken (1979)	Antarctic & sub-Antarctic	Non-pelagic
Pellilitorina pellita	Picken (1979)	Antarctic	Non-pelagic
Laevilacunaria antarctica	Picken (1979)	Antarctic	Non-pelagic
Laevilacunaria bennetti	Picken (1979)	Antarctic	Non-pelagic
Laevilitorina coriacea	Picken (1979)	Antarctic	Non-pelagic
Laevilitorina caliginosa	Simpson (1977)	Antarctic & sub-Antarctic	Non-pelagic
Macquariella hamiltoni	Simpson (1977)	Sub-Antarctic	Non-pelagic
Diacolax cucumariae	Mandahl-Barth (1946)	Sub-Antarctic	Non-pelagic
Trophon species A	Picken (1979)	Antarctic	Non-pelagic
Trophon minutus	Picken (1979)	Antarctic	Non-pelagic
Two unidentified species	Picken (1979)	Antarctic ?	Non-pelagic

REPRODUCTION OF ANTARCTIC PROSOBRANCH GASTROPODS

Arctic and Northern Hemisphere prosobranch gastropods were called the "barometer of ecological conditions in the sea" by Thorson (1950), and were the principal example for his theory of reproductive adaptations. The prosobranchs have now been shown to be an equally good example of non-pelegic reproduction in the Antarctic. Of the seventeen Antarctic and sub-Antarctic species whose reproduction is now known, only three have free development, and all of these have distributions extending outside the Antarctic (Table 1). Several reproductive adaptations of Antarctic prosobranchs introduce and illustrate topics concerning polar benthic invertebrate reproduction in general.

Most of the Antarctic prosobranchs which are oviparous lay a small number of large yolky eggs — of the order of tens or hundreds of eggs per adult, rather than thousands or millions as with planktotrophic development. Both the number and size of the eggs of Antarctic species is comparable with that of similar Arctic species (Picken, 1979). Low numbers of eggs reflect the reduced mortality of protected development, but may also be due to the greater energy content of each egg (Spight, 1976), and to some extent the small size of the adult (Sellmer, 1967). Studies by Chia (1970) and Vance (1973), have shown that it is energetically more economical for the parent to produce a few yolky eggs than numerous non-yolky planktotrophic eggs. This may be an important consideration in high latitudes where food availability is low for much of the year.

Secondly, and here the Antarctic prosobranchs differ from the Arctic prosobranchs investigated by Thorson (1935), there appears to be only a vague seasonality in the timing of reproduction. The periods of spawning, development and recruitment of eight shallow sub-littoral prosobranchs at Signy Island, South Orkney Islands, are all prolonged (Fig. 1). Unlike Arctic prosobranchs, the reproduction of Antarctic prosobranchs is not confined to the summer months; however, there is evidence to suggest that in some species recruitment increases

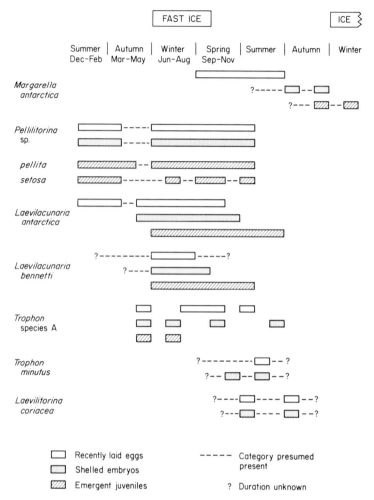

Figure 1. Synopsis of the reproductive patterns of eight Antarctic prosobranch gastropods from Signy Island, South Orkney Islands (from Picken, 1979).

during the Austral spring. The littorinid *Laevilacunaria antarctica,* for example, has a definite peak of recruitment in September, but even in this species spawning and recruitment last for seven or eight months, with a development time of about five months. In two other Antarctic littorinids. *Pellilitorina setosa* and *P. pellita,* newly emerged juveniles can be found in the sub-littoral in every month of the year (Picken, 1979).

Conversely, the limpet *Nacella concinna* produces free larvae and has a highly synchronous reproductive cycle. Spawning occurs over a brief period in summer, around late November to early December, and is timed so that larvae are produced at the peak of the phytoplankton bloom (Shabica, 1976; Picken, 1980).

The seasonality of reproduction in Antarctic marine invertebrates is an intriguing question. White (1977) proposed that the timing of reproduction is largely controlled by the degree to which adults or juveniles are dependent on the summer primary production. Primary production in the Antarctic Ocean is highly seasonal and of short duration. The onset of summer production is

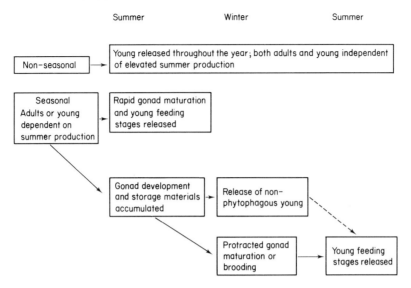

Figure 2. A model of Antarctic poikilotherm breeding cycles (from White, 1977).

predictable in off-shore waters, but in shallow coastal waters the presence of ice may drastically affect the timing of production (White, 1977). Reproductive activities such as gametogenesis, spawning and the liberation of juveniles may either be synchronized with the cycle of primary production in one way or another, or they may be independent of it (Fig. 2). The evidence for Antarctic prosobranchs with protected development suggests that neither the adults nor juveniles of any species are totally dependent on the summer production, variable as it is in onset and duration in the nearshore waters. However, the spring peak of recruitment in some species may be timed so that juveniles will derive maximum benefit from the elevated summer production whenever it occurs. We need to know the energetics of some representative species in greater detail before reproductive seasonality can be properly interpreted in the light of White's hypothesis.

COLONIZATION, DISPERSION AND ENDEMISM

Protected development has been considered to be a handicap to dispersion and colonization (Mileikovsky, 1971). The apparently high degree of endemism among various taxa in the shallow water fauna of the Antarctic Peninsula and the Islands of the Scotia Arc has been used to support this view. There are two methods of dispersion for shallow benthic species with protected development in which the adults are unable to migrate across the deep sea bottom. Adults or egg masses may be carried on algal fronds and holdfasts which become detached and float away with the prevailing currents, or they may be lifted from the sea bed by anchor ice and transported until the ice melts. The frequency of protected development appears to be roughly the same in both the Arctic and Antarctic Ocean (Arnaud, 1974); in the Arctic, protected development is achieved mainly by means of large yolky eggs deposited in the benthos, whereas in the Antarctic it is accomplished predominantly by brooding and viviparity. Thorson (1950) suggested that brooding and viviparity were rare in the Arctic because the fauna was still 'young' (in evolutionary terms) and had not had sufficient time to evolve these more advanced types of development. Arnaud (1974) discounted this idea and supported the hypothesis proposed by Dell (1972), that groups susceptible to brood protection have been preferentially selected in the Antarctic from original stock. He noted that dispersion and colonization by algae was of little significance in the Arctic, since macrophytes were rare and did not float. Species which brood will, therefore, have their dispersion limited in the Arctic, but not in the Antarctic; they may even have been aided in their initial colonization of the Antarctic Ocean by transport on macrophytes.

ACKNOWLEDGEMENTS

I would like to thank all my companions on Signy Island from 1974 to 1977 for their help and encouragement throughout the prosobranch study. I thank Dr A. Clarke, Dr J. R. Seager and Mr M. G. White for many useful discussions and comments on some of the topics covered in this paper.

REFERENCES

ARNAUD, P. M., 1972. Invertébrés marins des 12ᵉ et 15ᵉ Expéditions Antarctiques Françaises en Terre Adélie, 8. Gastéropodes Prosobranchs. *Téthys*, suppl. *4*: 105–134.
ARNAUD, P. M., 1974. Contribution à la bionomie marine benthique des regions Antarctiques et sub-Antarctiques. *Téthys, 6*: 465–656.
BONE, D. G., 1972. Aspects of the biology of the Antarctic amphipod *Bovallia gigantea* Pfeffer at Signy Island, South Orkney Islands. *British Antarctic Survey Bulletin*, No. *27*: 105–122.
BREGAZZI, P. K., 1972. Life cycles and seasonal movements of *Cheirimedon femoratus* (Pfeffer) and *Tryphosella kergueleni* (Miers) (Crustacea: Amphipoda). *British Antarctic Survey Bulletin*, No. *30*: 1–34.
CHIA, F. S., 1970. Reproduction of Arctic marine invertebrates. *Marine Pollution Bulletin, 1(5)*: 78–79.
CLARKE, A. & LAKHANI, K. H., 1979. Measures of biomass, moulting behaviour and the pattern of early growth in *Chorismus antarcticus* (Pfeffer). *British Antarctic Survey Bulletin*, No. *47*: 61–88.
DELL, R. K., 1964. Antarctic and sub-Antarctic mollusca: Amphineura, Scaphopoda and Bivalvia. *'Discovery' Report, 33*: 93–205.
DELL, R. K., 1972. Antarctic benthos. In S. Russell & C. M. Yonge (Eds.), *Advances in Marine Biology, 10*: 1–216. New York & London: Academic Press.
EINARSSON, H.; 1948. Echinoderma. *Zoology of Iceland, 4*: 1–67.
HARDY, P., 1977. *Scoloplos marginatus mcleani*: life cycle and adaptations to the Antarctic marine environment. In G. A. Llano (Ed.), *Adaptations within Antarctic ecosystems. Proceedings of the 3rd. SCAR symposium on Antarctic Biology*: 209–226. Houston, Texas: Gulf Publishing Company.
JOHN, D. D., 1938. Crinoidea. *'Discovery' Report, 18*: 121–222.
JOHN, D. D., 1939. Crinoidea. *British, Australian and New Zealand Antarctic Research Expedition 1901–1904*, Rep. (B) 4(6): 189–212.
MACKINTOSH, N. A., 1934. Distribution of the macroplankton in the Atlantic sector of the Antarctic. *'Discovery' Report, 9*: 67–160.
MANDAHL-BARTH, G., 1946. *Diacolax cucumariae* n.gen., n.sp., a new parasitic snail. *Videnskabelige Meddelelser fra Dansk Naturhistorisk Forening i Kjøbenhavn, 109*: 55–68.
MILEIKOVSKY, S. A., 1971. Types of larval development in marine bottom invertebrates, their distribution and ecological significance: a re-evaluation. *Marine Biology, 10*: 193–213.
MORTENSEN, T., 1936. Echinoidea and Ophiuroidea. *'Discovery' Report, 12*: 199–348.
OCKELMANN, W. K., 1958. Marine Lamellibranchiata. The Zoology of East Greenland. *Meddelelser om Grønland, 122*: 1–256.
OCKELMANN, W. K., 1965. Development types in marine bivalves and distribution along the Atlantic coast of Europe. In L. R. Peake & J. F. Cox (Eds.), *Proceedings of the First European Malacological Congress, 1962*: 25–35, London: Conchology Society of Great Britain and the Malacology Society.
OSTERGREEN, H., 1912. Uber die Brutpflege der Echinodermen in den sudpolaren Kustengebeiten. *Zeitschreiffe wissenschaftliche Zoologische, 101*: 325–341.
PEARSE, J. S., 1969. Slow developing demersal embryos and larvae of the Antarctic sea star *Odontaster validus*. *Marine Biology, 3*: 110–116.

PEARSE, J. S. & GIESE, C., 1966. Food, reproduction and organic constitution of the common Antarctic echinoid *Sterechinus neumayeri* (Meissner). *Biological Bulletin, 130:* 387–401.

PICKEN, G. B., 1979. Non-pelagic reproduction of some Antarctic prosobranch gastropods from Signy Island, South Orkney Islands. *Malacologia, 19:* 109–128.

PICKEN, G. B., 1980. The distribution, growth and reproduction of the Antarctic limpet *Nacella (Patinigera) concinna* (Strebel, 1908). *Journal of Experimental Marine Biology and Ecology, 42:* 71–85.

RICHARDSON, M. G., 1980. The ecology and reproduction of the brooding Antarctic bivalve *Lissarca miliaris* *British Antarctic Survey Bulletin*, No. *49:* 91–115.

SEAGER, J. R., 1979. Reproductive biology of the Antarctic opisthobranch *Philine gibba* Strebel. *Journal of Experimental Marine Biology and Ecology, 41:* 51–74.

SELLMER, G. P., 1967. Functional morphology and ecological life history of the gem clam, *Gemma gemma* (Eulamellibranchia, Veneridae). *Malacologia, 5:* 137–223.

SHABICA, S. V., 1975. *Reproductive Biology of the Brooding Antarctic lamellibranch* Kidderia subquadratum *Pelseneer.* M.Sc. Thesis, Oregon State University. Summary only seen.

SHABICA, S. V., 1976. *The Natural History of the Antarctic Limpet* Patinigera polaris *(Hombron & Jacquinot).* Ph.D. Thesis, Oregon State University, 294 pp.

SIMPSON, R. D., 1972. *The Ecology and Biology of Molluscs in the Littoral and Sub-littoral Zones at Macquarie Island, with Special Reference to* Patinigera macquariensis *(Finlay, 1927).* Ph.D. Thesis, University of Adelaide, 360 pp. Summary only seen.

SIMPSON, R. D., 1977. The reproduction of some littoral molluscs from Macquarie Island (sub-Antarctic). *Marine Biology, 44:* 125–142.

SOOT-RYEN, T., 1951. Antarctic pelecypods. *Scientific Results of the Norwegian Antarctic Expedition 1927–1928, 32:* 1–46.

SPIGHT, T. M., 1976. Ecology of hatching size for marine snails. *Oecologia, 24:* 283–294.

THORSON, G., 1935. Studies on the egg capsules and development of Arctic marine prosobranchs. *Meddelelser om Grønland, 100:* 1–71.

THORSON, G., 1936. The larval development, growth and metabolism of Arctic marine bottom invertebrates, compared with those of other seas. *Meddelelser om Grønland, 100:* 1–155.

THORSON, G., 1950. Reproductive and larval ecology of marine bottom invertebrates. *Biological Reviews, 25:* 1–45.

THURSTON, M. H., 1972. The Crustacea Amphipoda of Signy Island, South Orkney Islands. *British Antarctic Survey Scientific Report, 71:* 127 pp.

VANCE, R. R., 1973. On reproductive strategies in marine benthic invertebrates. *American Naturalist, 107:* 339–352.

WALKER, A. J. M., 1972. Introduction to the ecology of the Antarctic limpet *Patinigera polaris* (Hombron & Jacquinot) at Signy Island, South Orkney Islands. *British Antarctic Survey Bulletin*, No. *28:* 49–71.

WHITE, M. G., 1970. Aspects of the breeding biology of *Glyptonotus antarcticus* (Eights) (Crustacea: Isopoda) at Signy Island, South Orkney Islands. In M. W. Holdgate (Ed.). *Antarctic Ecology, 1:* 279–285. New York London: Academic Press.

WHITE, M. G., 1977. Ecological adaptations by Antarctic poikilotherms to the polar marine environment. In G. A. Llano (Ed.), *Adaptations within Antarctic ecosystems. Proceedings of the 3rd. SCAR symposium on Antarctic Biology:* 197–208. Houston, Texas: Gulf Publishing Company.

A reappraisal of the concept of metabolic cold adaptation in polar marine invertebrates

ANDREW CLARKE

Life Sciences Division, British Antarctic Survey,
Natural Environment Research Council,
Madingley Road, Cambridge CB3 0ET, England

Accepted for publication January 1980

The concept of 'metabolic cold adaptation', namely that polar marine ectotherms are adapted in having an elevated basal metabolic rate, has been examined in the light of recent biochemical, physiological and ecological data for Antarctic marine organisms. It is now clear that marine invertebrates from Antarctic waters are characterized by slow growth rates, low basal metabolism and reduced annual reproductive effort, and there is thus no clear evidence of the traditional view of an elevated metabolic rate. By analogy with fish, protein synthesis rates are probably also low. This suggests that the major feature of cold adaptation is a reduction in the individual total annual energy intake in comparison with ecologically similar organisms from warm water. This allows a high standing crop of suspension feeders to develop, and low temperature is thus a significant factor in the successful widespread adoption of typical K-strategies in Antarctic marine invertebrates.

KEY WORDS: – polar – marine – invertebrate – metabolism – physiology – enzyme – protein – cold-adaptation – K-strategies.

CONTENTS

INTRODUCTION

The purpose of this paper is to examine the concept of 'metabolic cold adaptation' in the light of recent biochemical and physiological data, and to see whether these can be combined into a coherent picture of adaptation to low temperature.

The concept of metabolic cold adaptation, namely that polar ectotherms are characterized by an elevated metabolic rate, has a long history which has been summarized succinctly by Dunbar (1968). As early as 1916, Krogh speculated that an elevated metabolic rate was to be expected in polar ectotherms, but from the 1930s to 1950s a number of comparative studies of marine organisms from arctic and tropical waters produced evidence both for and against such an elevation of metabolic rate in arctic marine invertebrates. One problem highlighted clearly by these studies was the degree to which the chosen comparative organism influenced the outcome of the comparison. Scholander, Flagg, Waters & Irving (1953) undertook detailed comparisons of Arctic and tropical fish, and this work together with that of Wohlschlag (1960, 1964) on Antarctic fish firmly established the concept of an elevated metabolic rate in the literature.

Wohlschlag (1960, 1964) found that the routine rates of oxygen consumption of polar fish were considerably higher (five to ten fold) than would have been expected on the basis of extrapolation to polar temperatures of the oxygen consumption rates of temperate water fish. This elevated metabolic rate was taken as indicating adaptation to the polar environment, although some fish such as lipariids had more or less the expected oxygen consumption rates. The concept of metabolic cold adaptation was thus purely empirical, but nevertheless useful. In particular it afforded an obvious explanation for the slow growth rates of many polar ectotherms; if metabolic cold adaptation meant that more energy was required for maintenance, less was obviously available for activities such as growth (Dunbar, 1968). Elevated metabolic rates have subsequently been described for a number of marine invertebrates including the amphipod *Paramoera walkeri* (Rakusa-Suszczewski & Klekowski, 1973) and the euphausiid *Euphausia superba* (McWhinnie, 1964).

Holeton (1973, 1974), however, demonstrated that polar fish were far more sensitive to physiological stress than had previously been realized, and suggested that Scholander *et al.* (1953) and Wohlschlag (1960, 1964) had not measured true routine metabolism. In a careful series of measurements Holeton (1973, 1974) demonstrated that true routine oxygen consumption rates in Arctic fish were very low.

Subsequent careful experimental work has demonstrated that routine metabolic rates in many polar marine invertebrates are also very low (see for example, White, 1975), and the empirical concept of metabolic cold adaptation is now generally abandoned (Everson, 1977).

There is now an increasing body of data on the biochemistry and physiology of marine ectotherms. In this paper I hope to relate these data to the ecology of the organisms by investigating the question of why polar marine invertebrates grow slowly. This will require examination of data on growth rates, metabolism, enzyme adaptation and protein synthesis, though it will be useful first to describe the important features of the Antarctic marine environment.

THE ANTARCTIC MARINE ENVIRONMENT

To the casual observer the dominant feature of the Antarctic marine environment is ice; indeed pack-ice covers between 11 and 60% of the surface of the sea south of the Antarctic convergence, depending on the season (Mackintosh, 1973). However, with the exception of the shallower areas where scour governs the distribution of benthos, anchor-ice development encases organisms, with consequent risk of their death by tissue freezing, and supercooled fish run the risk of freezing, ice has little direct effect on animals in Antarctic waters (White, 1973). Ice can, however, have a pervasive effect through its control of light availability for primary productivity.

The temperature in Antarctic water is low and seasonally stable in comparison with temperate waters. The annual temperature range in water close to the sea bed at South Georgia is about 0–3°C at South Georgia (54°S),–1.8 to +2°C at

Signy Island (61°S) and −1.9° to −1.8°C at McMurdo Sound (78°S) (Littlepage, 1965; Everson, 1977). Marine animals are found abundantly at all such temperatures and low temperatures *per se* are thus no bar to life. For hypo-osmotic marine invertebrates freezing is not a problem, and those fish living in waters below the freezing point of teleost blood and which regularly come into contact with ice have a glycoprotein antifreeze to enable them to exploit these waters (DeVries & Lin, 1977).

The major seasonal variable in Antarctic waters is primary production and the consequent standing crop of phytoplankton. This seasonality is remarkably predictable, particularly in higher latitudes (Hart, 1942; Littlepage, 1965; Horne, Fogg & Eagle, 1969; Whitaker, 1977); there is also a strong seasonal cycle in benthic diatoms (Arnaud, 1977). As a result food for benthos is superabundant in summer during the bloom, but can be very scarce in winter.

The standing crop of benthic invertebrates in Antarctic waters is generally comparable to temperate waters, and may be very high (Platt, 1978; Arnaud, 1977). Where valid comparisons have been made, the diversity of these polar communities also appears to be comparable with warmer waters (Richardson & Hedgpeth, 1977). Over large areas of the seabed the benthos is dominated by suspension feeders, particularly hexactinellid sponges, demosponges, hydroids, tunicates, polyzoa, sedentary polychaets, actinarians, scleractinian corals and holothurians. Many of these organisms are reported to go into 'winter dormancy' during the winter food shortage (Arnaud, 1977). For necrophagous or scavenging errant benthos, however, food although still seasonally variable is more likely to be available in winter and these organisms have life histories tied less strictly to the annual cycle of primary production (White, 1977).

Much of the work to be discussed below has been performed on these more active organisms, including fish; the results may thus not necessarily be typical of the benthos as a whole, which is predominantly sessile and suspension feeding. Care must therefore be exercised in extending the discussion of ecological adaptations to the maritime Antarctic benthos as a whole (Clarke, 1979).

RESULTS: THE OBSERVATIONAL AND EXPERIMENTAL DATA

Growth rate

Although it is generally accepted that polar marine invertebrates grow slowly, there are nevertheless well documented reports of species which appear to grow rapidly, for example the mollusc *Adamussium colbecki* (White, 1975). It is therefore reasonable to ask whether polar marine invertebrates really do grow slowly.

A random selection of species of, for example molluscs, from the inshore marine Antarctic, will show a wide range of absolute growth rates. Figure 1 shows the growth rates reported for six species of Antarctic mollusc. It can be seen that growth rates vary widely, since size at four years varies from < 0.5 cm to > 6 cm. Three of these species grow faster than the temperate species *Venus striatula* plotted for comparison. The six species of Antarctic molluscs plotted, however, come from a wide variety of ecological niches, from the small weed-dwelling *Lissarca miliaris* to the large burrowing *Laturnula elliptica*. If the relatively rapidly growing *Adamussium colbecki* is compared with temperate water species of similar ecology and maximum size rather than *Venus striatula,* it is found that the polar species grow more slowly than their temperate water counterparts (Table 1).

A. CLARKE

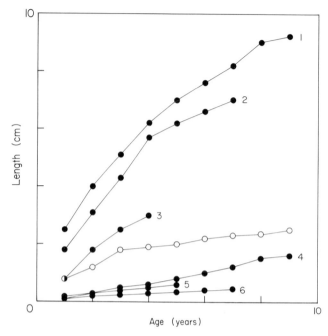

Figure 1. Growth rates of six polar and one temperate mollusc. O, *Venus striatula* at Millport, U.K.;
●, polar species: 1, *Laternula elliptica*; 2, *Adamussium colbecki*; 3, *Gaimardia trapesina*; 4, *Yoldia eightsii*;
5, *Kidderia bicolor*; 6, *Lissarca miliaris*. Data from Everson, 1977.

There are no comparative data for the small species *Kidderia bicolor* or *Lissarca miliaris*, but growth in these species appears to be very slow, as it does in the gastropod *Laevilacunaria antarctica* (Picken, 1979) and the burrowing opisthobranch *Philine gibba* (Seager, 1979).

A detailed study of the growth rate of the caridean shrimp *Chorismus antarcticus* at South Georgia showed that this species grows more slowly than in any other caridean so far studied (Clarke & Lakhani, 1979).

There are other indications of slow growth in Antarctic marine invertebrates

Table 1. Growth rates of polar and temperate water molluscs (data
from Ralph & Maxwell, 1977a)

Species	Locality	Von Bertalanffy growth coefficient, K (from Ford-Walford plots)
Polar		
Adamussium colbecki	Stonington Island	0.24
Laternula elliptica	Signy Island	0.16
Temperate		
Pecten maximus	Port Erin	
	spring spawned	0.46
	autumn spawned	0.35
	Irish West Coast	0.47
	Holyhead	0.44
Placopecten magellanicus	Georges Bank	0.31
	Bay of Fundy	0.30
Mya arenaria	Roskilde Fjord,	
	Denmark	0.28

(for example *Odontaster validus:* Pearse, 1965; see also reviews by Everson, 1977; Arnaud, 1977; Clarke, 1979), but in many cases the significance is hard to assess because of the lack of suitable comparative data. Nonetheless those comparisons it is possible to make would suggest that:

(1) cold water *per se* is no bar to fast absolute growth rates;
(2) growth rates are often markedly seasonal, suggesting that availability of food is a major regulating factor;
(3) wherever it is possible to make valid comparisons, polar species tend to grow more slowly than related species of similar ecology and maximum size from warmer waters.

In many species slow growth is coupled with deferred maturity, and gametogenesis is also slow, often taking more than 12 months (Clarke, 1979). It is also noticeable that the rate of embryonic development in many polar invertebrates is very slow. Wear (1974) has demonstrated a relationship between temperature and embryonic development rate in carideans. Antarctic caridean shrimps, however, hatch at a more advanced stage of development than would be expected due to a shortening of certain larval stages within the egg (abbreviated development: Gurney, 1937; Makarov, 1968, 1973; Clarke, 1979), and this may be a general feature in crustaceans.

Basal metabolism

Metabolic activities may be split into those concerned with reproduction, growth, feeding or activity, and those which serve to keep the organism alive; the latter may be termed basal metabolism. The concept of basal metabolism is critical to any discussion of metabolic cold adaptation, since it is basal metabolism and not the cost of feeding or scope for activity which is believed to be elevated in classical metabolic cold adaptation (Dunbar, 1968). It is therefore necessary to define exactly what processes constitute basal metabolism, and then decide whether it is theoretically possible, or practically feasible, to measure this.

If basal metabolism is defined as the sum of those activities which are necessary to maintain the internal environment of the organism in the face of external environmental constraints, then it will consist of:

(1) ATP generation for protein and nucleic acid turnover;
(2) ATP generation to fuel membrane pumps;
(3) ATP and NADPH generation for basal lipid turnover;
(4) in more complex organisms, also ATP for the cost of circulating oxygen-carrying fluids and maintenance of basal neurocircuitry function.

It is not currently possible to estimate the relative importance of these four processes, although it has been estimated that in various mammalian organs the cost of ATP for Na^+-dependent ATPase varies from 30 to 70% of the resting metabolism (Coulson, Hernandez & Herbert, 1977).

Although this ignores the case of organisms with a significant capacity for anaerobic metabolism, such as some intertidal molluscs, the latter adaptations are usually measures for circumventing short-term oxygen deficiency, the animals returning to aerobic pathways when oxygen once more becomes available. A requirement for oxygen to fuel the basic metabolic processes appears to be universal in multicellular organisms.

Since ATP generation requires oxygen, an obvious approach would be to estimate basal metabolism by measuring basal oxygen consumption. Unfortunately almost all activities such as digestion, feeding, movement, gametogensesis or preparation for moulting also require oxygen and so these processes must either be eliminated or allowed for before basal metabolism (as defined above) can be measured. In practice this is difficult, if not impossible. Although an organism such as a fish can be starved and its spontaneous activity either measured and allowed for, or prevented by anaesthetics, it is not always possible to stop either growth or gametogenesis. Both of these processes are greatly diminished in winter, but they are not necessarily negligible; gametogenesis in many Antarctic organisms, for example, takes over one year (Clarke, 1979).

There are also problems of definition; for example very careful analyses have revealed differences in oxygen consumption rates between crabs which are actively pumping water over their gills, and those which have ceased pumping. Similar considerations apply to bivalves where respiration and feeding are intimately linked. These factors make comparison of oxygen consumption rates between systematic groups difficult to interpret.

It is clear that it is not possible to measure basal metabolism as defined above. A reasonable approximation, however, can be made by measuring the oxygen consumption of a quiescent organism where all feeding and spontaneous activity have ceased; this is often referred to as routine oxygen consumption. This measure is essentially that of basal metabolism together with the instantaneous contribution from any growth or gametogenesis taking place during the period of the experiment. Since these cannot be controlled for, and because most organisms in respirometry chambers show at least some spontaneous activity, routine metabolic rate data can be very variable. Nonetheless, such data are of value in approximating basal metabolism, and much useful comparative information has been obtained by the use of careful experimental technique and experimentally resilient animals.

The problems of technique have been well outlined by Holeton (1973, 1974), who demonstrated that many of the data on which the original empirical concept of metabolic cold adaptation was based were almost certainly abnormally high. Careful experiment (in particular taking care over acclimation to the experimental apparatus and avoidance of physiological shock following capture and handling) suggested that the routine oxygen consumption rates of polar fish were much lower than originally thought.

There is now sufficient reliable data on routine metabolic rate in marine invertebrates to decide whether the oxygen consumption of polar species is higher, equal to, or lower than would be expected. It is at this point that a severe difficulty of interpretation appears, namely the need to define precisely the expected relationship between routine metabolism and temperature, before it can be used as reference against which to judge the presence or absence of an elevated metabolic rate in polar species. As was pointed out by Holeton (1974), the extrapolation to low temperatures of Krogh's (1914) metabolism-temperature curve is suspect. Such extrapolation however, was integral to the original suggestion that marine ectotherms had elevated routine metabolic rates (Scholander et al., 1953; Wohlschlag, 1960, 1964). Holeton (1974) has further shown that refinements of the routine metabolism-temperature curve reduce the

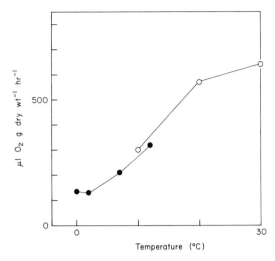

Figure 2. Oxygen consumption of caridean decapods. ●, *Chorismus antarcticus* (polar); ○, *Palaemonetes varians* (temperate, = *P. vulgaris*). Data from Maxwell, 1977.

apparent elevation of metabolic rate in polar fish from sevenfold to twofold. An alternative approach is to define the metabolism-temperature curve by taking a Q_{10} value of, say 2 (Holeton, 1974). However, in a system as complex as an organism there can be little justification in applying a fixed Q_{10} across the temperature range.

A common experimental technique is to compare the routine oxygen consumption rates of polar organisms acclimated to high temperatures with those of warmer water species acclimated to lower temperatures. This procedure of overlapping acclimation temperature ranges, however, is suspect in that many polar organisms are very stenothermal and oxygen consumption rates from thermally stressed animals are of limited value. In polar organisms, for example, very high (and obviously meaningless) Q_{10} values can be obtained for thermally stressed animals. Nonetheless, although the ideal approach would be to construct an overall routine metabolic rate-temperature curve solely from organisms analysed at their environmental temperature, temperature acclimation studies are an accepted part of respiratory physiology and most comparative studies utilize such data.

A number of such studies are now available for Antarctic marine invertebrates. These have been summarized recently by Everson (1977), and so will only be outlined here. Plotting routine oxygen consumption for the polar shrimp *Chorismus antarcticus* alongside that for the grass shrimp *Palaemonetes varians* suggests that there is a general relationship between oxygen consumption and temperature extending through both species (Fig. 2), although the upper temperatures plotted for *C. antarcticus* are well outside the range normally experienced by the animal. There is no sign of any elevation of routine metabolic rate in the polar species.

A careful study of the oxygen consumption in the giant marine isopod *Glyptonotus antarcticus* by White (1975) also indicated no elevation of metabolic rate in that the observed routine oxygen consumption rates fell within the region of extrapolation to polar temperatures of reliable temperate water data. Similar

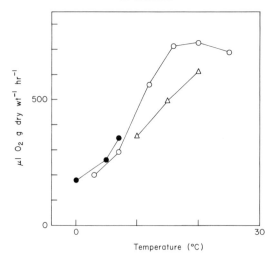

Figure 3. Oxygen consumption of bivalve molluscs. ●, *Gaimardia trapesina* (polar); ○, *Mytilus edulis* (temperate) and △, *Donax vittatus* (temperate). Data from Maxwell, 1977.

data were obtained by Belman (1975), though interpreted differently, but George (1977) reported considerably higher data, highlighting the varied problems of technique and comparability in oxygen consumption studies.

Several studies of Antarctic bivalve molluscs have also indicated no elevation of routine metabolic rate. The kelp-dwelling bivalve *Gaimardia trapesina* has a low routine metabolic rate in comparison with more temperate water bivalves (Fig. 3; Ralph & Maxwell, 1977c), and there is no sign of any elevation in the polar limpet *Nacella concinna* (Ralph & Maxwell, 1977b).

A number of studies of polar marine organisms do appear, however, to have indicated an elevated basal metabolism. In particular studies of krill, *Euphausia superba*, by McWhinnie (1965) reveal an apparently elevated metabolism. Strict comparison with benthos, however, is invalid since zooplankton are unlikely to cease moving in a respirometer and no control was made in these experiments for the effect of handling, state of feeding, and so all the sources of potential error in respiration data are liable to be presented. A small number of reports of an elevated metabolic rate in benthos (data plotted in White, 1975) are probably due, at least in part, to the use of closed-bottle respirometry.

It is therefore concluded that there is no detectable elevation in routine metabolism, and by inference basal metabolism, in Antarctic marine invertebrates (White, 1975; Everson, 1977; Ralph & Maxwell, 1977c). Although it is possible that a small elevation (or depression) in routine metabolism from the expected metabolism-temperature curve is hidden within the experimental variance, it is clear that an elevation of the magnitude originally suggested by Scholander *et al.* (1953) or Wohlschlag (1960, 1964) is not present.

Two conclusions follow: firstly since protein synthesis for turnover is an integral part of basal metabolism, this too must be low; secondly, with a reduced growth rate and low basal metabolism, for a given food intake there should be more energy available for reproduction and activity. This second point will be examined in the discussion.

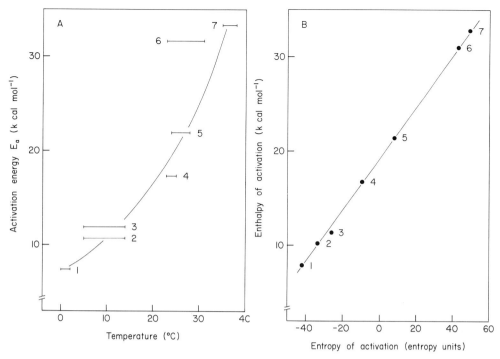

Figure 4. A. Arrhenius activation energies of ATPase in seven species of fish from a range of habitat temperatures. B. Relationship between the enthalpy of activation and entropy of activation for ATPase in 7 species of fish from a range of habitat temperatures. 1, *Notothenia rosii*; 2, *Gadus virens*; 3, *Gadus morhoa*; 4, *Amphiprion sebea*; 5, *Carassius auratus*; 6, *Tilapia nigra*; 7, *Tilapia grahami*. Data from Johnston and Goldspink, 1975.

Temperature adaptation in enzymes

It has long been known that if metabolism is to proceed at comparable rates in ectothermic organisms from different environmental temperatures, some form of compensation for cell temperature must evolve. It is equally clear that such molecular compensation has been achieved. One way of compensating for a decreased cell temperature, and hence the decrease in the mean kinetic energy of the reacting substrate molecules, is to lower the energy barrier to the reaction (see discussion in Hochachka & Somero, 1973, and Hazel & Prosser, 1974). A detailed study of the thermodynamic activation parameters of myofibrillar ATPase from fish adapted to a wide variety of environmental temperatures has shown that the Arrhenius activation energy E_a is positively correlated with habitat temperature (Fig. 4A). E_a is essentially a measure of the enthalpy of activation $\Delta H\ddagger$, and investigation showed that the Gibbs free energy of activation, $\Delta G\ddagger$, remains fairly constant across the range of habitat temperatures. There is however a change in the relative importance of the enthalpy, $\Delta H\ddagger$, and entropy, $\Delta S\ddagger$, of activation (Fig. 4B). This increase in the entropic contribution to the free energy of activation at lower cell temperatures greatly reduces the temperature sensitivity of the rate limiting step in forming the activated enzyme-substrate complex (Johnstone & Goldspink, 1975; Johnston, Walesby, Davidson & Goldspink, 1977).

Although this is a particularly clear example, not all enzymes that have been studied behave similarly with respect to temperature. Feeney & Osuga (1976) have outlined a variety of ways that enzymes could theoretically adapt to temperature, and compared these with data for a number of enzymes isolated from Antarctic fish.

Although not a universal trend (Feeney & Osuga, 1976), it is common for adaptation to low temperature involving a decrease in the enthalpic contribution to the free energy of activation to be accompanied by a decrease in the thermal stability of the molecule, possibly as a result of a more open molecular structure (Johnston & Goldspink, 1975). Although this means that at any given temperature the cold water enzyme variant will degrade faster than the warm water variant, this is not necessarily so at the temperatures to which the enzymes are adapted. This correlation does, however, suggest a reason for the frequent incidence of stenothermy in cold water ectotherms (DeVries, 1977).

Protein synthesis and temperature

Total protein synthesis may be divided, in a manner analogous to metabolism, into basal protein synthesis and that required for growth and gametogenesis. Although measurements of routine metabolism suggest that basal protein synthesis will be slow in polar ectotherms, measurements of protein synthesis are affected by errors similar to those encountered in trying to measure basal metabolism, specifically the inability to separate basal from the total observed synthesis. The observed total rates of synthesis will thus be a summation of growth, gametogenesis, requirements for feeding or digestion and the turnover requirement.

Mathews & Haschemeyer (1978) investigating the thermal dependence of protein synthesis in the toadfish, *Opsanus tau,* found a variation in protein synthesis rate with temperature which extrapolated well to the data for mammalian systems (Fig. 5). This suggests the possibility that protein synthesis does not compensate for temperature. Although there are obvious upper limits to the rate of protein synthesis (rate of supply of tRNA derivatives, ATP supply, number of ribosomes per cell) it is difficult to see why protein synthesis alone should be so strictly temperature dependent.

Rates of protein synthesis vary greatly from organ to organ in fish, and fish from a variety of habitats, but at the same environmental temperature, show wide variations in the activities of the enzyme PEF–1 in liver (Nielsen, 1979). Nonetheless a comparison of rates of liver protein synthesis in fish from a wide range of habitat temperatures revealed a decrease in rate with temperature similar to that for acclimated toadfish, that is a Q_{10} of about 2.4 (Smith & Haschemeyer, in press). A small deviation from this apparent strict thermal dependance was, however, noted in polar fish from McMurdo Sound, whose liver protein synthesis rates were elevated about twofold above the extrapolated $Q_{10} = 2.4$ line.

The latter indicates that adaptation to very low temperatures (that is 5°C and below) carries a slightly increased burden of degradation relative to the $Q_{10} = 2.4$ line, but that rates are still less than in temperature fish. The data also suggest the possibility of a slightly elevated basal oxygen consumption rate in polar fish; although such an increase (about twofold) is probably not excluded by the variability of the oxygen consumption data available, it is considerably less than that proposed by Wohlschlag (1960, 1964). Without knowledge of variations in

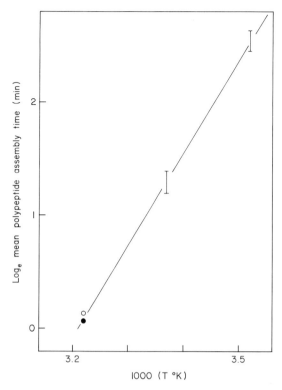

Figure 5. Arrhenius plot of protein synthesis rates in acclimated toadfish, *Opsanus tau,* liver (vertical bars) extrapolated to data for mouse (●) and rat (O) livers. Data from Haschemeyer, 1978.

the other parameters of basal metabolism, however, it is not possible to say whether this increase in protein synthesis at low temperatures will actually be reflected in an elevated metabolic rate.

DISCUSSION

Reconciling the data

Although the data described above derive from diverse animals, a picture emerges of reduced growth rate, reduced basal metabolism, reduced protein synthesis and many enzymes showing subtle molecular adjustments to compensate for the effect of temperature on rate.

This picture poses two immediate questions:

(1) Why isn't growth and/or protein synthesis also compensating for temperature?

(2) Are the remaining areas of energy utilization (scope for activity, reproduction) also decreased?

There are few data for reproductive effort in polar marine invertebrates, but a comparison of polar and temperate water shrimps indicated that individual annual reproductive effort, RE, is reduced in the polar species (Clarke, 1979). There are also strong indications of a reduced RE in the polar opisthobranch *Philine gibba* (Seager, 1979) and the brooding bivalve *Lissarca miliaris* (Richardson, 1977). There are no data available on scope for activity in polar marine invertebrates, but there is no reason to believe that the range of activities (although not necessarily their cost) is any different from related temperate water species. Since myofibrillar ATPase at least appears to compensate for temperature, it would seem reasonable to assume that the cost of activity is not wildly different from that in warmer water.

Despite widespread evolution of mechanisms to compensate the rate of metabolism for decreasing temperature, protein synthesis and growth are nevertheless slow in cold water ectotherms. Although the protein synthetic machinery presumably adapts in the sense that the thermodynamics of the system compensate for the decrease in cell temperature, the overall rates of protein synthesis and growth are slower in cold water. The wide range of growth rates observed in polar benthos (measured as absolute weight increase per animal per unit time) and the demonstration that some rates are faster than in some temperate water species (Fig. 1) suggest, however, that such compensation is theoretically possible. The implication is that the constraints leading to a reduced growth rate are not physico-chemical, but ecological.

The same conclusion follows from consideration of the protein synthesis data. Although the basal rate of protein synthesis is dictated by the requirements for protein turnover, there remains a theoretical capacity for normal, or even enhanced protein synthesis for growth. The data of Smith & Haschemeyer (in press) for polar fish indicate that there is no absolute temperature dependence of protein synthesis, but it is always possible that a reduced basal metabolism (advantageous because of the consequent reduced energy requirement) brings with it a concomitant reduced growth rate. This is not inconceivable, since (presumably) the same set of ribosomal machinery is used for both basal and growth protein synthesis.

Further evidence for a connection between low basal protein synthesis and slow growth comes from rates of embryonic development. There is a marked correlation between habitat temperature and developmental rate in marine invertebrates (see for example the data of Wear, 1974, for decapods). This may not necessarily, however, be a causal relationship, since the amount of yolk per egg also varies with habitat temperature (Clarke, 1979) and this may slow the rate of embryonic development independently of temperature (Clark & Goetzfried, 1978).

There is at the moment insufficient evidence to decide whether slow growth is related directly to the low basal protein metabolism, or whether it has evolved in response to the problems posed by living in the Antarctic environment. It has previously been argued that many of the characteristic features of the Antarctic benthos may be interpreted as the consequences of the widespread evolution of typical K-strategies (Clarke, 1979) and slow growth may be regarded as one part of such strategy. This leads to a re-appraisal of cold adaptation.

Ecological constraints: cold adaptation

It is now clear that the original concept of metabolic cold adaptation, namely that there is a large increase in basal metabolic rate in cold water resulting in less energy being available for growth and reproduction (Dunbar, 1968), does not stand up in the face of recent biochemical and physiological data. Instead, evidence for a reduced basal metabolism, reduced growth, reduced reproductive effort,

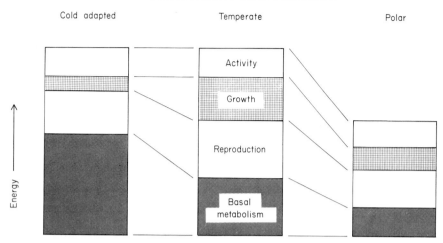

Figure 6. Diagramatic representation of the effects of 'metabolic cold adaptation' (*sensu* Dunbar, 1968; left hand diagram) and cold adaptation as postulated in this paper (right hand diagram) on the total annual individual energy intake of a temperate water benthic marine invertebrate. The size of the various boxes representing metabolism, growth, reproduction and activity are arbitrary.

and the assumption that the energetic costs of feeding, movement and other activities are at least comparable, leads to a concept of cold adaptation shown diagrammatically in Fig. 6. In this diagram the centre block shows the fate of the total annual energy input in a typical temperate water marine invertebrate. The box on the left shows the effect of metabolic cold adaptation, *sensu* Dunbar (1968), on a related organism of similar size and ecology but living in polar waters, and that on the right shows the effect of the concept of cold adaptation advanced here. It can immediately be seen that the major consequence is a reduction in the overall energy intake.

Some indication of the size of the benefit to be obtained can be gauged from data available for caridean shrimps. Taking 0°C and 10°C as typical temperatures for polar and temperate waters respectively, basal metabolism is reduced by about 55% (Fig. 2), growth by about 40% (data for *Chorismus antarcticus* and *Pandalus montagui*; Clarke & Lakhani, 1979) and annual reproductive effort by about 30% (data for same species pair: Clarke, 1979).

Many of the features of the Antarctic marine benthos may be interpreted as the result of the widespread evolution of typical K-strategies, that is deferred maturity, reduced reproductive effort, production of large yolk-rich eggs, mature newly-hatched larvae, iteroparity and increased longevity (Clarke, 1979). Slow growth and reduced basal metabolism may thus be seen as part of a suite of adaptations, conveniently labelled K-strategies, which adapt marine invertebrates to the particular conditions of the Antarctic marine environment, particularly seasonal availability of food.

It has been postulated that K-strategies will evolve where the major determining factors in the environment are either homogeneous in time and space, or else variations in these factors are predictable (Southwood, 1977). This is the case in the Antarctic, where temperature is relatively very stable but the marked seasonal variations in food availability are very predictable (Clarke, 1979).

The importance of low temperature is that the necessary rates of basal metabolism are greatly reduced in cold water, which allows a reduced food intake and also (perhaps necessarily) reduced growth rate and reproductive effort. This does not mean that K-strategies will be limited to cold water, but that the effects of cold water are such that in most cases they are the most efficient ways of adapting to a cold seasonally-productive environment (Clarke, 1979).

The marked seasonal variation in food availability dictates that many processes such as growth and gametogenesis are limited to summer. This seasonality will be particularly severe for suspension feeders, and the winter cessation of all but basal metabolism probably accounts for reports of winter dormancy in Antarctic benthos (Arnaud, 1977).

Since individual annual food intake is greatly reduced, for a given food availability considerably greater standing crop is possible, hence the high biomass figures reported for Antarctic benthos (Dell, 1972; Arnaud, 1977). Food is probably superabundant in summer and so competition for food will largely occur in winter, though it is not possible to predict whether this will be more or less severe than in a temperate or tropical suspension feeding community.

Although the generalized picture advanced here for cold adaptation is based on data for fish or largely active errant benthos, it is felt that it is probably a valid picture for the Antarctic marine benthos as a whole. That is not to say that all such benthos will turn out to have similar basal metabolic rates, protein synthesis rates or reproductive effort, but that when valid comparisons are made between polar and warmer water species, the data will tend to fit the picture advanced in Fig. 6.

Postscript: metabolic cold adaptation and the terrestrial environment

Although originally formulated from observations on marine animals, the concept of metabolic cold adaptation (sensu Dunbar, 1968) has also been applied to terrestrial invertebrates. In spite of an increasing weight of evidence that metabolic cold adaptation does not occur in marine animals, there is still good evidence for an elevated metabolic rate in terrestrial ectotherms.

The protocol for establishing such an elevation is identical to that used for marine animals, and is subject to criticism similar to that levelled at such measurements on marine animals, making it extremely difficult to achieve convincing measurements of basal metabolism. As with marine invertebrates, the oxygen consumption data show enormous variability and the only available technique for respirometry for many organisms (Cartesian diver microrespirometry) is far from ideal. Nonetheless, extensive comparative work indicates strongly that basal metabolic rate is elevated in some polar groups of terrestrial ectotherms (Block & Young, 1978).

It is possible that this will prove to be an artefact of experiment, as with marine animals, but more likely it is a real phenomenon. A possible reason for the difference between the marine and terrestrial data may lie in the great difference in temperature range (both diurnal and seasonal) to which invertebrates living in these two environments are subject. It is possible that a metabolic rate that slavishly follows a diurnal variation in temperature of up to 15°C (Block, 1980, this volume) may pose too severe a problem for an invertebrate, and that the only viable strategy is to elevate all aspects of basal metabolism, accepting a concomitant increased food requirement. Seasonal studies of the energy budgets of marine and terrestrial invertebrates would obviously be valuable.

ACKNOWLEDGEMENTS

The ideas expressed in this paper are the result of many discussions with other members of the British Antarctic Survey, to whom I am most grateful. I would particularly like to thank A. E. V. Haschemeyer, I. A. Johnston, J. G. H. Maxwell, G. B. Picken, R. Ralph, J. R. Seager and N. J. Walesby for access to data, some of it unpublished, during the course of preparing this paper, and A. E. V. Haschemeyer and E. L. Mills for their valuable criticism of the manuscript.

REFERENCES

ARNAUD, P. M., 1977. Adaptations within the Antarctic marine benthic ecosystem. In G. A. Llano (Ed.) *Adaptations within Antarctic Ecosystems:* 135–157. Houston, Texas: Gulf Publishing Co.

BELMAN, B. W., 1975. Oxygen consumption and ventilation of the Antarctic isopod *Glyptonotus. Comparative Biochemistry and Physiology, 50A:* 149–151.

BLOCK, W. & YOUNG, S. R., 1978. Metabolic adaptations of Antarctic terrestrial micro-arthropods. *Comparative Biochemistry and Physiology, 61A:* 363–368.

CLARK, K. B. & GOETZFRIED, A., 1978. Zoogeographic influences on development patterns of north Atlantic Ascoglossa and Nudibranchia, with a discussion of factors affecting egg size and number. *Journal of Molluscan Studies, 44:* 283–294.

CLARKE, A., 1979. On living in cold water: K-strategies in Antarctic benthos. *Marine Biology, 55:* 111–119.

CLARKE, A. & LAKHANI, K. H., 1979. Measures of biomass, moulting behaviour and the pattern of early growth in *Chorismus antarcticus* (Pfeffer). *British Antarctic Survey Bulletin,* No. *48:* 61–88.

COULSON, R. A., HERNANDEZ, T. & HERBERT, J. D., 1977. Metabolic rate, enzyme kinetics *in vivo. Comparative Biochemistry and Physiology, 56A:* 251–262.

DELL, R. K., 1972. Antarctic benthos. *Advances in Marine Biology, 10:* 1–216.

DeVRIES, A. L., 1977. The physiology of cold adaptation in polar marine poikilotherms. In M. J. Dunbar (Ed.) *Polar Oceans:* 409–420. Calgary: Arctic Institute of North America.

DeVRIES, A. L. & Lin, Y., 1977. The role of glycoprotein antifreezes in the survival of Antarctic fishes. In G. A. Llano (Ed.) *Adaptations within Antarctic Ecosystems:* 439–458. Houston, Texas: Gulf Publishing Co.

DUNBAR, M. J., 1968. *Ecological Development in Polar Regions:* 119 pp. Englewood Cliffs, N. J.: Prentice Hall.

EVERSON, I., 1977. Antarctic marine secondary production and the phenomenon of cold adaptation. *Philosophical Transactions of the Royal Society of London (B), 279:* 55–66.

FEENEY, R. E. & OSUGA, D. T., 1976. Comparative biochemistry of Antarctic proteins. *Comparative Biochemistry and Physiology, 54A:* 281–286.

GEORGE, R. Y., 1977. Dissimilar and similar trends in Antarctic and Arctic marine benthos. In: M. J. Dunbar (Ed.) *Polar oceans:* 392–407. Calgary: Arctic Institute of North America.

GURNEY, R., 1937. Larvae of decapod Crustacea. *'Discovery' Reports, 14:* 351–404.

HART, T. J., 1942. Phytoplankton periodicity in Antarctic surface waters. *'Discovery' Reports, 21:* 263–348.

HASCHEMEYER, A. E. V., 1978. Protein metabolism and its role in temperature acclimation. In D. C. Malins & J. R. Sargent (Eds), *Biochemical and Biophysical Perspectives in Marine Biology, 4:* 3–84, London & New York: Academic Press.

HAZEL, J. R. & PROSSER, C. L., 1974. Molecular mechanisms of temperature compensation in poikilotherms. *Physiological Reviews, 54:* 620–670.

HOCHACHKA, P. W. & SOMERO, G. N., 1973. *Strategies of Biochemical Adaptation:* 358 pp. Philadelphia: W. B. Saunders.

HOLETON, G. F., 1973. Respiration of arctic char (*Salvelinus alpinus*) from a high arctic lake. *Journal of the Fisheries Research Board Canada, 30:* 717–723.

HOLETON, G. F., 1974. Metabolic cold adaptation of polar fish: fact or artefact? *Physiological Zoology, 47:* 137–152.

HORNE, A. J., FOGG, G. E. & EAGLE, D. J., 1969. Studies *in situ* of the primary production of an area of inshore Antarctic sea. *Journal of the Marine Biological Association U.K., 49:* 393–405.

JOHNSTON, I. A. & GOLDSPINK, G., 1975. Thermodynamic activation parameters of fish myofibrillar ATPase enzyme and evolutionary adaptations to temperature. *Nature, 257:* 620–622.

JOHNSTON, I. A., WALESBY, N. J., DAVIDSON, W. & GOLDSPINK, G., 1977. Further studies on the adaptation of fish myofibrillar ATPases to different cell temperatures. *Pflügers Archiv, 371:* 257–262.

KROGH, A., 1914. The quantitative relation between temperature and standard metabolism in animals. *Internationale Zeitschrift für Physikalisch-Chemische Biologie, 1:* 491–508.

KROGH, A., 1916. *The Respiratory Exchange of Animals and Man:* 173 pp. London: Longmans, Green.

LITTLEPAGE, J. L., 1965. Oceanographic investigations in McMurdo Sound, Antarctica. *Antarctic Research Series, 5:* 1–37.

MACKINTOSH, N. A., 1973. Distribution of postlarval krill in Antarctic. *'Discovery' Reports, 36:* 95–156.

MAKAROV, R. R., 1968. The abbreviation of the larval development in decapods (Crustacea, Decapoda). (In Russian). *Zoologicheskii Zhurnal, 47:* 348–359.

MAKAROV, R. R., 1973. Larval development of *Notocrangon antarcticus* (Decapoda, Crangonidae). (In Russian). *Zoologicheskii Zhurnal, 52:* 1149–1155.

MATHEWS, R. W. & HASCHEMEYER, A. E. V., 1978. Temperature dependency of protein synthesis in toadfish liver in vivo. *Comparative Biochemistry and Physiology, 61B:* 479–484.

MAXWELL, J. G. H., 1977. *Aspects of the Biology and Ecology of Selected Antarctic Invertebrates:* 131 pp. Ph.D. thesis. University of Aberdeen.

McWHINNIE, M. A., 1964. Temperature responses and tissue respiration in Antarctic crustaceans with particular reference to the krill *Euphausia superba. Antarctic Research Series, 1:* 63–72.

NARITA, J. & HORIUCHI, S., 1979. Effect of environmental temperature upon muscle lactate dehydrogenase in the crayfish, *Procambarus clarki* Girard. *Comparative Biochemistry and Physiology, 64B:* 249–253.

NIELSEN, J. B. K., 1979. Levels of polypeptide elongation factor 1 in relation to adaptation of protein synthesis in tropical fishes. *Marine Biology Letters, 1:* 15–22.

PEARSE, J. S., 1965. Reproductive periodicities in several contrasting populations of *Odontaster validus* Koehler, a common Antarctic asteroid. *Antarctic Research Series, 5:* 39–85.

PICKEN, G. B., 1979. Growth, production and biomass of the Antarctic gastropod *Laevilacunaria antarctica* Martens 1885. *Journal of Experimental Marine Biology and Ecology, 40:* 71–79.

PLATT, H. M., 1978. Assessment of the macrobenthos in an Antarctic environment following recent pollution abatement. *Marine Pollution Bulletin, 9:* 149–153.

RAKUSA-SUSZCZEWSKI, S. & KLEKOWSKI, R. Z., 1973. Biology and respiration of the Antarctic amphipod (*Paramoera walkeri* Stebbing) in the summer. *Polskie Archiwrm Hydrobiologii, 20:* 475–488.

RALPH, R. & MAXWELL, J. G. H., 1977a. Growth of two Antarctic lamellibranchs: *Adamussium colbecki* and *Laternula elliptica. Marine Biology, 42:* 171–175.

RALPH, R. & MAXWELL, J. G. H., 1977b. The oxygen consumption of the Antarctic limpet *Nacella (Patinigera) concinna. British Antarctic Survey Bulletin,* No. *45:* 19–23.

RALPH, R. & MAXWELL, J. G. H., 1977c. The oxygen consumption of the Antarctic lamellibranch *Gaimardia trapesina trapesina* in relation to cold adaptation in polar invertebrates. *British Antarctic Survey Bulletin,* No. *45:* 41–46.

RICHARDSON, M. D. & HEDGPETH, J. W., 1977. Antarctic soft-bottom macrobenthic community adaptations to a cold, stable, highly productive, glacially affected environment. In G. A. Llano (Ed.), *Adaptations within Antarctic Ecosystems,* 181–196. Houston, Texas: Gulf Publishing Co.

RICHARDSON, M. G., 1977. *The Ecology (including Physiological Aspects) of Selected Antarctic Marine Invertebrates Associated with Inshore Macrophytes:* 211 pp. Ph.D. thesis. University of Durham.

SCHOLANDER, P. F., FLAGG, W., WATERS, V. & IRVING, L., 1953. Climatic adaptation in arctic and tropical poikilotherms. *Physiological Zoology, 26:* 67–92.

SEAGER, J. R., 1979. Reproductive biology of the Antarctic opisthobranch *Philine gibba* Strebel. *Journal of Experimental Marine Biology and Ecology, 41:* 51–74.

SMITH, M. A. K. & HASCHEMEYER, A. E. V., in press. Protein metabolism and cold adaptation in Antarctic fishes. *Physiological Zoology.*

SOUTHWOOD, T. R. E., 1977. Habitat, the templet for ecological strategies? *Journal of Animal Ecology, 46:* 337–365.

WEAR, R. G., 1974. Incubation in British decapod Crustacea, and the effects of temperature on the rate and success of embryonic development. *Journal of the Marine Biological Association, U.K., 54:* 745–762.

WHITAKER, T. M., 1977. *Plant Production in Inshore Waters of Signy Island, Antarctica:* 196 pp. Ph.D. thesis. Univeristy of London.

WHITE, M. G., 1973. Aspects of the biological significance of ice in the marine environment. *Proceedings of the Challenger Society, 4:* 145–146.

WHITE, M. G., 1975. Oxygen consumption and nitrogen excretion by the giant Antarctic isopod *Glyptonotus antarcticus* Eights in relation to cold-adapted metabolism in marine polar poikilotherms. *Proceedings of the 9th European Marine Biology Symposium:* 707–724 (Ed. H. Barnes, Aberdeen).

WHITE, M. G., 1977. Ecological adaptations by Antarctic poikilotherms to the polar marine environment. In G. A. Llano (Ed.), *Adaptations within Antarctic Ecosystems:* 197–208. Houston, Texas: Gulf Publishing Co.

WOHLSCHLAG, D. E., 1960. Metabolism of an Antarctic fish and the phenomenon of cold adaptation. *Ecology, 41:* 287–292.

WOHLSCHLAG, D. E., 1963. An Antarctic fish with an unusually low metabolism. *Ecology, 44:* 557–564.

WOHLSCHLAG, D. E., 1964. Respiratory metabolism and ecological characteristics of some fishes in McMurdo Sound, Antarctica. *Antarctic Research Series, 1:* 33–62.

Aspects of Scotia Sea zooplankton

INIGO EVERSON AND PETER WARD

Life Sciences Division, British Antarctic Survey,
Natural Environment Research Council, Madingley Road,
Cambridge CB3 0ET, England

Accepted for publication January 1980

Information on small scale distributions of three species of Antarctic zooplankton is reviewed. Aggregations of the euphausiid *Euphausia superba,* the tunicate *Salpa thompsoni,* and the amphipod *Parathemisto gaudichaudii* are compared, and the manner in which such aggregations may arise is discussed. A possible relationship between swarming and feeding activity in *E. superba* is suggested in which krill are thought to be dispersed whilst feeding but that on repletion they swarm. It is thought that this may account for this species' irregular spatial distribution as recorded by previous expeditions. A further consequence of this theory is that during the Winter swarming will be minimal.

KEY WORDS:– Antarctic – zooplankton – Southern Ocean – *Euphausia superba* – swarming – feeding cycle.

CONTENTS

INTRODUCTION

In recent years there has been an upsurge of interest in the biology of the Southern Ocean due very largely to the realization that the Antarctic krill, *Euphausia superba,* is a resource having a very high annual production and as such could form the basis for a major fishery. Although the annual production of krill is undoubtedly large (almost certainly several times the current total world fish catch) it is the dominant food of a large proportion of the animals present in the Southern Ocean and any fishery would therefore almost certainly be at the expense of some of these consumers. This factor is one of the major reasons why the Scientific Committee on Antarctic Research through its Group of Specialists on Living Resources of the Southern Ocean has organized a Biological Investigation of Marine Antarctic Systems and Stocks (BIOMASS) with the express purpose of studying the biology of krill and its interactions within the Southern Ocean ecosystem.

A major component of the U.K. input to BIOMASS is being made by the British Antarctic Survey through its Offshore Biological Programme. Some preliminary field work has been carried out for this programme during the 1977/78 field season whilst the main field work is planned to start in the 1979/80 season and in most years thereafter. It is intended that the field programme will enable sampling to be carried out in all months of the year. This paper reviews some of the information on small scale distributions of zooplankton in order to identify topics which we hope to undertake as part of our programme and also in collaboration with colleagues from abroad.

SMALL SCALE AGGREGATIONS IN THREE SELECTED SPECIES

The three species that have been selected for comparison, *Salpa thompsoni* (Tunicata), *Parathemisto gaudichaudii* (Amphipoda) and *Euphausia superba* (Euphausiacea), are all known to occur commonly in the Southern Ocean and all are said to occur in swarms (Foxton, 1966; Kane 1966; Marr, 1962). Swarm is a term commonly used to describe aggregations of zooplankton although beyond specifying the term as a 'very dense concentration of individuals' there seems little consistency in its usage. This is largely because of the inherent difficulties in, firstly, seeing dense zooplankton concentrations in the field, and, secondly in gaining some idea of the behaviour patterns of the individual creatures.

A direct consequence of a highly aggregated distribution, such as is the result of swarming, is that the variance of a series of net hauls, even those made in close proximity to each other at more or less the same time, will be quite high. A standard statistical technique for normalizing the data and thus reducing the variance is to apply a fairly strong transformation such as

$$x_{\text{transformed}} = \tfrac{1}{2}(\log x + \log (x + 1))\ \text{(Gerard \& Berthet, 1966)}.$$

This transformation has been applied to the results for four series of net hauls (Table 1). Two of the series are set out in Hardy & Gunther (1936) and were sequential series made at the surface whilst steaming in a line from South Georgia. The results of Mackintosh (1973) refer to a large number of net hauls over much of the Southern Ocean all of which caught krill. The fourth series is a sequence of hauls on a grid pattern we made at a depth of about 3 m during the hours of darkness on 22/23 January 1978.

As expected the very high variance associated with the untransformed data is greatly reduced when the transformation is applied. However, although in the case of *Salpa thompsoni* the variances have been reduced to a more or less acceptable level those for *Euphausia superba* are still in most cases much larger than the mean. The reasons for this almost certainly lie in the manner in which the aggregations occur and are thus linked with the respective definitions of swarms.

Considering first of all the situation in *Salpa thompsoni,* a species whose life history has been described in detail by Foxton (1966). During the winter months the population is composed almost entirely of the solitary form which in the spring produces large numbers of asexually budded aggregate forms and these in turn give rise to the solitary form at the end of the summer. There is thus a very

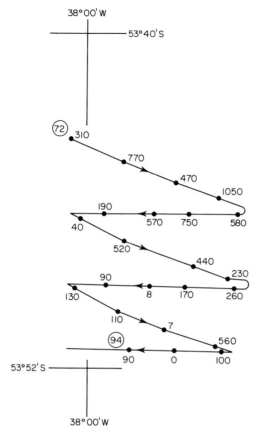

Figure 1. Grid worked by High Speed Tow Net on the night of January 22/23 1978 off the north east coast of South Georgia. Numbers of *Parathemisto gaudichaudii*/10m³ are shown at the respective sampling stations 72–94 (●). Station 72, started at 21.02 hours (G.M.T.); station 94, completed 02.33 hours (G.M.T.). Arrows indicate direction of ships tack.

clearly marked alternation of generations in this species. The production of aggregates begins in the spring soon after the start of the phytoplankton bloom and is probably triggered by it (Foxton, 1964). Since each solitary form is itself potentially capable of producing around 800 aggregates even a moderate concentration of solitaries during the winter could give rise to an enormous number of aggregates very quickly in the summer. Dense concentrations of salps are therefore present only during the summer and these concentrations will have arisen as a result of a response to high phytoplankton densities. Thus swarms of salps are to be expected in water masses which have had solitaries present in them and in addition experienced a recent phytoplankton bloom.

By contrast, the amphipod *Parathemisto gaudichaudii* is a carnivore which is present all year round and has a normal life cycle of one year (Kane, 1966). The annual cycle is geared to producing juvenile stages during the spring at about the same time that the herbivores are producing their young. Although this produces an influx of juvenile stages in the spring the effect is not nearly as numerically great as the production of salps. *Parathemisto* is also known to have a very marked diurnal vertical migration pattern (Hardy & Gunther, 1936; Kane, 1966), but although Kane (1966) considered that avoidance may have been a major and un-

Table 1. Log transformation applied to catch values for *Euphausia superba*, *Salpa thompsoni* and *Parathemisto gaudichaudii* from four series of net hauls

Species	Haul series	Mean catch	Variance catch	Mean (Log catch)	Variance (Log catch)
Euphausia superba	A–AAA (H + G)	1738	11,552,734	4.485	9.954
	A–X (H + G)	294	161,652	4.242	5.46
	O–D (Mac)	51.7	86.436	0.45	68.64
	J–M (Mac)	519	12,434,206	1.296	176.7
Salpa thompsoni	A–AAA (H + G)	183.6	204,500	1.272	1.061
	A–X (H + G)	59.5	21,158	1.093	0.622
Parathemisto gaudichaudii	A–AAA (H + G)	265	275,250	4.186	3.452
	A–X (H + G)	54.5	6,531	3.13	2.025
	72–94 (Present study)	338	87,702	5.278	1.758

A–AAA, Data from Hardy & Gunther (1935: table IV).
A–X, Data from Hardy & Gunther (1935: table V).
Mac, Data from Mackintosh (1973).

quantifiable problem in comparing day and night hauls our results suggest that this may not be the case. Using a Lowestoft pattern High Speed Tow Net at 3 m depth towed at 8 knots we also found an enormous difference in abundance between day and night hauls which are comparable to those reported by Kane (Table 2). It is unlikely that our net had a bias which would weight night-time hauls due to a lessened effect of avoidance since the speed of tow was such that this factor would be minimized. The diurnal vertical migration pattern is almost certainly the cause of the night-time surface aggregations and this is almost certainly part of a feeding cycle as suggested by Kane (1966). The migration of nearly all the individuals present in the top 100 m to the surface 5 m will inevitably cause concentrations there although these will be quite widespread within a given locality. This is indicated in Fig. 1 which although showing that high densities of *Parathemisto* do occur also indicates a not abnormally high degree of variation between net hauls (this is confirmed by the results in Table 1). Thus *Parathemisto gaudichaudii* although present in greater concentration at the surface at night than during the day does not have an abnormally high degree of aggregation with regard to its small scale distribution.

Table 2. Average day and night abundance of *Parathemisto gaudichaudii*

	Average number per 20 min haul (Kane 1966)	Average number per 10 m^3 (present study)
Day	13.7	0.36
Night	780	338

Table 3. Estimated densities of krill swarms

Numerical	Density By weight	Reference
1 per in³		Marr, 1962
1 per 8 in³		
	10–16 kg/m³	Moiseev, 1970
	up to 15 kg/m³	Makarov et al., 1970
	generally up to 5 kg/m³	
	max 6–33 kg/m³	Nemoto & Nasu, 1975
2000–8000/m³	Mean 1.5 kg/m³	Nemoto et al. (in press)
(max. 40,000/m³)		

Krill, *Euphausia superba,* by contrast occur in an enormous range of density as is indicated by Table 1. This range is far greater than is normally encountered in zooplankton ecology. Having a lifespan of more than two years means that the dense aggregations (swarms) are very unlikely to have arisen purely as a result of rapid multiplication. Current evidence suggests that swarming is an activity that is related to feeding and vertical migration; this is discussed more fully later.

Although no comparative figures are available for *Salpa thompsoni* or *Parathemisto gaudichaudii* it is fairly certain that their maximum densities do not approach that of *Euphausia superba.* Some estimates of density in krill swarms are given in Table 3.

Krill swarms have also been observed by eye (Marr, 1962) and also, more frequently, using echosounders (Fischer & Mohr, 1978), and when good visual observations have been made the impression given is that the individuals constituting the swarm are acting in unison with their immediate neighbours (Hardy & Gunther 1936; Semenov, 1969). Harmonious activity has not, so far as we are aware, been described for *Salpa* or *Parathemisto* although it may well be a characteristic of other species such as *Antarctomysis.*

In general parlance, swarming in krill can be considered as more or less synonymous with schooling in fish. However, such a comparison is almost certainly not valid for either *Parathemisto* or *Salpa* and we would therefore recommend that such a term should not be used to define their concentrations unless the aggregations can be shown to exhibit the characteristics of high density and harmonious activity.

SWARMING AND FEEDING CYCLES IN KRILL

Most of the observations on krill swarms have been made during the summer months and these indicate some slight tendency for them to be present nearer to the surface at night and to be spread out in the top 100 m or so during the day (Makarov, Naumov & Shevtsov, 1970; Fischer & Mohr, 1978). Pavlov (1969), based on observations he made in South Orkney and South Georgia regions, suggested krill swarms occur as part of a feeding cycle. In brief he noted that the krill are dispersed during feeding but when replete they come together and swarm. The swarms then slowly sink whilst the animals digest the food in their gut after which they disperse again and feed. Although Pavlov did not observe this cycle under all conditions of phytoplankton density it does offer a reasonable

4

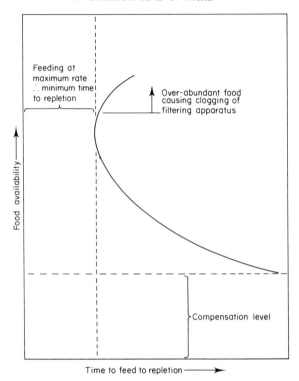

Figure 2. Suggested relationship between food availability and time required to feed to repletion for *Euphausia superba*.

explanation for events and we have used it as the basis for developing a hypothesis to explain some at least of the observed phenomena.

In Fig. 2 a postulated relationship is shown between food availability and the time taken for an individual to feed to repletion. Under conditions of low phytoplankton abundance the feeding time to repletion may be very long and below the compensation level will be infinite. This is because digestion is proceeding as fast as or faster than ingestion. At the other extreme, in areas of higher food density the feeding time to repletion will reach a minimum which will depend on the maximum rate that the animal can ingest the food. Above this level of food concentration the filtering apparatus will become less efficient due to clogging and the ingestion rate will fall.

The positions of the threshold levels and the curve in Fig. 2 will depend on the size of the individual krill. For a given food concentration we anticipate that larger krill would tend to take longer to feed to repletion than smaller ones. (This would not necessarily alter the compensation level but rather the rate at which the curves approach this asymptote.)

Once the animals have become replete providing they stop feeding, as Pavlov suggests, the time taken for digestion should, for a given temperature, be independent of food availability but dependent on the size of the krill. Since the digestion phase is also the swarming phase we now have the basic information necessary to postulate a series of rhythms involving feeding and swarming and related to size. (Fig. 3A, B).

The cycle indicated in Fig. 3B will mean that smaller krill will tend to go

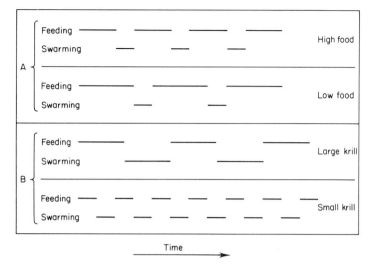

Figure 3. A, B. Suggested periodicity of feeding and swarming cycles for large and small krill *Euphausia superba* at different levels of food availability.

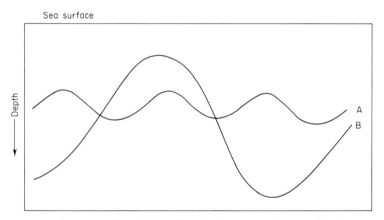

Figure 4. Suggested range and periodicity of vertical migration in A, small and B, large krill *Euphausia superba.*

through a complete cycle of feeding and swarming more rapidly than larger krill. Since the swarming phase is the time when the krill are sinking the smaller krill will tend to sink less than larger krill. Thus both the vertical extent of the migration and the periodicity depend on the size of the krill (Fig. 4). The results of such an arrangement would be that separation between large and small krill should occur and also that swarms of large krill are just as likely to occur above as well as below those of small krill.

This type of situation has frequently been reported (see Shevtsov & Makarov, 1969; Nast, 1979) and has been the cause of much confusion in the past with the result that no clear relationship could be recognized between vertical migration and time of day (see Marr, 1962; Everson, 1977).

Another consequence of this theory is that since it considers swarming as being related to food availability the natural consequence is that during the winter when food is scarce swarming will be minimal. There is very little year-round

Table 4. Catch frequencies versus time of year for *Euphausia superba*

| Time | N | Catch frequency distribution | |
		Arithmetic mean	Mode
Oct–Dec	142	54	10–18 (also 1–2)
Jan–March	243	518	3.2–5.6
April	25	42	3.2–5.6
Oct–April	410	325	3.2–5.6

information to provide confirmation of this although the results of Mackintosh (1973) (Table 4) do tend to indicate that this is the case. The fact that the mode of the catch frequencies is the same for most of the time indicates that the overall amount of krill present is more or less the same throughout the period. However, the arithmetic mean is very high during the middle of summer and this indicates that at that time the distribution is strongly skewed to the right (a small number of very large samples having a disproportionately large effect on the mean). Large samples would indicate that swarms had been sampled and since the effect is greatest in the middle of summer that must be the period when swarms are the most frequent.

A further and more serious implication of the theory is that fishing, by reducing the krill stocks, will have the effect of increasing the food available per individual which will in turn increase the tendency to swarm. Thus fishing may have little effect on the amount of krill present in swarms until a significant amount of the stock has been fished out (Everson, 1978).

Clearly the next step must be to test this theory and this it is hoped to do during the coming field season.

ACKNOWLEDGEMENTS

We gratefully acknowledge the assistance given by the officers and crew of the R.R.S. John Biscoe in our field sampling programme, and M.A.F.F. Lowestoft for the loan of the High Speed Tow Nets.

REFERENCES

EVERSON, I., 1977. The living resources of the Southern Ocean. Rome. FAO; UNDP. Southern Ocean Fisheries Survey Programme GLO/SO/77/I.

EVERSON, I., 1978. Antarctic krill (*Euphausia superba*) as an acoustic target. *Proceedings of the Conference Acoustics in Fisheries, 2.2:* 26 pp. University of Bath.

FISCHER, W. & MOHR, H., 1978. Verhallensbeobachungen an krill (*Euphausia superba* Dana). *Archiv fur Fischereiwissenschaft, 29:* 71–79.

FOXTON, P., 1964. Seasonal variations in the plankton of Antarctic waters. In R. Carrick, M. Holdgate & J. Prevost (Eds), *Biologie Antarctique.* Paris: Hermann.

FOXTON, P., 1966. The distribution and life-history of *Salpa thompsoni* Foxton with observations on a related species *Salpa gerlachei* Foxton. *'Discovery' Report 34:* 1–116.

GERARD, G. & BERTHET, P., 1966. A statistical study of microdistribution of Oribatei. Part III. The transformation of the data. *Oikos, 17:* 142–149.

HARDY, A. C. & GUNTHER, E. R., 1935. The plankton of the South Georgia whaling grounds and adjacent waters, 1926/27. *'Discovery' Report 11:* 1–456.

KANE, J. E., 1966. The distribution of *Parathemisto gaudichaudii* (Guer), with observations on its life-history in the 0–20 degree sector of the Southern Ocean. *'Discovery' Report, 34:* 163–198.

MACKINTOSH, N. A., 1973. Distribution of post larval krill in the Antarctic. *Discovery' Report, 36:* 95–156.

MAKAROV, R. R., NAUMOV, A. G. & SHEVTSOV, V. V., 1970. The biology and distribution of Antarctic krill. In M. W. Holdgate (Ed.), *Antarctic Ecology, 1:* 173–176. New York: Academic Press.

MARR, J. W. S., 1962. The natural history and geography of the Antarctic krill (*Euphausia superba* Dana.) *'Discovery' Report, 32:* 33–464.

MOISEEV, P. A., 1970. Some aspects of the commercial use of the krill resources of the Antarctic Seas. In: M. W. Holdgate (Ed.) *Antarctic Ecology, 1:* 213–216. New York: Academic Press.

NAST, F., 1979. The vertical distribution of larval and adult krill (*Euphausia superba* Dana.) on a time station south of Elephant Island, South Shetlands. *Meeresforsch, 27* (1978/79): 103–108.

NEMOTO, T. & NASU, K., 1975. Present status of exploitation and biology of krill in the Antarctic. *Oceanology International Conference Papers, Brighton:* 353–360.

NEMOTO, T., DOI, T. & NASU, K. (in press). Biological characteristics of krill shown by their study of the krill caught by fisheries operation in the Antarctic. In *Biological Investigations of Marine Antarctic Systems and Stocks (BIOMASS)*, Vol. 2.

PAVLOV, V. Ya., 1969. Pitanie krilya i nekotorye osobennosti ego povedeniya. (The feeding of krill and some features of its behaviour). *Trudy VNIRO, 66:* 207–222 (MAFF Translation No. NS94).

SEMENOV, V. N., 1969. Akvarial nye nablyudeniya za povendenium krilya. (Observations of krill behaviour in aquarium). *Trudy VNIRO, 66:* 235–239. (MAFF Translation No. NS93).

SHEVTSOV, V. V. & MAKAROV, R. R., 1969. K biologii Antarkticheskogo krilya. (On the biology of the Antarctic krill). *Trudy VNIRO, 66:* 177–206. (MAFF Translation No. NS91).

Food, feeding ecology and ecological segregation of seabirds at South Georgia

J. P. CROXALL AND P. A. PRINCE

Life Sciences Division, British Antarctic Survey,
Natural Environment Research Council, Madingley Road,
Cambridge CB3 0ET, England

Accepted for publication January 1980

At the sub-Antarctic island of South Georgia 25 of the 29 breeding species are seabirds. Fifteen of these have recently been studied in some detail. By examining the timing of their breeding seasons and their diet and feeding ecology (especially feeding techniques and potential foraging ranges), the nature of their ecological isolating mechanisms, and in particular the way in which they partition the resources of the marine environment, are reviewed.

Although breeding season adaptations occur (winter breeding in Wandering Albatross and King Penguin; out of phase breeding in two species-pairs of small petrels) these are less important than differences in food and feeding ecology. There is a fundamental distinction between the niche of pursuit-diving species (mainly penguins) and the remainder which are basically surface-feeders. The two abundant krill-eating penguins show clear differences in feeding zones. Three albatrosses and a petrel feed mainly on squid and there are differences in both the species and size of the prey of each. The remaining seabirds chiefly take krill (although the giant petrels are extensive scavengers and some smaller petrels specialize on copepods) and utilize different feeding methods and areas to do so.

Various adaptations related to inshore and offshore feeding zones are discussed. Although most species possess a combination of ecological isolating mechanisms additional evidence for the particular importance of dietary differences is presented.

CONTENTS

INTRODUCTION

While the nature of ecological isolating mechanisms operating in multi-species seabird communities has received some attention in north temperate and tropical regions (e.g. Belopolskii, 1957; Ashmole & Ashmole, 1967; Ashmole, 1968; Pearson, 1968; Cody, 1973) there has been no similar detailed investigation of any south temperate, sub-Antarctic or Antarctic situation although Carrick & Ingham (1967, 1970) summarized much general information for Antarctic areas.

The southern oceans, particularly in the last two regions, are well known to be rich in plant and animal plankton and nekton and to support an extensive array of vertebrate predators including vast numbers of seabirds. At high latitudes, such as the periphery of the Antarctic continent, the exceptional seabird biomass is not matched by a comparable species diversity. At the sub-Antarctic islands, however, most of the considerable diversity of seabird species are present in substantial numbers. This circumstance is probably due to a combination of the rich upwelling areas around the islands' continental shelves and their proximity to the highly productive area of water mixing known as the Antarctic Convergence and to the very restricted amount of suitable land areas for breeding in these latitudes.

Although South Georgia is a little further south than the other islands usually classified as sub-Antarctic (e.g. Prince Edward Islands, Crozet Islands, Kerguelen Island, Macquarie Island) it still lies only 300 km south of the Antarctic Convergence. Of its 29 species of breeding birds (Prince & Payne, 1979) there are 16 procellariforms (albatrosses, petrels etc.) five penguins and four other species (shag, skua, gull and tern) which derive all or part of their food from the sea.

In the last few years the biology and ecology of many of the albatrosses, petrels and penguins have been studied at Bird Island (a small island of c. 500 ha off extreme north-west South Georgia) usually with particular emphasis on diet and feeding ecology. Although much of the research is still in progress this would seem a useful stage to summarize our present ideas on the morphological, behavioural, ecological and temporal mechanisms by which these species partition the resources of the surrounding marine environment.

SPECIES

A list of the main species to be discussed and an estimate of the size of their current breeding population at South Georgia and Bird Island is given in Table 1; selected measurements of these species appear in Appendix 1 and 2.

The Table, and most of what follows, is confined to procellariforms and penguins. We have only anecdotal information on the four species thus excluded; three (shag, gull and tern) breed only in very small numbers on Bird Island and all four appear to have very distinct ecological roles, each typical of its group, which overlap hardly at all either with each other or with the other seabirds. The Antarctic Tern feeds very close inshore, usually in sheltered water, by contact dipping (picking prey from the sea surface while momentarily halting flight) or shallow plunging; Southern Black-backed Gull feeds mainly on marine organisms in the intertidal zone or close inshore waters; the Brown Skua is part scavenger (at fur seal and penguin colonies), part predator of small petrels, mainly at night; Blue-eyed Shag is chiefly piscivorous in water close inshore,

Table 1. Estimated breeding population size (pairs) of seabirds at South Georgia and Bird Island

	Species	South Georgia	Bird Island	Reference
King Penguin	*Aptenodytes patagonica* J. F. Miller	22,000	–	Smith & Tallowin, 1980
Chinstrap Penguin	*Pygoscelis antarctica* (Forster)	2000 +	10	Prince & Payne, 1979
Gentoo Penguin	*Pygoscelis papua* (Forster)	c. 100,000	1200–6500	Croxall & Prince, 1979
Rockhopper Penguin	*Eudyptes crestatus* (J. F. Miller)	10–50	1–2	Prince & Payne, 1979
Macaroni Penguin	*Eudyptes chrysolophus* (Brandt)	5 million +	175,000	Croxall & Prince, 1979
Wandering Albatross	*Diomedea exulans* L.	4300	2600	Croxall, 1979
Black-browed Albatross	*Diomedea melanophris* Temminck	60,000	12,600	Prince & Payne, 1979
Grey-headed Albatross	*Diomedea chrysostoma* Forster	60,000	14,500	Prince & Payne, 1979
Light-mantled Sooty Albatross	*Phoebetria palpebrata* (Forster)	8000–13,000	150	–
Southern Giant Petrel	*Macronectes giganteus* (Gmelin)	20,000–30,000	600	S. Hunter, 1979
Northern Giant Petrel	*Macronectes halli* (Mathews)	5 000–15,000	1100	S. Hunter, 1979
Cape Pigeon	*Daption capense* (L.)	1000–5000	100	Prince & Payne, 1979
Snow Petrel	*Pagodroma nivea* (Forster)	1000–5000	2	
Dove Prion	*Pachyptila desolata* (Gmelin)	millions	500,000 +	
Blue Petrel	*Halobaena caerulea* (Gmelin)	50,000–100,000	10,000 +	
White-chinned Petrel	*Procellaria aequinoctialis* (L.)	20,000–60,000	5000 +	
Wilson's Storm Petrel	*Oceanites oceanicus* (Kuhl)	100,000 +	2000 +	
Black-bellied Storm Petrel	*Fregetta tropica* (Gould)	scarce	100 +	
Grey-backed Storm Petrel	*Garrodia nereis* (Gould)	scarce	?	
South Georgia Diving Petrel	*Pelecanoides georgicus* Murphy & Harper	100,000 +	5000	
Common Diving Petrel	*Pelecanoides urinatrix exsul* Salvin	50,000 +	5000 +	
Blue-eyed Shag	*Phalacrocorax atriceps* King	2000–5000	100	
Brown Skua	*Catharacta lonnbergii* (Mathews)	2000–5000	350	
Southern Black-backed Gull	*Larus dominicanus* Lichtenstein	500–1000	20	
Antarctic Tern	*Sterna vittata* Gmelin	1000 +	25	

Figures without reference are based on the current information in B.A.S. files. They will be fairly accurate for Bird Island, less so for South Georgia.

particularly around kelp beds although the population at Shag Rocks, 200 km west of South Georgia, must be considerably more oceanic in habit. These species will not be treated subsequently except where their ecological role appears relevant to the remaining species.

Table 1 shows also that there are six other species (Chinstrap and Rockhopper Penguins, Snow and Cape Petrels, Black-bellied and Grey-backed Storm Petrels) that are at best scarce breeding species at South Georgia. Except for Chinstrap Penguin we have little information even on their diet. Attention will therefore be focussed chiefly on the remaining 15 species, comprising three penguins, four albatrosses, five petrels, two diving petrels and a storm petrel.

BREEDING HABITAT

The existence of nest site preferences has been well described for northern hemisphere auks (e.g. Lack, 1934; Sergeant, 1951) and noted for other seabirds. Together with evidence for interspecific competition for nest sites (e.g. Belopolskii, 1957; Bedard, 1959a) such habitat segregation has been recognized as a significant ecological isolating mechanism, at least in situations where available breeding sites are in limited supply.

Some South Georgia seabirds show distinct habitat preferences when breeding and these are summarized, together with information on the nature of their breeding aggregations, in Table 2. The ubiquity of the tussock grass *Poa flabellata* (Lam.) Hook. f. habitat, the dominant vegetation type, and its suitability as a substrate for burrowing petrels ensures that most species breed in this habitat. With the petrels and particularly the two diving petrels (see Payne & Prince, 1979, for full details) it is possible often to recognize certain preferences of aspect, slope and microhabitat (cf. Richdale, 1965) and these are being investigated at Bird Island while census work on the burrow-dwelling species is in progress.

With no species has any form of interspecific nest site competition been observed. For all species there appear to be available extensive areas of fully suitable breeding habitat as yet unexploited and it is very difficult to believe that nest site availability has any significant effect on breeding population numbers. It is particularly notable that few species at South Georgia breed on cliffs. The absence of predators may be responsible for this contrast with the northern hemisphere where cliff nesting is such a feature of seabird biology.

There seem to be no obvious disadvantages attending the choice of particular breeding habitats as even the most inland sites are seldom more than a few hundred metres from the sea and most species-specific differences in site topography are probably interpretable in relation to species' morphological, behavioural and ecological adaptations.

TIMING OF BREEDING SEASON

Most South Georgia seabird species show very high synchrony of breeding events both within and between seasons. Egg laying is usually completed within two to three weeks and variation in laying date from season to season is often much less than this. This is not true for King Penguin (discussed in detail below), nor for Gentoo Penguin where, although each colony is fairly well synchronized, there may be considerable intercolony variation and a four to five week season to

Table 2. Breeding habitat and dispersion of South Georgia seabirds

Species	Breeding sites	Breeding dispersion and size	Inter-nest distance
King Penguin	flat beaches	usually large colonies (10^3)	1 m
Chinstrap Penguin	beaches, slopes	medium colonies (10^2–10^3)	0.75 m
Gentoo Penguin	flat beaches, tussock	small colonies (10^2)	1 m
Macaroni Penguin	steep coastal slopes	very large colonies (10^4+)	0.5 m
Wandering Albatross	tussock flats	loose aggregations	10–20 m
Grey-headed Albatross	tussock slopes	medium colonies (10^2–10^3)	1–2 m
Black-browed Albatross	steep tussock slopes	medium colonies (10^2–10^3)	1–2 m
Light-mantled Sooty Albatross	tussock cliffs	solitary-small groups (< 10)	5–10 m
Southern Giant Petrel	tussock flats	loose aggregations	5–10 m
Northern Giant Petrel	tussock flats (often coastal)	loose aggregations	5–10m
Cape Pigeon	ledges of coastal cliffs	small groups	–
Snow Petrel	crevices of high (300 m a.s.l.) inland cliffs	small groups	–
Dove Prion	tussock flats, slopes	dense colonies	1400/1000 m^2
Blue Petrel	tussock flats, slopes	locally dense colonies	720/1000 m^2
White-chinned Petrel	tussock ridges, hills, slopes	locally dense colonies	40/1000 m^2
Wilson's Storm Petrel	coarse scree, rubble, cliff crevices	medium colonies (10^2–10^3+)	
South Georgia Diving Petrel	fine, high (100–250 m a.s.l.) scree	small colonies (10^2)	200/1000 m^2
Common Diving Petrel	very steep coastal tussock slopes	local medium colonies (10^2–10^3)	

For burrow-dwelling species (below horizontal line) values are breeding densities (occupied burrows/1000m^2) for optimum habitats (data from I. Hunter (1979) and pers. comm.).

season variation in laying date has been recorded. The storm petrels are probably also poorly synchronized, as at Signy Island (Beck, 1970), but there are insufficient data.

The average duration of the breeding season, from egg-laying to chick fledging, of South Georgia penguins and petrels is shown in Fig. 1. This shows clearly that for most species the onset of breeding is October–November with fledging February–March–April. The relative consistency of this pattern is, of course, a reflection of the strong seasonality of the environment with phytoplankton production virtually restricted to the period October–May with a single pronounced peak in the South Georgia area around early December (Hart, 1942) and mean zooplankton biomass in the 0–50 m depth zone rising steadily from October to a peak in April and returning to very low levels by July (Foxton, 1956; 1964).

In general terms the larger seabirds (e.g. albatrosses, giant petrels), with

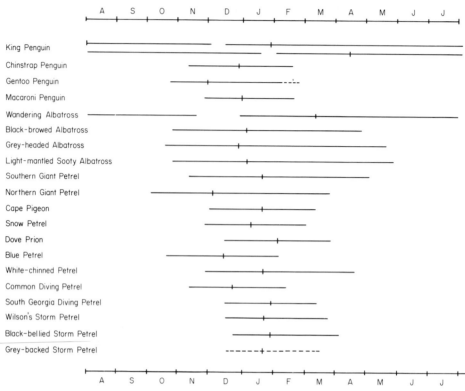

Figure 1. Breeding seasons of South Georgia seabirds. Horizontal lines run from mean laying to mean fledging date. Vertical bar is mean hatching date. Broken line indicates dates or period uncertain.

inevitably longer incubation and fledging periods, appear to commence breeding as soon as practicable (usually in October) apparently in order to ensure that chicks are fledged while rich supplies of zooplankton remain available. For smaller seabirds, with a shorter breeding season, it is clearly possible for its onset to be considerably delayed and fledging at an optimum period maintained.

In spite of the considerable similarities referred to there are two anomalous species and several other features of particular interest. At South Georgia Stonehouse (1960) found that breeding King Penguins usually follow a sequence of early breeding (laying in November–December, chick fledging following November), late breeding (laying February–April, chicks fledging January–February) and non-breeding in three successive seasons, raising, at best, two chicks in this period. At Iles Crozet a somewhat similar situation prevails, although it appears that birds there may only breed successfully in alternate seasons (Barrat, 1976).

It has been suggested (Stonehouse, 1960) that this system has been adopted due to the inability of King Penguins to lay eggs before November which thus prevents chicks being fledged before June (at a time when food resources are dwindling to a minimum). The chicks are therefore sustained with sporadic feeds through the winter and fledge in early summer when food is plentiful; the parents can then return to breeding condition and lay in late summer but this chick, if it survives the high winter mortality, does not fledge until mid-summer and the parents are now unable to commence breeding again that season.

Similar arguments (long chick fledging period in relation to resource availability) can be advanced to account for the Wandering Albatross rearing its chick with regular feeds throughout the winter. The chicks fledge in late November and adults that successfully raise a chick (and those that lose it after June) can only breed biennially (Tickell, 1968). In this context it should be noted that such greater than annual breeding periodicity is not associated solely with winter breeding species; Grey-headed and Light-mantled Sooty Albatrosses are both biennial breeders when successful (Tickell & Pinder, 1967; Prince, unpublished data; Kerry, pers. comm. and in prep.).

The flexibility in timing of breeding season available to the smaller petrels has already been mentioned. In two cases it appears that this may have been used to reduce interspecific competition, particularly with respect to the time of greatest demands for food, i.e. when raising chicks. Thus, both for Dove Prion and Blue Petrel and for South Georgia and Common Diving Petrels, chick-rearing periods are virtually mutually exclusive.

Unfortunately, there are no data on timing of the breeding season for sites at which only one member of these 'species-pairs' breed, to indicate if an alternative breeding schedule is possible. At Signy Island, in the absence of Blue Petrel, Dove Prion commences breeding at a date similar to that on South Georgia (Tickell, 1960). However Signy Island is much further south and breeding probably starts as early as conditions permit (Beck, 1970). Other subspecies of Common Diving Petrel in the New Zealand area are likewise early breeders (Richdale, 1965; Thoresen, 1969) but there are several small petrels (though no other diving petrel) that breed later. While the staggered breeding seasons of the two sibling species of giant petrels, which consistently lay about six weeks apart, may chiefly function as a reproductive isolating mechanism (and even so hybrid pairs are occasionally reported (Burger, 1978; S. Hunter, 1979) it will be seen that this may also play a part in restricting the extent of direct competition for food.

DIET

A summary of the results of quantitative studies on the diet of South Georgia seabirds is presented in Table 3. Also included are estimates derived from earlier qualitative analyses where these have been confirmed by current observations. Data obtained farther south have been used for three species as our observations indicate that a similar situation prevails at South Georgia, where we lack fully quantitative information.

More comprehensive information can be found in the references indicated, in most of which details of the frequency of occurrence and number of individuals in each prey class are given. For the present purpose the weight data were thought to provide the most straightforward and relevant picture. Details of the various sampling and analytical techniques employed are given, principally in Prince (1980 a, b) and Croxall & Prince (1980). In particular it should be noted that most samples were obtained from adults just about to feed their chicks, thus avoiding the problems of food accumulation that result if samples are taken from chicks.

Table 3. Percentage composition by weight of diet of South Georgia seabirds

Species	Main prey classes					Crustacean prey				Reference
	Squid	Fish	Lamprey	Crustacea	Carrion	Euphausiids	Decapods	Amphipods	Copepods	
King Penguin	(90)	(10)								unpublished data
Chinstrap Penguin		4**		96**		100**		+		Croxall & Furse, 1980
Gentoo Penguin		32		68		100		+		Croxall & Prince, 1980
Macaroni Penguin		2		98		100		+		Croxall & Prince, 1980
Wandering Albatross	(80)	(10)		(+)	(+)					Tickell, 1968; Clarke et al., in press
Black-browed Albatross	21	38	1	40	+	95	2.5	2.5		Prince, 1980b
Grey-headed Albatross	49	24	11	16		96	2	2		Prince, 1980b
Light-mantled Sooty Albatross	47	11		41	+	89	10	1		Thomas, unpublished data
Southern Giant Petrel	(10)			(50)	(40)	(100)				S. Hunter, unpublished data
Northern Giant Petrel				(30)	(70)	(100)				S. Hunter, unpublished data
Cape Pigeon		(15)*		(80)*	+	(80)*		(12)*	+	Beck, 1969
Dove Prion	1	2		97		60		8	32	Prince, 1980a
Blue Petrel	1	8		91		90	1	5	4	Prince, 1980a
White-chinned Petrel	47	24		80		96	2	2		Prince, unpublished data
Wilson's Storm Petrel				(95)*		(95)*		+		Beck, 1972
South Georgia Diving Petrel				100		15	17		68	Payne & Prince, 1979
Common Diving Petrel				100		76	4		20	Payne & Prince, 1979

* Data for Signy Island, South Orkney Islands.
** Data for Elephant Island group, South Shetland Islands.
() Values derived from qualitative analysis.
+ Present in small quantities.

The basic breakdown of consumers in respect of the major prey classes can now briefly be summarized before the further segregation that may be achieved by feeding ecology is considered.

Fish

Fish are taken by many species in the Table but are the principal prey of none, although they almost certainly predominate in the diet of Blue-eyed Shag. Fish are important in the diet of Black-browed Albatross, Grey-headed Albatross, Gentoo Penguin and White-chinned Petrel and also for Blue Petrel. This last is not apparent from the table but Prince (1980a) noted that fish occurred in 83% of samples and if the components of the highly digested totally unidentifiable material are (reasonably) attributed to fish then they would contribute 50% by weight to the diet and the crustacean contribution would be commensurately reduced.

Except in Gentoo Penguin, the condition of fish material has usually been insufficient for identification, other than at the family level of Myctophidae and Notothenidae and *Pseudochaenichthys georgianus* Norman (Chaenichthyidae) in some albatross samples. In the Gentoo Penguin material specimens of *Notothenia rossii* Richardson, *N. larseni* Lonnberg and *Champsocephalus gunnari* Lonnberg *c.* 25 cm long were identified (Croxall & Prince, 1980); *N. gibberifrons* Lonnberg 9–12 cm long has been recorded in a stomach examined at Signy Island (Conroy & Twelves, 1972). Blue Petrels take very small fish (and probably mainly myctophids) but it is not possible to discern any differences between the fish portion of the diet in the other species.

The presence of lampreys in the diet of Grey-headed Albatross (and hardly at all in Black-browed Albatross) is particularly noteworthy. The specimens were nearly mature individuals, probably just about to return to their South American breeding rivers (Potter, Prince & Croxall, 1979), of *Geotria australis* Gray, a species only recorded hitherto in the diet of one other seabird, Black Petrel *Procellaria parkinsoni* Gray (Imber, 1976).

Squid

Squid appear fundamental to the diet of King Penguin and Wandering Albatross and very important as a food for Grey-headed Albatross, Light-mantled Sooty Albatross and White-chinned Petrel.

While we have no squid material for King Penguin and that for White-chinned Petrel is still being analysed it is possible to compare in more detail the composition of the squid portion of the diet of four albatrosses (the three mentioned above plus Black-browed Albatross) in Table 4. This table includes details of all squid species which formed more than 5% by numbers or weight of the squid diet of any of the albatrosses.

Some clear differences are apparent. Many squid species were recorded from Wandering Albatross but the bulk of its diet is made up by *Kondakovia longimana* of mean weight just over 3 kg. Grey-headed and Black-browed Albatrosses mainly took *Todarodes sagittatus* of mean weight just under 200 g. *Mesonychoteuthis* species (mean weight 80 g) was the most abundant squid in Light-mantled Sooty Albatross samples but *Discoteuthis* (mean weight *c.* 700 g) made up the bulk by weight. It would seem therefore that, with the exception of the very similar (in

Table 4. Composition of squid component of albatross diets

	Wandering Albatross (N = 534)			Grey-headed Albatross (N = 190)			Black-browed Albatross (N = 97)			Light-mantled Sooty Albatross (N = 191)		
	No	Wt %	Mean Wt (g)	No	Wt %	Mean Wt (g)	No	Wt %	Mean Wt (g)	No	Wt %	Mean Wt (g)
Cranchidae												
Mesonychoteuthis sp. A	5	<1	84	12	5	74	25	13	81	56	17	81
Taonius pavo Lesueur	5	6	319	–	–		–	–		–	–	
Crystalloteuthis sp.	15	3	276	–	–		–	–		2	1	c. 270
Onychoteuthidae												
Kondakovia longimana Filippova	36	78	3170	–	–		1	1	203	<1	2	c. 1000
Histioteuthidae												
Histioteuthis ? eltaninae (Voss)	10	<1	71	–	–		–	–		<1	<1	c. 70
H. atlantica (Hoyle)	3	1	192	–	–		–	–		–	–	
Gonatidae												
Gonatus antarcticus Lönnberg	4	1	330	–	–		–	–	186	5	6	c. 300
Gonatus sp.	2	<1	162	–	–		–	–		8	5	c. 150
Cycloteuthidae												
Discoteuthis sp.	–	–		–	–		–	–		21	60	726
Octopoteuthidae												
Taningia danae Joubin	2	8	6520	–	–		–	–		–	–	
Enoploteuthidae												
Ancistrocheirus lesueuri (d'Orbigny)	2	2	1476	–	–		1	7	1110	–	–	
Psychroteuthidae												
Psychroteuthis sp.	–	–		–	–		–	–		5	9	570
Ommastrephidae												
Todarodes sagittatus (Lam.)	1	<1	350	95	<1	183	67	76	189	2	<1	c. 180
Other species	(14) 11	<2		(1) 4	<1		(1) 3	2		(1) <1	<1	

1. Number of additional species is in parenthesis on bottom row of table.
2. References: Clarke et al., in press; Prince, 1980b; Clarke & Prince, in press; unpublished data.

body and bill dimensions) Grey-headed Albatross and Black-browed Albatross (and squid is of small importance in the diet of the latter) the albatrosses take squid of both different species and sizes. There are, however, differences in the provenance of the samples. Although the Grey-headed Albatross and Black-browed Albatross data are directly comparable and largely comprise information from nearly complete squid from fresh samples, those for the two other species are derived from examination of regurgitated beaks, which in the case of Wandering Albatross must derive mainly from squid fed to the chick during the austral winter. Thus we do not know what squid this albatross feeds on when the other three are breeding (and vice versa). Nevertheless, even with these qualifications, the pattern of segregation of squid prey by species and size amongst three types of albatrosses seems a convincing one. White-chinned Petrels, not surprisingly, take mainly much smaller prey amongst which histioteuthids predominate and one or two larger genera like *Taonius* and *Gonatus* occur. They too would seem to be reasonably distinct from the other species in their squid prey.

Elsewhere giant petrels have been recorded to regurgitate squid (Conroy, 1972; Johnstone, 1977) and it was surprising that none were found in the small number of samples collected at Bird Island in 1978–79 (although a few beaks had been found in previous seasons). At Macquarie Island Johnstone (1977) reports *Kondakovia longimana, Taonius, Gonatus* and *Histioteuthis ? eltaninae,* a combination that is reminiscent of Wandering Albatross squid diet, as well as *Nototodarus sloani* Gray, a species apparently particularly common in Australasian waters, and various less certainly identified taxa.

Crustacea

In contrast to squid, where the variety of species available may make it easier to achieve a degree of dietary segregation, the principal crustacean taken by nearly all birds is krill *Euphausia superba* Dana. Only in three species (Dove Prion and the two diving petrels) does it represent much less than 90% of crustacean biomass. For these three species copepods are the other main prey; they predominate by numbers in the diet of Dove Prion and even by weight in that of Common Diving Petrel, the latter thus contrasting quite strongly with the situation in South Georgia Diving Petrel where copepods are much less, and euphausiids much more, important.

Amphipods are ubiquitous, but probably often derive from the stomach contents of larger prey items; only in the smaller petrels are they probably a regular feature of the diet. Large decapods (chiefly *Acanthephyra* spp.) are taken mainly by albatrosses and larger petrels and appear to make a significant contribution to the diet of Light-mantled Sooty Albatross.

In squid the size of prey varied between predators but, in spite of the many bird species of different dimensions to which krill is important, most take mature krill of mean length *c.* 53–55 mm. Blue Petrel and Dove Prion both took smaller Krill (mean length 45 and 41 mm respectively; (Prince, 1980a) and Macaroni Penguin took large numbers (but only 18% by weight) of small, probably 1st year krill of mean length *c.* 20 mm (Croxall & Prince, 1980). The broad picture, however, is clearly one of mature krill being of basic importance to the diet of all species (including Snow Petrel and Cape Pigeon which are not in Table 3) except

King Penguin, Wandering Albatross, Grey-headed Albatross and perhaps Common Diving Petrel.

Nevertheless the minor components of the diet should not always be dismissed as totally insignificant. Careful analysis of the amphipods in the diet of Blue Petrel and Dove Prion showed that there were significant differences in the proportions taken of nearly all of the six species common to the diet of both birds (Prince, 1980a). This also provided some additional evidence for suggestions that some of the dietary differences might be due to prey selection (resulting from different feeding techniques) rather than changes in prey availability.

Carrion

Several seabirds are well known ship-followers, notably giant petrels, Wandering and Black-browed Albatrosses, Cape Pigeons and Wilson's Storm Petrels and the last two and Snow Petrel were common scavengers at whaling stations. It is doubtful nowadays if any of these species subsist to any significant extent upon items scavenged around ships.

Wandering Albatrosses may obtain some of their squid from material regurgitated by Sperm Whales *Physeter catodon* L. (see feeding ecology) and giant petrels certainly derive substantial food from around seal beaches and penguin colonies.

At South Georgia, and Bird Island in particular, the recent population explosion of Antarctic Fur Seal *Arctocephalus gazella* Peters (Payne, 1977) has had some interesting effects on the giant petrel population. Between 1973/74 and 1978/79 the *M. halli* population has increased from fewer than 500 pairs to 1100 pairs, while *M. giganteus* has increased little, if at all (S. Hunter, 1979). This has coincided with the Bird Island fur seal beaches reaching maximum density and with a correlated substantial availability of placentae and pup carcasses in December–January. The difference in the timing of the breeding seasons of these two giant petrels means that such food is available during the chick rearing period only to *M. halli* and may be significantly implicated in the numerical increase of this species. The greater dependence of *M. halli* on beach carrion may also account for indications that *M. giganteus* feeds more at sea and takes a greater proportion of free-living food.

FEEDING ECOLOGY

With the small number of basic prey types available it is not surprising that the distinctions indicated in the previous section between the diet of most species relate to differences in the proportions of these main prey classes taken rather than to absolute prey-specific differences. There are several ways in which information on feeding ecology can contribute to further the picture of resource division and ecological segregation during the breeding season.

First, it may be possible to distinguish differences in species' feeding location, whether in terms of depth or area. Second, the use of particular feeding techniques may reinforce the dietary segregation by being closely correlated with predation of particular organisms. The main feeding methods of the seabirds involved are shown in Table 5.

Table 5. Feeding methods of South Georgia seabirds

Species	Pursuit dive	Plunge	Dive	Methods Surface seize	Dip	Filter	Scavenge
King Penguin	xxx						
Chinstrap Penguin	xxx						
Gentoo Penguin	xxx						
Macaroni Penguin	xxx						
Wandering Albatross				xxx			xx
Black-browed Albatross		x	x	xxx			xx
Grey-headed Albatross		x	x	xxx			x
Light mantled Sooty Albatross		x	?	xxx			x
Southern Giant Petrel				xxx			xxx
Northern Giant Petrel				xxx			xxx
Cape Pigeon				xxx			xx
Snow Petrel				xxx			x
Dove Prion				xx		xxx	
Blue Petrel			xx	xx	xx		
White-chinned Petrel			xxx	xxx			
Common Diving Petrel	xxx	xx	xx	xx			
South Georgia Diving Petrel	xxx	xx	xx	xx			
Wilson's Storm Petrel		x			xxx		x
Black-bellied Storm Petrel		xx			xxx		x
Grey-backed Storm Petrel		xx			xxx		
Blue-eyed Shag	xxx						
Brown Skua							xxx
Southern Black-backed Gull				xxx			xx
Antarctic Tern		xxx			xxx		

xxx: common, xx: occasional, x: rare

Feeding methods

The major division here is between the pursuit-diving species, whether wing-propelled like penguins and diving petrels or foot-propelled like Blue-eyed Shag, and the remainder which are essentially restricted to feeding at the surface of the water.

The penguins are clearly pre-eminently adapted for life as aquatic pursuit-divers. This ability to exploit the water column to a considerable depth must be a substantial advantage over surface restricted species, amply compensating for any reduction in horizontal foraging area consequent on their inability to fly. There are few data on diving depths e.g. Gentoo Penguin caught at 100 m in a trammel net; (Conroy & Twelves, 1972) but it seems likely that the smaller species can easily feed at 100 m. This would be consistent with the depth distribution of large krill concentrations (mainly above 150 m even during the day) and of the fish species taken by Gentoo Penguin (see p. 111). Recent experiments suggest that King Penguins may be able to reach 215 m (G. L. Kooyman, pers. comm.) which compares favourably with a maximum of 265 m recorded for Emperor Penguin (Kooyman, Drabek, Elsner & Campbell, 1971). Blue-eyed Shag has been caught in nets at 25 m (Conroy & Twelves, 1972) and although diving times of up to 2.5 min have been recorded (Kooyman, 1975), comparable with some of those for the smaller penguins (see Conroy & Twelves, 1972; Kooyman, 1975), it is doubtful if they have the same capacity for prolonged diving. The diving petrels are also specialized for diving and swimming underwater, chiefly by reduction in wing

Table 6. *Feeding frequency, flight speed and potential foraging range of South Georgia seabirds*

Species	Feeding frequency* (days)	Flight speed† (Vmp: m s^{-1})	Foraging range‡ (km)
Southern Giant Petrel	< 1	12.5	c. 350
Northern Giant Petrel	< 1	12.5	c. 350
Gentoo Penguin	1	1.9	31.5
South Georgia Diving Petrel	1 +	7.6	330
Common Diving Petrel	1–1½	8.4	360
Wilson's Storm Petrel	? 1–2	5.7	250
Dove Prion	1–2	6.9	300
Macaroni Penguin	2	1.9	115
Black-browed Albatross	2	10.7	925
Grey-headed Albatross	2	11.0	950
Blue Petrel	2–3	7.0	600
Light-mantled Sooty Albatross	3	9.7	1250
White-chinned Petrel	4	9.5	1650
Wandering Albatross	5–6	12.2	2650
King Penguin	? 5–6	1.9	c. 500

* Feeding frequency is interval between successive feeds to chick by same parent.
† Flight and swimming speeds calculated as described in text.
‡ Foraging range calculated on basis of higher feeding frequency.

length so that a 'paddle-like' condition for underwater propulsion is attained (Kuroda, 1967). This has decidedly impaired their flying ability and the species have very high flight speeds (Table 6) and wing loadings, a low buoyancy index (Appendix 2) and a relationship between wing areas and body mass very different from other procellariforms but similar to that of auks Alcidae which they so closely resemble (Warham, 1977: fig. 1). They are certainly not deep divers and may penetrate only a few metres below the sea surface. White-chinned Petrel is probably the only other species that regularly feeds below the surface and then only on very shallow surface dives.

In essence then only penguins, diving petrels and a shag depend on sub-surface foraging techniques. In contrast nearly all albatrosses and petrels take prey at the surface but there are so few field observations that it is not possible to say if there are any variations in the techniques used by different species. There are, however, a few species which mainly detect prey while in flight and either execute a shallow plunge to catch it (Antarctic Tern) or stoop to secure it while still in flight. In the latter category come the very different feeding methods of Wilson's Storm Petrel (pattering over the wave tops) and Blue Petrel (stooping from some height in a manner more typical of the gadfly petrels *Pterodroma* spp.).

Ainley (1977) has indicated that feeding methods may broadly relate to buoyancy indices (see Appendix 2). In Antarctic seabirds there is a much smaller range of such values (2.5–4.0) compared with temperate and tropical species (2.0–5.5). The low values for diving petrels are an integral part of the adaptations for diving and the high ones for storm petrels accord well with the association of such values with the 'dipping' method of feeding (see Ainley, 1977: table 1). Rather surprisingly Blue Petrel has a relatively low buoyancy value but its very low wing loading may be a compensation.

Giant petrels and albatrosses show uniformly low values, except for Light-mantled Sooty Albatross which is recognized as the most aerially adapted of

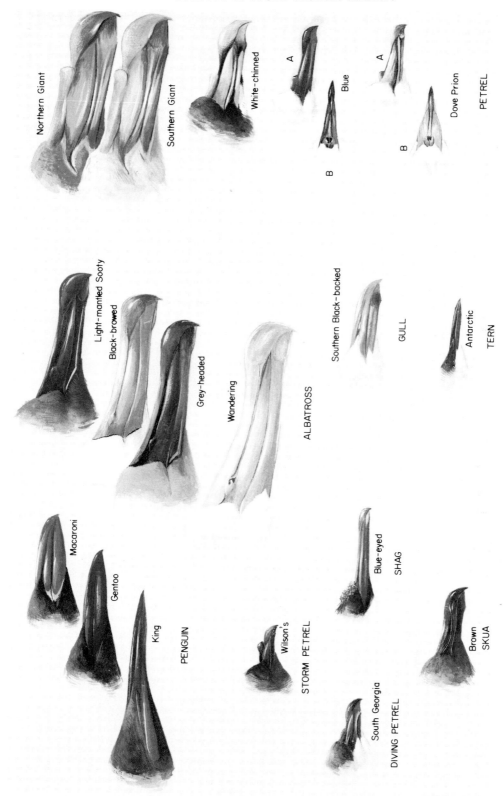

Figure 2. Bills of South Georgia seabirds. King Penguin (x 0.24); Gentoo Penguin (x 0.6); Macaroni Penguin (x 0.24); Wandering Albatross (x 0.5); Grey-headed Albatross (x 0.3); Black-browed Albatross (x 0.3); Light-mantled Sooty Albatross (x 0.3); Southern Giant Petrel (x 0.3); Northern Giant Petrel (x 0.42); White-chinned Petrel (x 0.42); Blue Petrel (x 0.6), A lateral view, B dorsal view; Dove Prion (x 0.6), A lateral view, B dorsal view; Wilson's Storm Petrel (x 0.9); South Georgia Diving Petrel (x 0.9); Blue-eyed Shag (x 0.36); Southern Black-backed Gull (x 0.36); Brown Skua (x 0.3); Antarctic Tern (x 0.48).

albatrosses, although it is unknown what relationship, if any, this has to its feeding methods. It may be noteworthy that the two small fulmarine petrels, Cape Pigeon and Snow Petrel, have rather different indices.

Finally the distinctive feeding technique of Dove Prion is particularly notable whereby, whether hydroplaning (wings outstretched, head just below the surface, propulsion from the feet) or swimming, small prey organisms are filtered by expelling the volume of water taken into the broad, deep bill (see Appendix 2, Fig. 2) through the lamellae fringing the inside of the upper mandible (see Prince, 1980a: plate I). It is this technique that makes it possible to capture vast quantities of small organisms—for example the 41,000 copepods in a food sample weighing only 16 g (Prince, 1980a). The employment of a specialized feeding apparatus thus permits Dove Prion to take substantial quantities of a vastly abundant prey that is clearly quite uneconomic for the other petrels, with bills adapted for picking and seizing, to exploit. In turn a feeding strategy like dipping is probably associated with the capture of larger prey, i.e. those which can be seen while the seabird is in flight. For nearly all prey items Blue Petrel was indeed shown to take larger (and usually significantly so) individuals than Dove Prion (Prince, 1980a). There is also a striking difference in wing loading between Blue Petrel and Dove Prion (see Appendix 2) which is not offset by differences in estimated flight speed (Table 6) and suggests that Blue Petrel uses less energy per unit distance which would fit with its greater dependence on aerial feeding techniques.

Giant petrels, which feed extensively on carrion, seem well adapted for this with relatively short, deep and presumably very powerful bills for tearing flesh from carcasses and it is possible that the flattened occiput of their skull represents an adaptation for inserting the head into carcasses.

The species that mainly use surface seizing techniques show a wide variation in bill size and shape (see Appendix 2, Fig. 2). Ashmole (1968) discussed extensively the relationships between bill size and shape and prey size in five species of sympatric tropical terns. Four of these species had bills of very similar lengths but differed more in depth (and hence cross-section area) and there was some correlation between bill stoutness and prey size although this was complicated by the influence of body size whereby smaller birds (with bill not always in proportion) tended to take very much smaller prey.

Here, although there are probably some relationships between bill shape and prey type (e.g. Gentoo with its more dagger-shaped bill being the small penguin which takes significant fish in its diet), there is little indication of correlation between bill size and crustacean prey size, although large decapods (especially *Acanthephyra*) seem principally to be taken by the larger petrels and albatrosses and copepods by the smaller petrels. There is insufficient information on fish dimensions to do other than confirm that petrels take much smaller prey than penguins and albatrosses. The differences in the dimensions of squid taken by albatrosses have already been noted, with Wandering Albatrosses taking many squid of mean weight 3 kg, Grey-headed and Black-browed Albatrosses squid of *c.* 200 g (although some individuals of up to 1200 g were found) and Light-mantled Sooty Albatross a combination of squid weighing 80 g and *c.* 700 g. It is not clear why the latter, which is the smallest albatross, regularly takes squid substantially larger than those taken by the slightly larger mollymauks. Equally it has been noted elsewhere (Clarke *et al.,* in press) that 3 kg *Kondakovia* are themselves active, very well-armed predators and an albatross must be very adept to take such squid alive. It is certain that Wandering Albatrosses do scavenge the remains of some squid (e.g. of 6 kg + *Taningia*) probably from sperm whale vomit and it might be suggested that *Kondakovia* (and the *Discoteuthis* in Light-mantled Sooty Albatross diet) are taken in a similar manner. Evidence for and against this has been presented by Clarke *et al.* (in press) and we believe that, on balance, the long, powerful, razor-sharp and hook-tipped bills of these albatrosses are sufficiently effective to immobilize even quite large squid once they are impaled.

This in turn raises the question of how such active species as squid and fish can be approached by birds feeding at the surface and, apart from occasional records of surface plunging by mollymauks, there are no direct observations. It seems likely to us that squid and fish are often associated, as predators, with krill swarms and that as these rise to the surface (vertical migration) at night the predators accompany them and become available to petrels and albatrosses sitting, essentially invisible from below, on the surface.

The topic of nocturnal feeding by seabirds on vertically migrating marine organisms was reviewed by Imber (1973) who also drew attention to the high numbers of bioluminescent squid and fish (especially myctophids) taken by certain sea-birds and suggested that these prey were detected by their nocturnal light emissions. As more squid are bioluminescent than not and most have downwardly directed photophores, bioluminescent species may not, in fact, be especially vulnerable. Concentrations of bioluminescent krill may, however, be particularly visible and attractive to night-feeding seabirds—both krill-feeding species and those that gather in anticipation of catching the associated predators.

Although all seabirds will presumably take suitable prey at whatever time of day it is available, diurnal feeding on live prey has been recorded for few species. To judge either from times of chick feeding or actual observations it may be of some importance to Cape Pigeon, Snow Petrel, giant petrels (which are unusual in feeding chicks both by day and night (S. Hunter, 1979)), Dove Prion and Wilson's Storm Petrel, although these last two do not feed their chicks until after dusk, presumably to reduce predation by skuas.

Pursuit-diving species would be expected to be much less restricted to nocturnal feeding than the surface feeders. It is not surprising, therefore, that all penguins regularly spend the night ashore in the colony on the conclusion of a feeding trip and proportionately must spend much more time feeding diurnally than nocturnally, especially while raising chicks. Thus a fundamental difference in feeding ecology (diving versus surface feeding) may also be associated, to some extent, with different temporal patterns of predation.

Foraging range

Species with similar breeding seasons, diets and foraging methods may still be adequately separated ecologically, if there is sufficient difference in their feeding zones. Examples of this have been provided by Ashmole & Ashmole (1967) for two tropical terns *Anous stolidus* (L.) and *Sterna fuscata* L. and Cody (1973) for a number of northern hemisphere auks. In both these cases much of the evidence rested on field observations of feeding birds but, as noted earlier, there are few such observations of Antarctic seabirds and especially so for birds of known breeding status and provenance.

In the absence of such information the interval between successive feeds brought to a chick by one parent can be used as an index of the distance travelled to find food. In Table 6 the species are arranged in order of increased duration of foraging trips (and therefore decreased frequency of feeding chicks).

In this paper we have chosen to use rather broad time categories for feeding frequency. For a number of the species we have much more precise data on the frequency with which a chick is fed, either derived from direct observations or the use of electronic recording devices in burrows to record the visits of parents, or from series' of chick weighings at 3 h intervals to detect feeds more accurately. Unfortunately we do not yet have such information for all the species concerned, nor are data from each source fully compatible. Pending a more thorough evaluation of all features of relevant data we have used simplified categories here, which may well mask some interspecific differences.

The species range from those where each parent feeds the chick daily (Gentoo Penguin usually has two chicks; all other species have only one) to those in which each parent may be absent for nearly a week. If there is any discontinuity in the distribution of species by foraging range it probably lies between species in which both parents feed chicks daily (e.g. giant petrels, diving petrels, often Dove Prion and probably Wilson's Storm Petrel) and those where each parent tends to feed the chick no oftener than on alternate days. This might represent a distinction between inshore and offshore feeding species and what few field observations exist would tend to confirm this. Thus all species in the first group are not infrequently seen feeding by land-based observers; none of the other species have ever been so observed at South Georgia.

In the absence of additional information it is impossible to make further sub-division (e.g. into a coastal-inshore-offshore-pelagic sequence) that might relate to the location of certain hydrographic features, e.g. continental shelf (c. 75 km wide), Antarctic Convergence c. 300 km distant. It is clear that some species (e.g. Wandering Albatross, White-chinned Petrel, Light-mantled Sooty Albatross) have the capacity for highly pelagic foraging and this is certainly supported by the presence of a number of squid in the diet of Wandering Albatross associated with warmer waters to the north of the Antarctic Convergence (Clarke *et al.*, in press).

It is possible to gain a rough idea of potential foraging ranges of these species by considering the length of absence on a feeding trip together with flight (or swimming for penguins) speed. Using the method of Pennycuick (1969), values for minimum power speed, Vmp (essentially speed at which fuel is used most slowly and probably near the lower limits of a bird's flight speed range) have been derived using body weight data from Appendix 2 and wing span values mainly from Warham (1977) supplemented by unpublished data for Blue Petrel and South Georgia Diving Petrel. Kooyman (1975) suggested that penguins usually swim at $7-10$ km h^{-1} and the lower value has been used to obtain the range estimates given here.

It should be stressed that these estimates are probably far from accurate, perhaps especially for the inshore species, as they assume a straight, direct flight path and no stops for feeding. In spite of these deficiencies it is instructive to examine the findings for taxonomically and ecologically related species.

Feeding range information has not shown up any obvious distinctions between the two *Diomedea* mollymauks, the two giant petrels (although there is circumstantial evidence that *M. giganteus* spends more time at sea than *M. halli*) or the two diving petrels (although Payne & Prince (1979) from a detailed analysis of chick weight changes, noted that *P. georgicus* chicks are fed more assiduously than those of *P. u. exsul*). The largest and smallest albatrosses would appear to be more pelagic than the others.

The potential for Blue Petrel to feed further from the breeding site is indicated and this is supported (Prince, 1980a) by more detailed evidence from chick weighings, the occurrence of South Shetland Island derived pumice in the stomachs of 40% of Blue Petrels but only 2% of Dove Prions and the occurrence of twice as much oil (product of digestion of solid food) in Blue Petrel samples.

The difference between the two penguins is even more striking with average feeding trips of Gentoo usually lasting *c.* 9 h and those of Macaroni *c.* 33 h. This inshore: offshore distinction is supported by the fish taken by Gentoo (see p. 111) belonging to the size classes of species which are known to frequent inshore kelp beds during maturation and by the much greater degree of digestion of krill of the same size in Macaroni samples than in Gentoo (Croxall & Prince, 1980). It is also plausible that Gentoo, seeking to raise two chicks, should be more restricted in its foraging range than Macaroni with only a single offspring.

A little additional information can be deduced from general observations of birds at sea during the breeding season. The overall distribution of records indicates that Light-mantled Sooty Albatrosses, in contrast to the other albatrosses, are rarely seen to the north of South Georgia and that Blue Petrel also has a distinct southerly bias to its records. This may provide some indication of a directional bias in foraging activity that could not be deduced from information on mean foraging distance and it is interesting that the two most pelagic albatrosses should differ quite markedly in this respect.

We do not, of course, have any direct evidence of the use of different feeding areas or zones by those species with similar dietary requirements and breeding seasons and the possibility that the 'offshore' species merely collects food more slowly over the same general area as the 'inshore' one can only be regarded as inherently unlikely (and unsupported by the appropriate visual observations).

On the other hand Macaroni penguins certainly catch some krill close to land on their return trips as the top few krill in the stomach are usually hardly digested. Nevertheless they must be subject to less direct competition once out of the range of Gentoo Penguins and in terms of swimming efficiency it would make sense to do this journey with as little extra body weight as possible.

We have already noted that there are numerous warmer-water squid in the diet of Wandering Albatross, indicative of lengthier trips to the north of South Georgia, than in the food of the other *Diomedea* spp. With better knowledge of the local distribution of marine stocks we might be able to interpret the occurrence of small *E. superba* only in Macaroni samples or lampreys only in Grey-headed Albatross samples in terms of feeding areas.

DISCUSSION

In this paper we have tried to describe the biology and adaptations of South Georgia seabirds in relation to their ecological segregation in the breeding season and in particular to the way in which the resources of the marine environment are partitioned.

It seems clear that temporal, dietary and geographical distinctions are each important and, indeed, it seems unlikely that any one mechanism by itself is adequate to achieve a sufficient degree of reduction in direct competition, if all species in the seabird community are considered together. Thus although Wandering Albatross breeds in winter it is likely that it takes different squid from other albatrosses even at other times of year. The diving petrels and the Blue Petrel-Dove Prion species pair have non-overlapping periods of chick rearing but, in addition, they have some clear differences in diet and associated adaptations. The two smaller penguins differ partly in diet and partly in feeding range. In citing these examples we are looking at the most similar pairs of species and only for the giant petrels (which are presently being studied) can we not yet see well-marked ecological differences.

We would re-emphasize, however, that the species of the community employ all of the main mechanisms in different combinations and proportions and that as a whole the community makes up a complex, dynamic pattern of interacting adaptations many facets of which still remain to be understood. In Table 8 we have set out in simplified diagrammatic form what we consider to be the way in which the more important ecological isolating mechanisms operate.

Unlike tropical seabirds where substantial diversity in the timing of breeding seasons is shown (Harris, 1969; Schreiber & Ashmole, 1970), in high latitudes there is little room for manoeuvre. At South Georgia winter breeding is an unusual strategy with Wandering Albatross its chief exponent, as the time of principal demand for food by King Penguin populations is almost certainly in summer. At this time, however, it is the only real subsurface avian squid predator but it may well be in substantial competition earlier in the season with Southern Elephant Seal *Mirounga leonina* L. which also eats squid and fish. The feeding activity of the large South Georgia population of this seal (170,000 tonnes biomass by 1960 (Laws, 1960) and certainly over 200,000 tonnes nowadays) before and during its August–October breeding season may compel King Penguin to delay the onset of breeding.

The distinction between diving and surface feeding is clearly a fundamental one and it is doubtful if there is much competition between members of the two categories, particularly as there are likely to be differences in the time of day when much of the predation occurs.

The subsurface feeders appear segregated chiefly by diving capacity and diet but it would be interesting to know to what extent the large fur seal population (369,000 seals with a biomass of 14,500 tonnes (Payne, 1979) at South Georgia (and particularly Bird Island), compete with the small penguins. This fur seal seldom dives below 68 m (G. L. Kooyman, pers. comm.) and its prey is principally krill, some fish and a little squid.

For Gentoo and Macaroni Penguins, and a number of surface-feeding seabirds, differences in foraging range seem significant. The distinction between inshore and offshore feeding seabirds is often regarded as an important one and correlated with certain other biological adaptations of the species concerned. Thus Lack (1968) suggested that in many families of marine birds offshore feeders breed in larger more widely spaced colonies, have smaller clutches, longer incubation and fledging periods, longer incubation shifts, reduced chick feeding frequency but higher chick peak weights relative to adult weights and later sexual maturity compared with inshore feeders and that the differences are principally related to food availability. Cody (1973) added slower growth rates, and feed size a smaller proportion of adult body weight from his studies of northern hemisphere auks where he regarded differences in feeding zones as the principal ecological isolating mechanism.

In addition, on the basis of data for two storm petrels *Oceanodroma,* Ainley *et al.* (1975) suggested that the lower wing loadings of offshore feeders may be adaptive in reducing the energy used per unit distance flown. The wing loadings of Dove Prion and Blue Petrel (Appendix 2) are in line with this but Warham (1977) has noted that lower wing loading is usually correlated with slower flight speed which may be a countervailing disadvantage and the whole topic clearly needs critical re-investigation.

Finally it is worth noting that the poorly synchronized breeding species (Gentoo Penguin, storm petrels, see p. 106) all seem to be inshore feeders and perhaps worth speculating whether this asynchrony in breeding timetable may be an adaptive mechanism for reducing intraspecific competition in the restricted inshore waters by spreading the peak demand for food more evenly over a longer period.

It is of interest briefly to see to what extent the information presented here corroborate the general picture developed by Lack (1968). Some additional relevant data are given in Table 7, with the species still placed in order of feeding frequency. Although some of the meal size data are very approximate (and derived variously from interpretation of food sample and chick growth increment data) there is no indication of any fixed relationship between it and body weight (cf. Cody, 1973) and only the diving petrel values (derived from chick growth increment analysis) stand out as anomalous and it remains to be seen if this persists when other species' diets are analysed similarly.

Likewise there is no clear relationship between feeding zone and growth rate. However, if Cody's (1973) data are reanalysed relative to the size of the bird (rather than just as absolute weight increases), as his smaller species (with smallest absolute growth but high *relative* growth) were feeding farthest from land there is no correlation for his species either. Equally, nothing clear cut can be derived from the data on the amount by which chicks at peak weight exceed adult weight, a statistic reflecting the extent of fat reserves and hence the degree to which the chicks are insured against variations in feeding frequency, likely to be greatest in offshore foraging birds.

At the level of the 'species-pair', however, one is able to see some of the logic behind the earlier generalizations. Thus, in contrast to the inshore feeding Gentoo Penguin, the offshore feeding Macaroni Penguin breeds in few, vast colonies (no need to reduce the intraspecific competition that would be generated by excessive clumping of inshore feeders) has only one not two chicks, has month-long incubation periods not daily changeovers, makes fewer, longer feeding trips (though the single chick gets fed daily just as do those of Gentoo) and probably does not breed until at least six years of age (Carrick, (1972) on another subspecies, Royal Penguin *E. chrysolophus schlegeli* Finsch) whereas if Gentoo is similar to its congeners it may commence breeding at three years of age (Le Resche & Sladen, 1970; Ainley, 1975; Ainley & De Master, in press). On the other hand incubation periods are similar and Macaroni chicks have faster growth and much shorter fledging periods. Many of these adaptations probably relate to the different requirements imposed by trying to raise two chicks rather

Table 7. Meal sizes and chick growth statistics for South Georgia seabirds

Species	Meal size		Chick growth*		Peak wt as % adult wt	Reference
	Mean (g)	As % adult weight	Mean wt gain (g.d^{-1})	As % peak weight		
Southern Giant Petrel	c. 500	10	79	1.3	116	S. Hunter, 1979
Northern Giant Petrel	c. 500	10	66	1.2	108	S. Hunter, 1979
Gentoo Penguin	860	15	85	1.7	91	Croxall, unpublished data
South Georgia Diving Petrel	c. 40	30	4.8	3.3	136	Payne & Prince, 1979
Common Diving Petrel	c. 40	37	4.0	2.6	120	Payne & Prince, 1979
Wilson's Storm Petrel	c. 5	13	1.3/2.5	2.0/3.6	158/182	Beck, 1972/Lacan, 1971
Dove Prion	c. 25	15	6.5	3.1	128	Prince, unpublished data
Macaroni Penguin	690	15	70	2.2	67	Croxall, unpublished data
Black-browed Albatross	570	15	70	1.4	132	Prince, unpublished data
Grey-headed Albatross	600	16	63	1.3	124	Prince, unpublished data
Blue Petrel	c. 35	18	7	2.4	150	Prince, unpublished data
Light-mantled Sooty Albatross	510	18	45	1.3	121	Thomas, unpublished data
White-chinned Petrel	c. 150	11	24	1.3	135	Prince, unpublished data
Wandering Albatross	750	9	56	0.5	132	Tickell, 1968
King Penguin	c. 2000	13	c. 120	1.1	80	Stonehouse, 1960

* Growth calculated over period $t_{10} - t_{90}$: see Ricklefs (1973)

than one and can perhaps be seen as ecologically alternative strategies. It is not clear, however, what the significance is of the extremely long incubation and brooding shifts in Macaroni Penguin.

The later sexual maturity in Macaroni Penguin might be explained by postulating greater intraspecific competition for food amongst the breeding (and potentially breeding) population thus favouring a delay in first breeding attempts. A rough indication that this might be so is obtained by calculating the volume of ocean available to each individual of the breeding population of each species at South Georgia (see Table 1) within the estimated foraging range (Table 6) and for a feeding depth of 100 m, assuming a circular feeding area around a point source. For Gentoo the result is 1558×10^3 m^3 per bird whereas for Macaroni it is only 419×10^3 m^3 per bird. Thus although the Macaroni Penguin population has over 13 times the sea volume at its disposal their 50 times greater abundance more than offsets this advantage.

Comparing the inshore Dove Prion with the more offshore Blue Petrel is somewhat less convincing as, against predictions, the latter is less abundant, has shorter incubation and fledging periods (but does show longer incubation shifts) and less frequent chick feeding (but larger feeds). With the two mollymauks meal size, feeding frequency, incubation shifts and incubation periods and abundance are similar (at South Georgia: Black-browed Albatross is much more abundant on a world population basis), and only the duration of the fledging and pre-laying attendance periods are different. Nevertheless Black-browed Albatross breeds at an earlier age and annually thereafter whereas Grey-headed Albatross breeds later and biennially when successful in raising a chick.

Thus in examining more closely three species-pairs we find, compared with predictions, reasonably good fits (penguins), poor fits (petrels) and species where major biological differences are barely indicated by differences in the range of adaptations surveyed. This is not to challenge the theoretical basis on which the generalizations rest nor their heuristic value nor the fact that all of them are supported by some species in some situations. It is rather to emphasize that with some Antarctic species we may have reached the stage where it will be possible, and preferable, on the basis of improved knowledge of appropriate details of the species' biology, to understand some of the key interrelationships between adaptations and ecological strategies, rather than to generate modified generalizations.

There is, both throughout the paper and in Table 8, a considerable emphasis on the importance of diet and its associated adaptations. This is partly because feeding studies form much of our work at South Georgia and partly because we believe that insufficient detailed quantitative attention has been given to this topic. For instance we wonder whether, if Cody had had available comprehensive dietary information (of the kind produced by Bedard (1969b) for three Alaskan auklets), he would have still maintained the over-riding importance of feeding zone separation.

We recognize that our own dietary data derive, in most cases, only from a single season's work and it may therefore be premature to regard them as fully typical. Nevertheless we would affirm the view, implicit in many of Lack's (1968) seabird analyses, that a knowledge of feeding ecology may be the key to understanding many other adaptations; in particular we believe that detailed knowledge of dietary composition by weight and nutritive value, of meal size and

Table 8. Principal mechanisms for ecological segregation in the breeding season
for South Georgia seabirds

Winter		Summer
Diving		*Diving*
King Penguin	Inshore	
	Fish:	Blue-eyed Shag
		Gentoo Penguin
	Krill:	Gentoo Penguin
	Offshore	
	Krill:	Macaroni Penguin
	Squid:	King Penguin
Surface Feeding		*Surface Feeding*
Wandering Albatross	Squid:	White-chinned Petrel
		Light-mantled Sooty Albatross
		Grey-headed Albatross
	Copepods:	Common Diving Petrel
		Dove Prion
	Krill	
	Inshore:	Common Diving Petrel (early)
		South Georgia Diving Petrel (late)
		Wilson's Storm Petrel
		Dove Prion
	Offshore:	Blue Petrel
		Black-browed Albatross
	Carrion:	Giant Petrels

feeding frequency in relation to chick growth rates are fundamental elements within this.

In saying this we imply that there may be important relationships between the above factors and it is appropriate here briefly to mention how they relate to the main differences between the two mollymauks (see p. 125). Prince (in prep.) has shown, particularly by following the growth of chicks raised from eggs by parents of the opposite species, that the difference in fledging times between these two species is principally due to differences in the composition of the diet fed to the chicks (the squid that predominates in Grey-headed Albatross diet being a much less nutritive resource than the krill which forms the bulk of Black-browed Albatross diet). It is likely also that the predominantly squid diet is implicated in the inability of successful Grey-headed Albatrosses to regain breeding condition in time to lay the following season. Thus, differences in dietary composition may be involved in fundamental differences in breeding strategy.

It has been implicit throughout this paper that most of the identified differences between species are the result of competition in the past and subsequent attempts by the birds to minimize the continuing effects of this. Some authors (e.g. Salomonsen, 1955; Beck, 1970) have contended that the abundance of suitable food is such that seabirds do not compete but most workers have been more impressed by the consequences of seasons of food shortage (Belopolskii, 1957; Ashmole, 1963, 1971; Croxall & Prince, 1979) and have concluded that it is often the availability of appropriate prey rather than its actual existence or abundance that is the critical factor.

As with most similar analyses direct evidence of interspecific competition is lacking and much of the circumstantial evidence (the exact nature of the ecological differences, evidence for the selection of certain prey items when others are available and being taken by other species) has elements of circularity in its reasoning.

In 1977-78, however, commercial fishing operations around South Georgia were unable to locate krill in swarms and there was an unprecedented failure of krill-eating seabirds, especially Gentoo Penguin and Black-browed Albatross, to raise their chicks (Croxall & Prince, 1979). In contrast Grey-headed Albatrosses, feeding mainly on squid (which themselves may have been feeding extensively on the astonishingly abundant amphipod *Parathemisto gaudichaudii* Guérin Meneville) had their best breeding season. It would appear significant that Black-browed Albatrosses, which do take squid, were unable sufficiently to switch to this resource to improve their breeding success and not implausible that direct competition with predominantly squid-eating Grey-headed Albatrosses may have been responsible.

This analysis has been exclusively concerned with the ecological picture during the breeding season. The lack of data on diet in winter makes it difficult to comment on the basis of segregation at that season. All species undoubtedly range much more widely once breeding is concluded. Diversity in the area is reduced as several species depart, notably Wilson's Storm Petrel, a migrant to the northern hemisphere, and Black-browed Albatross, moving north to warmer waters, chiefly off South Africa (Tickell, 1967). Some species, e.g. giant petrels, diving petrels, Gentoo Penguins, as well as Cape Pigeon and Snow Petrel, are seen at South Georgia throughout the winter and others such as Grey-headed Albatross certainly remain in high latitudes. There are thus indications that one member of at least two species-pairs may be considerably more migratory than the other. In the case of the albatrosses and the penguins the species that remains is that least dependent on euphausiid prey, a resource of minimal availability in winter, in contrast to squid and fish which are able to sustain breeding Wandering Albatrosses and King Penguins.

None of this information gives any indication whether competition for food for any of these species is more intense in summer or winter. The heavy demands during chick rearing (and particularly for penguins where a complete moult necessitating the development of enormous fat reserves immediately follows), lead us to think that the summer period may be the most critical.

Finally, why are certain South Georgia seabirds distinctly uncommon as breeding species and why do some other species not occur there? Although Rockhopper and Macaroni Penguins are probably respectively warmer and colder water replacement species they co-exist at Macquarie Island and at Marion Island. It is not clear why Rockhopper is not commoner at South Georgia unless the large population of Gentoo Penguins offers too much competition in inshore areas. The abundance of the two small penguins may also be restricting the expansion of Chinstrap Penguin (see Croxall & Kirkwood, 1979) which takes krill and is probably somewhat intermediate in its foraging range (Croxall & Furse, 1980). It may be significant that Chinstrap is most abundant at the southeast end of the island, where there is a much smaller concentration of Macaroni Penguins.

The small fulmarine petrels (Cape Pigeon and Snow Petrel) and the other storm petrels are all at a limit of their breeding range at South Georgia but it is uncertain why they are not more abundant. Cape Pigeon is a particular puzzle as it is abundant in the area in both summer and winter yet the breeding population is very small.

At more northerly subantarctic islands (e.g. Crozet, Marion) a slightly greater diversity of seabirds than at South Georgia does occur. The additional species can be divided into three categories:

(a) warmer water congeners of the colder water species, e.g. Sooty Albatross *Phoebetria fusca* (Hilsenberg) and various prions *Pachyptila* (some with and some without the filtering lamellae), the prions often with some differences in breeding habitat and timing of the breeding season,

(b) gadfly petrels *Pterodroma* spp., a group typical of warmer water and specializing in in 'dipping' feeding techniques,

(c) winter breeding medium-sized petrels (e.g. Grey Petrel *Procellaria cinerea* Gmelin and Great-winged Petrel *Pterodroma macroptera* (A. Smith)).

All the additional species seem to derive from the greater proximity of these slightly more northerly islands to warmer waters and perhaps from the generally milder climate giving a longer effective breeding season and permitting a greater variety of species to breed in winter.

However it is probable that the marine environment surrounding these islands may not be as rich in food resources as the South Georgia area and it would be of great interest to know how the abundance and ecology of the typically sub-Antarctic species are affected under these circumstances.

ACKNOWLEDGEMENTS

We should like to thank Dr D. G. Ainley, Dr M. R. Clarke, I. Hunter, S. Hunter and G. Thomas for making available their unpublished data, Drs K. R. Kerry and G. L. Kooyman for allowing us to use their personal communications and Drs R. M. Laws and C. M. Perrins for comments on the manuscript. We are most indebted to Bruce Pearson for providing Fig. 2.

REFERENCES

AINLEY, D. G., 1975. Development of reproductive maturity in Adelie Penguins. In B. Stonehouse (Ed.), *The Biology of Penguins:* 139–157. London: Macmillan.

AINLEY, D. G., 1977. Feeding methods in seabirds: a comparison of polar and tropical nesting communities in the eastern Pacific Ocean. In G. A. Llano (Ed.), *Adaptations within Antarctic Ecosystems:* 669–685. Washington: Smithsonian Institution.

AINLEY, D. H. & DEMASTER, D. P., in press. Survival and mortality in a population of penguins. *Ecology.*

AINLEY, D. G., MORRELL, S., LEWIS, T. J., 1974. Patterns in the life histories of storm petrels on the Farallon Islands. *Living Bird, 13:* 295–312.

ASHMOLE, N. P., 1963. The regulation of numbers of tropical oceanic birds. *Ibis, 103b:* 458–473.

ASHMOLE, N. P., 1968. Body size, prey size, and ecological segregation in five sympatric tropical terns (Aves: Laridae). *Systematic Zoology, 17:* 292–304.

ASHMOLE, N. P., 1971. Seabird ecology and the marine environment. In D. S. Farner and J. R. King (Eds.) *Avian Biology, Vol. 1:* 112–286. New York: Academic Press.

ASHMOLE, N. P. & ASHMOLE, M. J., 1976. Comparative feeding ecology of sea birds of a tropical oceanic island. *Bulletin of the Peabody Museum of Natural History, 24:* 1–131.

BARRAT, A., 1976. Quelques aspects de la biologie et de l'écologie du Manchot royal (*Aptenodytes patagonica*) de l'ile de la Possession, archipel Crozet. *Comite National Français des Récherches Antarctiques,* No. 40: 9–52.

BECK, J. R., 1969. Food, moult and age of first breeding in the Cape Pigeon, *Daption capensis* Linnaeus. *British Antarctic Survey Bulletin,* No. 21: 33–44.

BECK, J. R., 1970. Breeding seasons and moult in some smaller Antarctic petrels. In M. W. Holdgate (Ed.), *Antarctic Ecology:* 542–550. London: Academic Press.

BECK, J. R. & BROWN, 1972. The biology of Wilson's Storm Petrel *Oceanites oceanicus* (Kuhl), at Signy Island, South Orkney Islands. *Scientific Report of the British Antarctic Survey,* No. 69: 1–54.

BEDARD, J., 1969a. Histoire naturelle du Gode, *Alca torda* L., dans le golfe Saint Laurent, Province de Québec, Canada. *Etude de Service Canadien de la Faune,* No. 7. Ottawa.

BEDARD, J., 1969b. Feeding of the Least, Creasted and Parakeet Auklets around St. Lawrence Island, Alaska. *Canadian Journal of Zoology, 47:* 1025–1050.

BELOPOLSKII, L. O., 1957. *Ecology of Sea Colony Birds of the Barents Sea.* Israel Program of Scientific Translations, 1961.

BURGER, A. E., 1978. Interspecific breeding attempts by *Macronectes giganteus* and *M. halli. Emu, 78:* 234–5.

CARRICK, R., 1972. Population ecology of the Australian Black-backed Magpie, Royal Penguin and Silver Gull. In *Population Ecology of Migratory Birds: A Symposium. U.S. Department of the Interior Wildlife Research Report,* No. 2: 41–99.

CARRICK, R. & INGHAM, S. E., 1967. Antarctic sea-birds as subjects for ecological research. *Proceedings of the Symposium on Pacific-Antarctic Sciences, Tokyo, 1966. JARE Scientific Report, Spec. 1:* 151–184. Tokyo: Department of Polar Research.

CARRICK, R. & INGHAM, S. E., 1970. Ecology and population dynamics of antarctic seabirds. In M. W. Holdgate (Ed.), *Antarctic Ecology:* 505–525. London: Academic Press.

CLARKE, M. R. & PRINCE, P. A., in press. Cephalopod remains in regurgitations of Black-browed and Grey-headed Albatrosses at South Georgia. *British Antarctic Survey Bulletin.*

CLARKE, M. R., CROXALL, J. P. & PRINCE, P. A., in press. Cephalopod remains in regurgitations of the Wandering Albatross at South Georgia. *British Antarctic Survey Bulletin.*

CODY, M. L., 1973. Coexistence, coevolution and convergent evolution in seabird communities. *Ecology, 54:* 31–44.

CONROY, J. W. H., 1972. Ecological aspects of the biology of the giant petrel *Macronectes giganteus* (Gmelin) in the Maritime Antarctic. *Scientific Report of the British Antarctic Survey,* No. 75: 1–74.

CONROY, J. W. H. & TWELVES, E. L., 1972. Diving depths of the Gentoo Penguin (*Pygoscelis papua*) and Blue-eyed Shag (*Phalacrocorax atriceps*) from the South Orkney Islands. *British Antarctic Survey Bulletin,* No. 30: 106–108.

CROXALL, J. P., 1979. Distribution and population changes in the Wandering Albatross *Diomedea exulans* L. at South Georgia. *Ardea, 67:* 15–21.

CROXALL, J. P. & FURSE, J. R., 1980. Food of Chinstrap Penguins *Pygoscelis antarctica* and Macaroni Penguins *Eudyptes chrysolophus* at Elephant Island group, South Shetland Islands. *Ibis, 122:* 237–245.

CROXALL, J. P. & KIRKWOOD, E. D., 1979. *The Breeding Distribution of Penguins on the Antarctic Peninsula and the Islands of the Scotia Sea.* Cambridge: British Antarctic Survey.

CROXALL, J. P. & PRINCE, P. A., 1979. Antarctic seabird and seal monitoring studies. *Polar Record, 19:* 573–595.

CROXALL, J. P. & PRINCE, P. A., 1980. The food of Gentoo Penguins *Pygoscleis papua* and Marcaroni Penguins *Eudyptes chrysolophus* at South Georgia. *Ibis, 122:* 245–253.

FOXTON, P., 1956. The distribution of the standing crop of zooplankton in the Southern Ocean. *'Discovery' Reports, 28:* 191–236.

FOXTON, P., 1964. Seasonal variations in the plankton of Antarctic waters. In R. Carrick, M. W. Holdgate & J. Prevost (Eds.), *Biologie Antarctique:* 311–318. Paris: Hermann.

HARRIS, M. P., 1969. Breeding seasons of seabirds in the Galapagos Islands. *Journal of Zoology, 159:* 145–165.

HART, T. J., 1942. Phytoplankton periodicity in Antarctic surface waters. *'Discovery' Reports, 21:* 261–356.

HUNTER, I., 1979. *Burrow-dwelling petrel survey and census, Bird Island, South Georgia. Progress Report 1978–79.* British Antarctic Survey unpublished manuscript.

HUNTER, S., 1979. *Report on giant petrel fieldwork 1978–79.* British Antarctic Survey unpublished manuscript.

IMBER, M. J., 1973. The food of Grey-faced Petrels *Pterodroma macroptera gouldi* (Hutton), with special reference to diurnal vertical migration of their prey. *Journal of Animal Ecology, 42:* 645–662.

IMBER, M. J., 1976. Comparison of the prey of the black *Procellaria* petrels of New Zealand. *New Zealand Journal of Marine and Freshwater Research, 10:* 119–130.

JOHNSTONE, G. W., 1977. Comparative feeding ecology of the giant petrels *Macronectes giganteus* (Gmelin) & *M. halli* (Mathews). In G. A. Llano (Ed.), *Adaptations within Antarctic Ecosystems:* 647–668. Washington: Smithsonian Institution.

KOOYMAN, G. L., 1975. The physiology of diving in penguins. In B. Stonehouse (Ed.), *The Biology of Penguins:* 115–137. London: Macmillan.

KOOYMAN, G. L., DRABEK, C. M., ELSNER, R. & CAMPBELL, W. B., 1971. Diving behaviour of the Emperor Penguin, *Aptenodytes forsteri. Auk, 88:* 775–795.

KURODA, N. H., 1967. Morpho-anatomical analysis of parallel evolution between diving petrel and ancient auk, with comparative osteological data of other species. *Miscellaneous Reports of the Yamashina Institute of Ornithology and Zoology, 5, 2(28):* 111–137.

LACAN, F., 1971. Observations écologiques sur le pétrel de Wilson (*Oceanites oceanicus*) en Terre Adélie. *Oiseau Revue de Française Ornithologie, 41,* Special number: 65–89.

LACK, D., 1934. Habitat distribution in certain Icelandic birds. *Journal of Animal Ecology, 3:* 81–90.

LACK, D., 1968. *Ecological Adaptations for Breeding in Birds.* London: Methuen.

LAWS, R. M., 1960. The Southern Elephant Seal *Mirounga leonina* on South Georgia. *Norsk Hvalfangsttidende, 49:* 520–542.

LeRESCHE, R. E., & SLADEN, W. J. L., 1970. Establishment of pair and breeding site bonds by young known-age Adelie Penguins *Pygoscelis adeliae. Animal Behaviour, 18:* 517–526.

5

PAYNE, M. R., 1977. Growth of a fur seal population. *Philosophical Transactions of the Royal Society (B), 279:* 67–79.

PAYNE, M. R., 1979. Growth in the Antarctic Fur Seal *Arctocephalus gazella. Journal of Zoology, 187:* 1–20.

PAYNE, M. R. & PRINCE, P. A., 1979. Identification and breeding biology of the diving petrels *Pelecanoides georgicus* and *P. urinatrix exsul* at South Georgia. *New Zealand Journal of Zoology, 6:* 299–318.

PEARSON, T. H., 1968. The feeding biology of seabird species breeding on the Farne Islands, Northumberland. *Journal of Animal Ecology, 37:* 521–552.

PENNYCUICK, C. J., 1969. The mechanics of bird migration. *Ibis, 111:* 525–556.

POTTER, I. C., PRINCE, P. A. & CROXALL, J. P., 1979. Data on the adult marine and migratory phases in the life cycle of the Southern Hemisphere lamprey, *Geotria australis* Gray. *Environmental Biology of Fishes, 4:* 65–69.

PRINCE, P. A., 1980a. The food and feeding ecology of Blue Petrel (*Halobaena caerulea*) and Dove Prion (*Pachyptila desolata*). *Journal of Zoology, 190:* 59–76.

PRINCE, P. A., 1980b. The food and feeding ecology of Grey-headed Albatross *Diomedea chrysostoma* and Black-browed Albatross *D. melanophris. Ibis, 122.*

PRINCE, P. A. & PAYNE, M. R., 1979. Current status of birds at South Georgia. *British Antarctic Survey Bulletin,* No. *48:* 103–118.

RICHDALE, L. E., 1965. Biology of the birds of Whero Island, New Zealand, with special reference to the diving petrel and the White-faced Storm Petrel. *Transactions of the Zoology Society of London, 27:* 1–86.

RICKLEFS, R. E., 1973. Patterns of growths in birds. II. Growth rate and mode of development. *Ibis, 115:* 177–201.

SALOMONSEN, F., 1955. The food production of the sea and the annual cycle of Faeroese marine birds. *Oikos, 6:* 92–100.

SCHREIBER, R. W. & ASHMOLE, N. P., 1970. Seabird breeding seasons at Christmas Island, Pacific Ocean. *Ibis, 112:* 363–394.

SERGEANT, D. E., 1951. Ecological relationships of the guillemots *Uria aalge* and *Uria lomvia. Proceedings of the International Ornithological Congress X, 1959 (1951):* 578–587.

SMITH, R. I. L. & TALLOWIN, J. R. B., 1980. The distribution and size of King Penguin rookeries on South Georgia. *British Antarctic Survey Bulletin,* No. *49:* 259–276.

STONEHOUSE, B., 1960. The King Penguin *Aptenodytes patagonica* of South Georgia. I. Breeding behaviour and development. *Scientific Report of the Falkland Islands Dependencies Survey,* No. *23:* 1–81.

STONEHOUSE, B., 1967. The general biology and thermal balances of penguins. *Advances in Ecological Research, 4:* 131–196.

THORESEN, A. C., 1969. Observations on the breeding behaviour of the diving petrel *Pelecanoides u. urinatrix* (Gmelin). *Notornis, 16:* 241–260.

TICKELL, W. L. N., 1962. The Dove Prion, *Pachyptila desolata* Gmelin. *Scientific Report of the Falkland Islands Dependencies Survey,* No. *33:* 1–55.

TICKELL, W. L. N., 1967. Movements of Black-browed and Grey-headed Albatrosses in the South Atlantic. *Emu, 66:* 357–367.

TICKELL, W. L. N., 1968. The biology of the great albatrosses, *Diomedea exulans* and *Diomeda epomophora.* In O. L. Austin, Jr. (Ed.) *Antarctic Bird Studies, Antarctic Research Series, 12:* 1–55. Washington: American Geophysical Union.

TICKELL, W. L. N. & PINDER, R., 1967. Breeding frequencies in the albatrosses *Diomedea melanophris* and *D. chrysostoma. Nature, 213:* 315–6.

WARHAM, J., 1977. Wing loading, wing shapes and flight capabilities of Procellariiformes. *New Zealand Journal of Zoology, 4:* 73–83.

APPENDICES

Appendix 1. Selected measurements of penguins breeding at South Georgia

Species	Body weight (kg)	Flipper area (cm²)	Culmen length (mm)	Culmen width (mm)	Culmen depth (mm)
King Penguin	15.0	159	133	40	37
Gentoo Penguin	5.8	103	52	43	44
Macaroni Penguin	4.8	78	57	33	39
Rockhopper Penguin	2.5	57	44	27	33
Chinstrap Penguin	4.1	73	49	31	39

All figures are mean values for both sexes combined. Flipper area from Stonehouse (1967). Culmen width and depth measured at base.

Appendix 2. Selected measurements of albatrosses and petrels at South Georgia

Species	Body weight (g)	Wing area (cm²)	Wing loading (g cm⁻²)	Aspect ratio	Buoyancy index	Culmen length (mm)	Culmen width (mm)	Culmen depth (mm)
Wandering Albatross	8727	4337	2.00	15.6	3.2	166	45	63
Black-browed Albatross	3788	2682	1.41	14.9	3.3	117	28	50
Grey-headed Albatross	3788	2389	1.59	15.3	3.1	114	27	44
Light-mantled Sooty Albatross	2840	3226	0.88	–	4.0	110	23	35
Southern Giant Petrel	5165	2748	1.87	–	3.2	95	40	39
Northern Giant Petrel	5212	2846	1.83	11.9	3.0	97	42	40
Cape Pigeon	433	630	0.69	9.2	3.3	31	16	13
Snow Petrel	259	583	0.44	–	3.8	20	10	12
Dove Prion	168	423	0.69	8.5	3.7	30	15	14
Blue Petrel	193	392	0.49	10.8	2.4	27	10	10
White-chinned Petrel	1368	1455	0.94	12.1	3.4	52	21	20
Wilson's Storm Petrel	38	151	0.25	–	3.8	13	8	7
Black-bellied Storm Petrel	53	226	0.23	6.5	4.0	15	8	6
Grey-backed Storm Petrel	29	140	0.24	6.4	3.9	13	5	5
South Georgia Diving Petrel	107	183	0.58	6.9	2.6	15	8	8
Common Diving Petrel	133	174	0.76	7.0	2.5	16	8	10

Body weights and bill measurements are mean values for both sexes combined. Wing areas and aspect ratios from Warham (1977), except for Blue Petrel and South Georgia Diving Petrel. Buoyancy Index is square root of wing area divided by cube root of weight. Culmen width and depth measured at base.

Population structure and social organization of Southern Elephant Seals, *Mirounga leonina* (L.)

T. S. McCANN

Life Sciences Division, British Antarctic Survey, Natural Environment Research Council, Madingley Road, Cambridge, CB3 0ET

Accepted for publication January 1980

The population structure and social organization of the Southern Elephant Seal, *Mirounga leonina*, were studied at South Georgia principally by extensive field census work and determination of age and reproductive history from sections of teeth taken from samples of bulls and cows.

The adult males of the South Georgia population were exploited from 1910 to 1964, mainly at the maximum sustainable yield for this population.

The present data are compared with similar information obtained from studies at South Georgia in 1951 during the exploitation phase and at Macquarie Island in the 1950's where sealing ended in 1919 and the population had stabilized.

Changes have been noted in the time of bull haul out, number of bulls ashore, cow: bull ratio, harem size and the age of harem bulls. These changes can all be attributed to the ending of exploitation. In contrast, the structure of the cow herd has not changed appreciably in the same period.

In addition, differences in growth, body size and population structure still persist between the South Georgia and Macquarie Island populations and it is likely that most of them may reflect differences in food availability at the two locations.

KEY WORDS:— population structure – social organization – exploitation – recovery.

CONTENTS

INTRODUCTION

The Southern Elephant Seal, *Mirounga leonina* (L.), is the world's largest phocid. Harem bulls are usually 14–15 feet (4.3–4.6 m) in length and weigh 2.5–3.0 tonnes of which up to 40% is skin and blubber (Laws, 1960). The females are smaller, between eight and 10 feet (2.4–3.0 m) long.

Adult elephant seals are pelagic and only come ashore to breed and moult

although immatures of both sexes often come ashore for short periods
throughout the year. The first breeding bulls haul out in August followed in
September and October by the pregnant cows. The cows are naturally gregarious
and form groups on the beaches. The largest bulls compete for exclusive possession of these 'harems'. Each cow produces a single pup which she feeds until
weaning at about 23 days post-partum. Oestrus occurs about 19 days post-
partum and lasts for about four days (McCann, unpublished data) during which
period the cow may be mated several times by one or more bulls. The dominant
bull usually remains with the harem until the last cow has been mated before
returning to sea. Most breeding seals have left the beaches by the end of
November. Juveniles haul out to moult in late November and December having
been absent from the beaches during the breeding season. Breeding cows moult
in January and February; adult bulls from March until May.

In the nineteenth century elephant seals were hunted for their blubber oil at all
of their breeding sites (Fig. 1A). Their populations were so drastically reduced
that the industry became unprofitable and sealing had virtually ceased by the
turn of the century. At South Georgia, which has the world's largest population
of elephant seals, sealing came under Government control in 1910 and for many
years between 5000 and 6000 adult bulls were taken each season, a figure which
approximated to the maximum sustainable yield of bulls for the South Georgia
population (Laws, 1960). Sealing ended in 1964 when shore based whaling on
South Georgia was terminated and since then the population has been
undisturbed.

Laws (1953a, b, 1956a, b) conducted detailed investigations into elephant seal
biology including growth, reproductive physiology and general, social and
reproductive behaviour. His studies were made on the small population at Signy
Island in the South Orkney Islands between 1948 and 1950 and at South Georgia
in 1951. Carrick, Csordas & Ingham (1962a), Carrick, Csordas, Ingham & Keith
(1962b) and Carrick & Ingham (1960, 1962a,b,c) presented the results of a long
term study of known-age branded elephant seals at Macquarie Island in the
Southern Indian Ocean, where sealing ended in 1919 and the population had
been stable for several years (Carrick & Ingham, 1960). Their studies revealed
many differences between the South Georgia and Macquarie Island populations,
especially in age structure and social organization of the breeding herd, and
growth rates, many of which were attributed to the effects of sealing on the South
Georgia population.

One of the main aims of this study was to examine the present-day population
structure and social organization of elephant seals at South Georgia, in order to
assess the nature and extent of the changes that have taken place there since
exploitation ceased, and to determine what differences, if any, now exist between
the South Georgia and Macquarie Island populations.

METHODS

The study was made at Dartmouth Point in Cumberland East Bay, South
Georgia (Fig. 1). Dartmouth Point is a peninsula bounded on both sides by
glaciers which calve into the sea. It is rarely visited so the population is
undisturbed and was the study site chosen by Laws in 1951 when it was a reserve

A

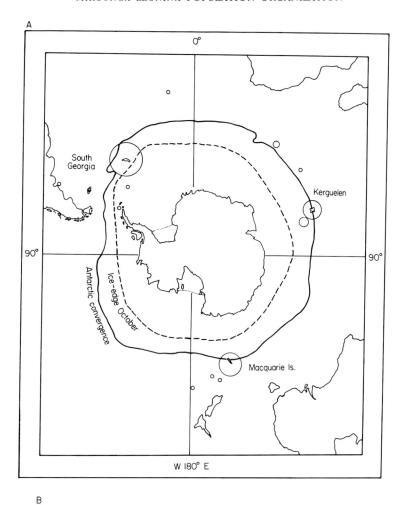

B

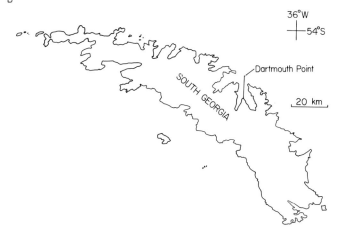

Figure 1. A. Distribution of elephant seal breeding populations. B. South Georgia showing location of study site at Dartmouth Point.

free from sealing. Most of the results presented were obtained in the 1976 and especially 1977 breeding seasons, but some data were also gathered in 1975 and 1978.

Counts

At Dartmouth Point the seals on 4 km of coastline were counted daily and occasional counts were made of the whole peninsula from the Nordenskjold glacier to the Harker glacier. During each count every bull was classified according to size, general appearance and proximity to cow aggregations (harems), as harem bulls, bachelor bulls or juveniles. Harem bulls were those bulls in harems with access to cows; bachelors were those excluded from harems by the agonistic activities of the harem bulls. Juveniles were seen ashore only at the begining and end of the breeding season.

Counts were also made of cows, live pups, dead pups and weaned pups. Also noted were the number and location of harems, number of cows and bulls per harem and the identity of the bulls where this was known. Bulls were individually marked with yacht enamel paint as soon as possible after hauling out and their movements recorded daily thereafter. A number of cows were also individually paint-marked and their movements recorded.

Collection of specimens

A small collection of bulls was made outside the daily census area. The purpose of the collection was to determine the age range of bulls ashore during the breeding season and the ages of animals representative of the harem bull and bachelor bull groups. If more than one bull was present in a harem then the dominant bull was taken. Bachelor bulls were selected from among those on the periphery of harems as well as from areas with no cow aggregations.

To determine the minimum age of recruitment to the breeding population at the time of the study 20 of the smallest, least-scarred breeding cows were collected.

Standard measurements were made on all specimens and the canine teeth were sawn off at the level of the gum (Laws, 1953a) for age determination.

Various methods of age determination were used on the teeth. The most satisfactory was to cut a transverse section from the canine tooth with a diamond-impregnated, water-cooled saw. The resulting sections were polished to a final thickness of 0.4 mm on fine grade (P360) wet and dry emery paper using water as a lubricant. They were then examined microscopically with transmitted light (Figs 2, 3). Polished tooth surfaces (Laws, 1953a) were examined by reflected light in some specimens and the silver nitrate staining method of Carrick & Ingham (1962b) was also used.

Pup weighing

In 1977 five pups of known age were weighed at approximately five day intervals from near birth to near weaning and in 1978 weights were obtained for 15 pups of known age. The pups were weighed in a net slung with block and tackle gear from a spring balance on a tripod.

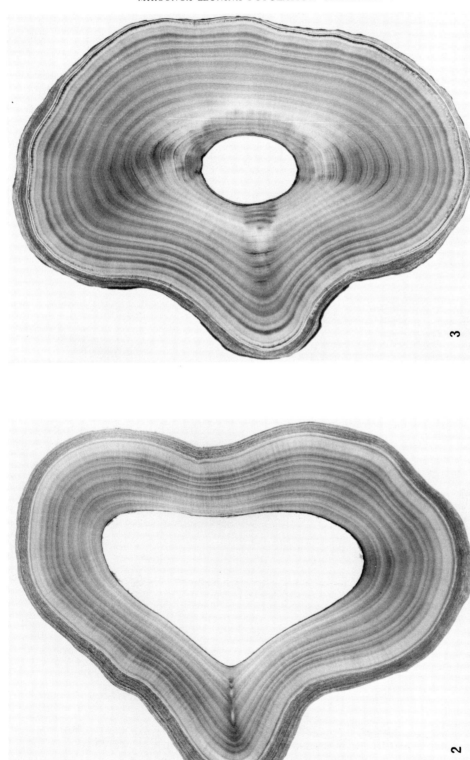

3

2

Figures 2, 3. Fig. 2. Canine tooth of six year old breeding female. Unstained transverse section viewed by transmitted light. Dark bands are dense dentine laid down while ashore to pup or moult, light bands indicate time spent at sea feeding. Fig. 3. Canine tooth of 14 year old breeding female. Unstained transverse section viewed by transmitted light.

RESULTS

Timing of the breeding season

The first bulls hauled out in mid-August and their numbers increased steadily from late August onwards (Fig. 4). The largest bulls, those which became dominant in the harems, were among the first bulls ashore. The number ashore fluctuated after early October and the greatest numbers were ashore from late October to mid-November after which numbers declined rapidly. The first cows hauled out around mid-September. The rate of increase and the date by which the maximum number of cows was ashore was closely similar in each of three seasons (Fig. 5).

The haul out to parturition interval for 67 marked cows (of the first 130 to haul out) was 6.4 ± 2.2 (s.d.) days but for the Dartmouth Point population as a whole (1000 cows) the census data (Fig. 4) show the interval to have been about eight days.

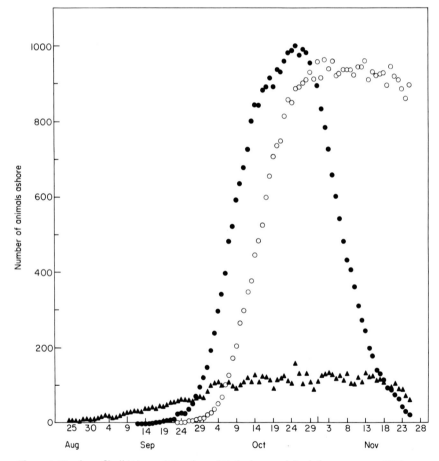

Figure 4. Number of bull (▲), cow (●) and pup (○) elephant seals in daily census area, 1977.

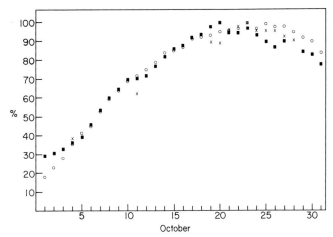

Figure 5. Number of cows ashore at Dartmouth Point on a given day expressed as a percentage of the maximum number of cows ashore. ■, 1976; O, 1977; ×, 1978.

Numbers of animals ashore

The maximum number of cows in the study area varied between 700 and 1000 over the four years for which data are available. The number of bulls varied in a similar manner and the overall cow:bull ratio remained fairly constant from season to season. However, the ratio varied with the area under study. In the daily census area it was 8.5:1 but on the peninsula from glacier to glacier 5.5:1 (at the time when the maximum numbers of cows were ashore). This is because the larger the area the more harem-free beach space there is. Bachelor bulls often gather in areas away from the more dominant bulls and their inclusion lowers the cow:bull ratio. This aspect of the social organization is better described by two ratios: (1) cows:total bulls ashore, (2) cows:bulls in harems (Fig. 6).

While harems tended to form in the same place each year and the total number formed varied little between seasons, the considerable variation in number of cows ashore caused the average maximum size to vary greatly between seasons. In each season the range in harem sizes was 6–*c.* 230.

The changes during a season in number of harems, cows per harem and harem bulls are shown in Fig. 7. The figure for number of cows per harem was calculated by dividing the number of cows in harems by the number of harems as was done by Laws (1956a). In late October as cows which had weaned their pups left the beaches in increasing numbers, some of the largest harems split into two, accounting for the increase in number of harems around this time. The number of bulls in a harem and therefore with access to the cows also varied with the size of the harem.

Age, size and weight

The age distribution and breeding status of the bulls collected is shown in Table 1. It should be remembered that the sample was selected to permit the range of ages of harem and bachelor bulls to be assessed and is not a random sample of all bulls hauled out. The age at first pupping of the selected sample of

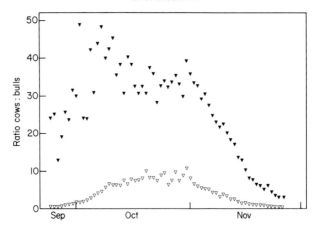

Figure 6. Ratio of cows: bulls, Dartmouth Point 1977. ▼, cows: harem bulls; ▽, cows: bulls ashore.

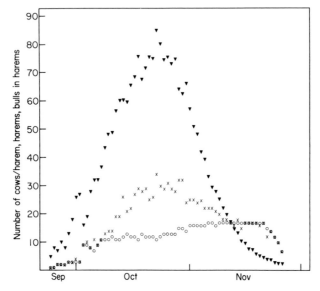

Figure 7. Number of harems (O), cows per harem (▼) and bulls in harems (×), Dartmouth Point 1977.

Table 1. Status, age distribution and number of bulls collected

Age	6	7	8	9	10	11	12	13	14	15	16	Mean
Harem bulls	—	—	2	3	8	4	—	2	—	—	1	10.5
Bachelor bulls	1	8	7	2	—	1	—	1	—	—	—	8.0

Table 2. Age at first pupping of cows collected

Age at first pupping	Number	%
3	5	25
4	11	55
5	4	20

Table 3. Age and mean (± 1 s.d.) curvilinear length of bulls collected

Age	Number	Curvilinear length	
		Mean	S.D.
6	1	4.22	—
7	8	4.10	0.18
8	9	4.33	0.38
9	5	4.73	0.25
10	8	4.78	0.20
11	5	4.94	0.12
12	0	—	—
13	3	4.83	0.18
14	0	—	—
15	0	—	—
16	1	4.86	—

Table 4. Age and mean (± 1 s.d.) curvilinear length of cows collected

Age	Number	Curvilinear length (m)	
		Mean	S.D.
3	5	2.43	0.05
4	9	2.50	0.12
5	6	2.48	0.09

cows is shown in Table 2. Of the 20 cows, 18 were primiparous and two were in their second breeding season.

The mean curvilinear length and standard deviation of the bulls and cows collected are shown in Tables 3 and 4.

The results of the 1978 pup weighings are shown in Fig. 8. Eight pups, including the six with the fastest growth rates, could not be located for weighing on the 20th day post-partum. The data point at day 20 is thus only for the four small pups remaining. Extrapolation on the basis of the mean growth rate of all pups for days 5–15 (4.7 kg day^{-1}) would give a value of 125 kg at day 20.

DISCUSSION

Laws (1956a) considered that the commercial sealing operations had had two main effects on the breeding population at South Georgia. Firstly, they had caused an extension in the length of the breeding season and a delay in its commencement when compared with the timings recorded by Matthews (1929). Secondly, and most noticeably, they had altered the adult sex ratio.

The studies of Carrick *et al.* (1962a) showed that animals at South Georgia grew faster, achieved a greater adult size and attained breeding status earlier than Macquarie Island elephant seals. They suggested that because of former over-exploitation and the (then) current sealing activities, the South Georgia population was below its natural limit with the result that intrasexual competition for food was reduced, resulting in better growth rates and the precocity in breeding observed by Laws.

Bryden (1968), however, proposed that disturbances to suckling in the large crowded harems at Macquarie Island, where there was probably a much greater level of male activity than at South Georgia, resulted in Macquarie pups receiving

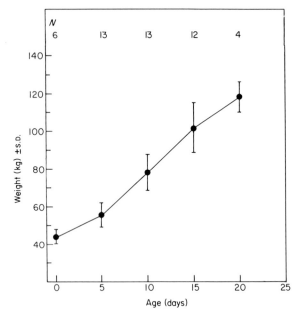

Figure 8. Weight increase of elephant seal pups, South Georgia 1978. N = number of pups weighed.

less milk, thereby failing to achieve their 'genetic growth competence' and becoming permanently stunted. Thus mature males at Macquarie Island were 94% of the size of mature males at South Georgia and mature females were only 60% of the size of South Georgia females (Bryden, 1968).

In the light of these suggestions it is interesting to see to what extent aspects of the breeding cycle, population structure and growth rates have changed at South Georgia in the 25 years since Laws' work (and presumably chiefly in the years since sealing ceased).

Timing and duration of the breeding season

The breeding season for bulls now begins at about the same time as in the early days of modern sealing (Table 5) i.e. before the level of exploitation had reached the maximum sustainable yield and while the population was believed to be expanding. Laws (1956a) proposed that the bulls tended to delay haul out because of the disturbances caused by sealing. It is unlikely that this could have

Table 5. Timing of breeding activities on South Georgia

Date	Bulls taken per season	Study date	Haul-out date Bulls	Cows	Max. No. cows ashore	References
1910 ⎫ 1927 ⎬ 1965 ⎭	2000–3000	1926	10 Aug	20 Aug	c. 27 Sep	Matthews (1929)
	5000–6000	1951 (D.Pt.)	25 Aug	10 Sep	18 Oct	Laws (1956a)
		1951 (S.G.)	5 Sep	19 Sep	26 Oct	Laws (1956a)
Present	No sealing	1975–77	10 Aug	12 Sep	25 Oct	

D.Pt., Dartmouth Point reserve; S.G., exploited beaches on South Georgia.

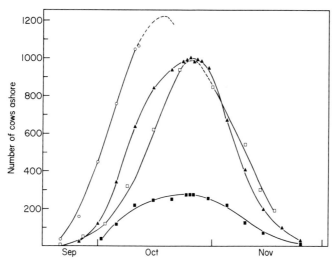

Figure 9. Time of cow haul out and maximum numbers ashore. Curves fitted by eye. O, Dartmouth Point, 1951; ▲, Dartmouth Point, 1977; □, Hestesletten, 1951; ■, Paul Beach, 1954.

been simply a response to a delay in cow haul out as bulls at present haul out very much earlier than cows.

The time of cow haul out and pupping in 1926 (Matthews, 1929) was very early, whether compared with the current situation at South Georgia or with that at other breeding places (Condy, 1979). Matthews recorded pups in late August and found that the majority were born in September, up to one month earlier than at other breeding locations.

At the Dartmouth Point reserve in 1951 the time of haul out and the date when the maximum number of cows was ashore were at least a week earlier than on the exploited beaches outside the reserve. Present counts show that the Dartmouth Point population is now in synchrony with those on the formerly exploited beaches and that on all of these the maximum numbers of cows are ashore in late October, as in the days of sealing (Fig. 9).

South Georgia and Macquarie Island are on the same line of latitude (54°S) and might be expected to show synchrony of events but the season at Macquarie Island is about ten days in advance of that at South Georgia. The three Scotia Sea populations for which data exist (South Georgia, Signy Island, South Shetland Islands (Muller-Schwarze, Waltz, Trivelpiece & Volkman, 1978)) breed at approximately the same time even though they cover an 8° range of latitude. If time of blastocyst implantation is determined by change in daylength then this does not appear to operate in a very subtle way.

Although numerous references to the length of the breeding season are found in the literature it is seldom stated whether they refer to the period of pupping, the period of pupping and mating, the period during which the cows are ashore or the time from when bulls first haul out until the last pup is weaned and the breeding adults return to sea. Thus precise comparisons are often difficult to make.

At South Georgia the harem-masters remain ashore until the last cows in the harem have been mated but most have left by the end of November. Thus the breeding season, from when the first bulls haul out until the last pup is weaned,

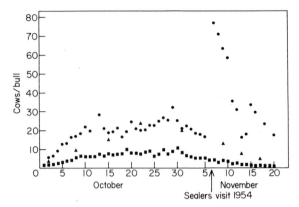

Figure 10. Ratio of cows: total bulls ashore. ▲, Hestesletten, 1951; ●, Paul Beach, 1954; ■, Dartmouth Point, 1978.

is now longer than in sealing days because of the earlier haul out of the bulls. It is, however, apparently no more lengthy than at Macquarie Island (Carrick *et al.*, 1962a). The period of pupping and mating is about the same as in 1951.

Sex ratio and harem size

The alteration in the adult sex ratio was the most obvious effect of the sealing operations. This resulted from killing the large breeding bulls (Laws, 1960) and may have been exaggerated by a possible increase in cow numbers coincident with the reduction of the male herd, as was thought to have occurred in the Alaska Fur Seal (*Callorhinus ursinus* (L.)) herd (Anon., 1962).

In 1951 the cow:bull ratio on the Dartmouth Point reserve was 13:1, similar to the ratio at Kerguelen (11.4:1 (Angot, 1954)) where sealing had not been attempted since the early thirties, and very different to that on the exploited beaches (about 28:1) (Fig. 10). Laws (1956a) considered therefore that the reserve population represented the unmodified state. It is now apparent that the Dartmouth Point population was unique; different from the herds on the exploited beaches but influenced by them to a marked extent. The cow:bull ratio then was relatively low because the bulls were not hunted, but, judging from the degree of mobility of bulls during the present study, it is likely that the herd would have been far from isolated and the age composition is likely to have been the same as on the exploited beaches.

The average age of South Georgia harem-masters in 1951 was eight (Laws, 1953b) and six and seven year olds made up the majority of bulls ashore during the breeding season. In the present study most harem bulls were found to be 10 or 11 years old (Table 1). They may be older still at Macquarie Island (Carrick *et al.*, 1962a). Presumably the younger harem bulls in 1951 lacked the size, experience and perhaps the aggression necessary to exclude other bulls from the cow aggregations, with the result that many small harems formed rather than a smaller number of large harems. On Dartmouth Point in 1951 there were 52 harems whereas the same area had 13 in 1977 with about the same total number of cows (Table 6). On the exploited beaches the smaller number of bulls relative to the cow population resulted in fewer and larger harems being formed. The average harem size has increased since the cessation of sealing because there are

Table 6. Comparison of exploited and non-exploited breeding rookeries

Locality	Date	Bulls	Cows	Harems	Cows/harem	Cows/bull		References
Hestesletten	1951	40	1000	20	46	24	sealing	Laws (1956a)
Maiviken	1951	7	200	6	30	28		Laws (1956a)
Paul Beach	1954	13	280	?	?	25		Bonner (unpubl.)
Dartmouth Point	1951	80	1200	50	24	13	no sealing	Laws (1956a)
Dartmouth Point	1977	120	1000	13	75	8		
Hestesletten	1977	130	1300	18	70	10		
Macquarie Is.	1962	500	5500	18	277	11		Carrick *et al.* (1962a)

now greater numbers of experienced, dominant bulls, able to exclude other bulls from a larger cow group.

At Macquarie Island the large open beaches on the isthmus study area encourage the formation of enormous 'composite harems' (Carrick *et al.*, 1962a) of up to 1000 cows and the mean harem size in the area was almost 300. Approximately 85% of the breeding cows at Macquarie island are found outside the isthmus area, scattered around the precipitous coast. It is likely that the average harem size will be smaller in these areas. As at Macquarie Island, harems where the peak size is less than 50 cows do not contain more than one harem bull at a time.

Bull age

Although the age distribution of the sample of bulls collected was not representative of the total population ashore (see Methods) the age range (6–16 years) probably is. In comparison with the random sample returned by the sealers (Bonner, 1956) there are many more older animals at present (Fig. 11). The majority of Laws' specimens were taken on the exploited beaches at South Georgia, although his oldest specimen 12 years) was taken at Signy Island and he found two bull skeletons at Signy Island whose ages at death he determined from

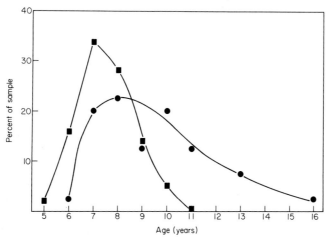

Figure 11. Age distribution of male elephant seals. ■, killed by sealers, South Georgia, 1956; ●, this study, South Georgia, 1976–77. Curves fitted by eye.

tooth analysis as 20 and 18 years, which is probably near the maximum for this species (Laws, 1953b).

The present absence of five year olds and the small proportion of six year olds ashore during the breeding season is probably a consequence of the increased intra-sexual competition associated with the increased numbers of bulls. Thus the smaller, and therefore younger animals are excluded and most remain at sea during the breeding season with the immatures. This would seem also to be the case at Macquarie Island where the youngest bulls ashore were six and only 51% of branded eight year olds were seen during the breeding season (Carrick *et al.*, 1962a).

Carrick *et al.* (1962a) thought that the majority of harem-masters at Macquarie Island were 14 years old or more, although Laws (1953b) believed that in an undisturbed population 9–12 year olds would provide the majority of harem bulls; a conclusion which certainly applies to the present South Georgia population.

Cow age and maturity

The 1976 sample of South Georgia breeding cows showed that there was variation in the age of recruitment, as with most large mammals, but that the majority of cows pupped for the first time at four years of age. Laws (1953b) determined the age at first pupping of South Georgia cows as three, with just a few pupping for the first time at four years of age. However, analysis of a recent random sample of 91 cows at South Georgia by back calculation from tooth annuli (Laws, 1977; Söderberg, 1977) failed to show any significant increase in age at first pupping between cows born while sealing operations were still in progress and cows born after sealing had ceased. The majority had pupped for the first time at four years of age (McCann *et al.*, 1979).

At Macquarie Island no cows aged three have been seen to pup, recruitment begins at four and was only about 70% complete by age six, 25% of known-age

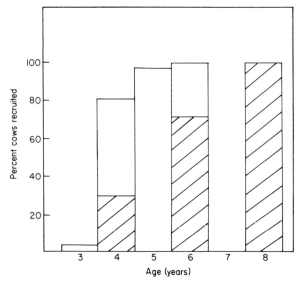

Figure 12. Percent recruitment of cows to the breeding population. There are insufficient data for 5 and 7 year old Macquarie Island cows. Unhatched, South Georgia; hatched, Macquarie Island.

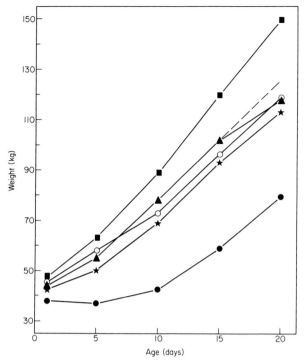

Figure 13. Comparison of growth of elephant seal pups from birth to 20 days of age. ■, Signy, 1948; ▲, South Georgia, 1978; ○, South Georgia, 1977; ★, Macquarie, 1965; ●, Macquarie, 1956.

cows having their first pup at age seven (Carrick *et al.*, 1962a). At South Georgia in 1978 recruitment was more than 75% complete by age four and 100% of cows examined had pupped by six years of age (Fig. 12).

Although the South Georgia population has had more than a decade to recover from the effects of exploitation of the male herd, and bull numbers have increased so that the cow:bull ratio is at least as low as at Macquarie Island, the majority of cows are still maturing and pupping earlier than those at Macquarie Island.

As noted previously, Carrick *et al.* (1962a) believed that the South Georgia female population was below its potential maximum, while Bryden (1968) thought that disturbance in the harems was reduced enabling pups to achieve their maximum potential growth.

Adult bull numbers have increased three to four fold since the ending of exploitation but no increase has been detected in the number of female elephant seals ashore to pup, although more extensive counts would be needed to verify this. Approximately the same number of pups were born in Cumberland Bay during the present study as were counted by Laws (1956a) in 1951.

With the cow:bull ratio at least as low as at Macquarie Island disturbance in the harems should be as great, other things being equal. However, pup growth rates at South Georgia were still faster than those obtained at Macquarie Island (Fig. 13), although less than those obtained by Laws (1953b) at Signy Island where disturbance in the small harems must have been minimal.

The mean curvilinear length-age data for bulls and cows collected at South Georgia in 1976–77 are shown in Tables 3 and 4. When compared with the data gathered by Laws (1953b) no significant differences were found. Furthermore the cows collected in 1976–77 were selected for their small size. Thus South Georgia animals are certainly as big as in sealing days and presumably still larger than Macquarie Island animals.

There is a possible analogous situation with the two North Atlantic populations of the grey seal (*Halichoerus grypus*). Canadian Grey Seals are larger and heavier throughout life than British Grey Seals and the females start pupping one year earlier than females in the British populations (Mansfield, 1977). Both the British and Canadian populations of grey seals are increasing by about 7% annually (Summers, 1978; Mansfield & Beck, 1977) so that neither population appears to be limited by food shortage. Harwood & Prime (1977) found no evidence for a change in age at first pregnancy with increasing population size in British Grey Seals and concluded that "ultimate population size in this population appears to be set by the number of potential breeding sites". This might be less important in the Canadian population approximately half of which breeds on ice in the Gulf of St. Lawrence (Mansfield & Beck, 1977).

Neither at Macquarie Island nor South Georgia is breeding space limiting and population size is probably set by the level of food availability.

CONCLUSIONS

It seems certain that some of the differences between the South Georgia and Macquarie Island elephant seal populations, noted while sealing was in progress, were intrinsic and persist today. These differences may be correlated with differences in food availability at the two sites. Marine production is higher around South Georgia than around Macquarie Island (Foxton, 1956), krill is more abundant (Marr, 1962) and as the area of continental shelf is much greater at South Georgia (Bakaev, 1966) it is likely that fish stocks are larger too. In addition, Chapman (1976) estimated that, prior to exploitation, population size of Fin Whales (*Balaenoptera physalus*), which feed on krill, was at least four times greater in Whaling Area II (60°W–0°), which includes South Georgia, than in Area V (130°E–170°W) which includes Macquarie Island.

Elephant seals feed on fish and squid (Murphy, 1914) which themselves presumably depend upon krill. The greater availability of these food organisms is also reflected in the size of the population of elephant seals at South Georgia (300,000 (Laws, 1960)) which is more than three times that at Macquarie Island (95,000 (Carrick & Ingham, 1960)).

In addition to differences in population size there is evidence that the age of sexual maturity of Fin whales prior to large-scale exploitation was lower in Area II than in Area V (Lockyer, 1979), which is consistent with the observations for the two elephant seal populations.

The apparent greater food availability may thus explain why South Georgia bulls and cows are larger age for age, breed earlier and why pups grow faster, perhaps through better milk transfer, than at Macquarie Island.

Another confounding variable is the reduction in the Antarctic krill-eating baleen whale stocks and squid-eating Sperm whale stocks which has been especially marked in the South Georgia area and Scotia Sea. This is thought to have made large amounts of krill, and probably squid, available to other predators. Increases have been observed in Adelie Penguin, *Pygoscelis adeliae,* and

Chinstrap Penguin, *P. antarctica* (recent evidence reviewed in Croxall & Kirkwood, 1979) and have been inferred in the krill-eating Crabeater Seal, *Lobodon carcinophagus* (Laws, 1977). An increase in available squid stocks may be indicated by the increase in King Penguins *Aptenodytes patagonica* (Smith & Tallowin, 1980).

Although, as noted previously, no increase has been detected in the number of female elephant seals, bull numbers have increased greatly so that elephant seal biomass has increased since the ending of exploitation, but it is not known how the present biomass compares with that of the population before exploitation began.

The situation is complicated by additional factors. The cessation of sealing has brought about a large change in the number of one sex with an unknown effect on the other sex. The absence of data on the extent of cow intrasexual competition then and now and complete absence of data on intersexual competition makes evaluation more or less impossible. Furthermore, while more food may be available, possible competition from man for food resources may be increasing. Trawlers have been very active around South Georgia and in 1970 more than 400,000 tonnes of fish were caught, an amount which is probably far in excess of the maximum sustainable yield (Everson, 1977).

To summarize:

(1) Since exploitation ended there has been a three to four fold increase in the number of adult bulls, an increase in the mean age of harem bulls and in mean harem size. Bulls haul out earlier and stay ashore longer than while sealing was in progress. The length of the breeding season and the social organization are now approximately the same as at Macquarie Island.

(2) This has been accompanied by little, if any, change in the number of breeding cows and the age structure of the breeding cow herd, which still differs from the Macquarie Island cow herd.

(3) Age at first breeding in cows is determined by intra- and inter-sexual competition which affects growth and development. Pup and adult growth may be better at South Georgia because of absolute differences in food availability.

ACKNOWLEDGEMENTS

I would like to thank the British Antarctic Survey personnel on South Georgia who assisted in various ways; in particular Tim Fogg, Steve Jones, Gerry Thomas and especially Lyndon Kearsley who assisted me throughout the study. My thanks also to W. N. Bonner and Dr J. P. Croxall for their help and encouragement.

REFERENCES

ANGOT, M., 1954. Observations sur les mammifères marins de l'Archipel de Kerguelen, avec une étude detaillée de l'éléphant de mer, *Mirounga leonina* (L.). *Mammalia, 18:* 1–111.
ANON., 1962. *North Pacific Fur Seal Commission Report On Investigations From 1958 to 1961.* Tokyo: Kenkyusha.
BAKAEV, V. G., 1966. (Ed.). *Sovetskaya Antarkticheskaya Ekspeditsiya Atlas Antarktiki. I:* 16–17. Moskva/Leningrad: Glavnoe Upravlenie Geodezii i Kartografii mg SSSR, 1966.
BONNER, W. N., 1957. *Report of the Sealing Industry at South Georgia 1956.* Unpublished mimeo.
BRYDEN, M. M., 1968. Control of growth in two populations of elephant seals. *Nature, 217:* 1106–08.
CARRICK, R., CSORDAS, S. E. & INGHAM, S. E., 1962a. Studies on the Southern Elephant Seal, *Mirounga leonina* (L.). IV. Breeding and Development. *CSIRO Wildlife Research, 7:* 161–197.
CARRICK, R., CSORDAS, S. E., INGHAM, S. E. & KEITH, K., 1962b. Studies on the Southern Elephant Seal, *Mirounga leonina* (L.). III. The Annual Cycle in Relation to Age and Sex. *CSIRO Wildlife Research, 7:* 119–160.

CARRICK, R. & INGHAM, S. E., 1960. Ecological studies of the southern elephant seal, *Mirounga leonina* (L.), at Macquarie Island and Heard Island. *Mammalia, 24:* 325–342.

CARRICK, R. & INGHAM, S. E., 1962a. Studies on the Southern Elephant Seal, *Mirounga leonina* (L.). I. Introduction to the series. *CSIRO Wildlife Research, 7:* 89–101.

CARRICK, R. & INGHAM, S. E., 1962b. Studies on the Southern Elephant Seal, *Mirounga leonina* (L.). II. Canine Tooth Structure in Relation to Function and Age Determination. *CSIRO Wildlife Research, 7:* 102–118.

CARRICK, R. & INGHAM, S. E., 1962c. Studies on the Southern Elephant Seal. *Mirounga leonina* (L). V. Population dynamics and utilization. *CSIRO Wildlife Research, 7:* 198–206.

CHAPMAN, D. G., 1976. Estimates of stocks (original, current, MSY level and MSY) as revised at Scientific Committee June 1975. *Report of the International Whaling Commission, 26:* 44–47.

CONDY, P. R., 1979. Annual cycle of the Southern Elephant Seal *Mirounga leonina* (Linn.) at Marion Island. *South African Journal of Zoology, 14:* No. 2.

CROXALL, J. P. & KIRKWOOD, E. D., 1979. *The Distribution of Penguins in the Antarctic Peninsula and Islands of the Scotia Sea.* Cambridge: British Antarctic Survey.

EVERSON, I., 1977. *The Living Resources of the Southern Ocean.* Rome: FAO. (FAO Report GLO/SO/77/1).

FOXTON, P., 1956. The distribution of the standing crop of zooplankton in the Southern Ocean. *'Discovery' Report, 28:* 191–235.

HARWOOD, J. & PRIME, J. H., 1978. Some factors affecting the size of British Grey seal populations. *Journal of Applied Ecology, 15:* 401–411.

LAWS, R. M., 1953a. A new method of age determination for mammals with special reference to the elephant seal, *Mirounga leonina* Linn. *Scientific Reports of the Falkland Islands Dependencies Survey,* No. *2:* 1–11.

LAWS, R. M., 1953b. The elephant seal (*Mirounga leonina* Linn.). I. Growth and age. *Scientific Reports of the Falkland Islands Dependencies Survey,* No. *8:* 1–62.

LAWS, R. M., 1956a. The elephant seal (*Mirounga leonina* Linn.). II. General, social and reproductive behaviour. *Scientific Reports of the Falkland Islands Dependencies Survey,* No. *13:* 1–88.

LAWS, R. M., 1956b. The elephant seal (*Mirounga leonina* Linn.). III. The physiology of reproduction . *Scientific Reports of the Falkland Islands Dependencies Survey,* No. *15:* 1–66.

LAWS, R. M., 1960. The Southern Elephant Seal (*Mirounga leonina* Linn.) at South Georgia. *Norsk Hvalfangst-Tidende, 49:* 446–476: 520–542.

LAWS, R. M., 1977. The significance of vertebrates in the Antarctic marine ecosystem. In G. A. Llano (Ed.) *Adaptations within Antarctic Ecosystems:* 411–438. Third Symposium on Antarctic Biology, Scientific Committee for Antarctic Research.

LOCKYER, C., 1979. Changes in a growth parameter associated with exploitation of Southern Fin and Sei Whales. *Report of the International Whaling Commission, 29:* 191–196.

MANSFIELD, A. W., 1977. *Growth and Longevity of the Grey Seal* Halichoerus grypus *in Eastern Canada.* International Council for the Exploration of the Sea. C. M. 1977/N:6. Mimeo.

MANSFIELD, A. W. & BECK, B., 1977. The grey seal in eastern Canada. *Fisheries and Marine Service, Technical Report,* No. *704:* 1–81.

MARR, J., 1962. The natural history and geography of the Antarctic krill (*Euphausia superba* Dana. *'Discovery' Report, 32:* 33–464.

MATTHEWS, L. H., 1929. The natural history of the elephant seal, with notes on other seals found at South Georgia. *'Discovery' Report, 1:* 233–256.

McCANN, T. S., BONNER, W. N., PRIME, J. H. & RICKETTS, C., 1979. *Age Distribution and Age at First Pregnancy of South Georgia Elephant Seals.* International Council for the Exploration of the Sea. C. M. 1979/N: 13. Mimeo.

MULLER-SCHWARZE, D., WALTZ, E. C., TRIVELPIECE, W. & VOLKMAN, N. J., 1978. Breeding status of southern elephant seals at King George Island. *Antarctic Journal of the United States, 13:* 157–58.

MURPHY, R. C., 1914. Notes on the sea elephant, *Mirounga leonina* Linn. *Bulletin of the American Museum of Natural History, 33:* 63–79.

SMITH, R. I. L. & TALLOWIN, J. R. B., 1980. The distribution and size of King penguin rookeries on South Georgia. *British Antarctic Survey Bulletin,* No. *49:* 259–276.

SÖDERBERG, S., 1977. *Falling Age at Sexual Maturity in Baltic seals.* Haikko, Finland: Proceedings of the Symposium on the Conservation of Baltic Seals.

SUMMERS, C. F., 1978. Trends in the size of British Grey Seal populations. *Journal of Applied Ecology, 15:* 395–400.